AF538548

AGRICULTURE, ECOLOGY AND ENVIRONMENT

AGRICULTURE, ECOLOGY AND ENVIRONMENT

Edited by

Dr. Pawan Kumar 'Bharti'

Centre for Agro-Rural Technologies (CART-India)
20, Jamaalpur Man, Raja Ka Tajpur
Bijnore (UP) - 246 735 (India)
E-mail: gurupawanbharti@rediffmail.com

&

Prof. Olubukola Oluranti Babalola

Department of Biological Sciences
Faculty of Agriculture Science & Technology
North-West University, Mahikeng Campus
Mmabatho 2735, South Africa

Associate Editor

Dr. Avnish Chauhan

Department of Applied Science
Phonics Group of Institutions
Roorkee, Haridwar (Uttarakhand)
(India)

DISCOVERY PUBLISHING HOUSE PVT. LTD.
NEW DELHI-110 002

Published by:
Tilak Wasan

DISCOVERY PUBLISHING HOUSE PVT. LTD.
4383/4B, Ansari Road, Darya Ganj
New Delhi-110 002 (India)
Phone : +91-11-23279245, 43596064-65
Fax : +91-11-23253475
E-mail : discoverypublishinghouse@gmail.com
sales@discoverypublishinggroup.com
parul.wasan@gmail.com
web : www.discoverypublishinggroup.com

***First Edition:* 2014**

ISBN: 978-93-5056-480-6

Agriculture, Ecology and Environment

Printed at:
Aditi Fine Art Press
Delhi

Preface

In recent past, air pollutants, responsible for vegetation injury and crop yield losses, are causing increased concern. Gaseous form of pollutants is absorbed through the leaves, while the particulate forms are generally absorbed on the outer surface of the plant. The particulate dust falling on the leaves is said to cause foliar injuries, reduction in yield, changes in the rate of photosynthesis, transpiration and uptake and accumulation of minerals elements from soil.

Because of intensive crop production practices with excessive use of agrochemicals, agricultural lands worldwide have become vulnerable to degradative processes. Chemical-based, conventional agricultural has created many sources of pollution that can contribute to degradation of the environment and destruction of our natural resource base directly or indirectly. Problems such as soil erosion, nutrient depletion and loss of organic matter, decline in soil productivity, contamination of surface and ground water, non target effect on natural enemies & beneficial microbes are associated with agrochemicals. Moreover, their residue when enter in food chain through fruits and vegetables leads to bio-magnification of residue. Consequently, there has been a growing public concern about adverse impacts of agrochemicals on agriculture, environment and on the safety and quality of food.

Strategies for increasing diversified agricultural productivity on sustainable basis have become imperative because of its role in poverty scale-up and economic development. Agriculture is expected to continue to be the engine of economic growth and other numerous ancillary benefits, by being increasingly more productive and more efficient to meet the needs of an increasing population but has often been plagued by climate, ecological, and socio-economic problems; weak institutional policy reforms and poor infrastructure for crop production, handling, and marketing, thus causing fluctuations in food availability, hunger as well as adverse effect on economies.

Present day we are facing excessive pollution caused by industrialized agriculture where variety of chemical fertilizers and pesticides belongs to diverse chemical class are being used. Hence, these chemical fertilizers and pesticides have emerged as indispensible tool in modern agriculture. Their residue is contaminating the environment, hampers the balance of the eco-system and pesticides also destroy predator and parasites of the target organisms, leading to the reduction of beneficial species. They contaminate the ground water by leaching. Pesticides enter the food chain and lead to bio-magnification as their residues are found on fruits and vegetables.

This book provides comprehensive coverage of the fundamental principles and current practices and trends in the field of agriculture, ecology and environmental biotechnology.

This book updates the subject matter, illustrations and problems to incorporate new concepts and issues related to agriculture, ecology, environment and biotechnology.

Particularly thanks are due to all contributors from Japan, South America, South Africa, Nigeria, India; and publisher also for their contribution and assistance.

I hope this book will be of benefit to both present and future colleagues, who teach, study and working in the field of environment, ecology, environmental pollution, agriculture and biotechnology.

Dr. Pawan Kumar 'Bharti'
(*gurupawanbharti@rediffmail.com*)

Contents

Agriculture and Environmental Pollution
Causes, Consequences and Control

Tunde Ezekiel Lawal and **Olubukola Oluranti Babalola***

ABSTRACT

Effect of environmental pollution on agriculture and *vice versa* is becoming a front burner of recent. Pollution is affecting agricultural productivities as the environment is one of the determinants of agricultural success. Once the environment (soil, water and atmosphere) is polluted, then agriculture cannot thrive. However, agricultural activities, if not well managed also add to environmental pollution. Therefore, farmers and the entire populace need to be sufficiently informed about the dangers and consequences of pollution on agriculture. This write up intends to shed light on causes and effects of pollution on agriculture, types of pollution, types of pollutants, and the possible panacea to pollution.

Key words: Agriculture, control, environment, pollution.

INTRODUCTION

It has become very important to be well informed about the influence of pollution on agriculture and environment. Agriculture and environment are inseparable because one influences the other. Notably, it has been observed that they influence each other positively and negatively. Pollution takes place

---

* Department of Biological Sciences, Faculty of Agriculture, Science and Technology, North-West University, Mahikeng Campus, Private Bag X2046, Mmabatho 2735, South Africa.

in urban centres, semi urban and rural areas. It takes place via so many ways and so many things can be polluted (Hansen et al 2010, Maher et al 2009). Governments and Non-Governmental Organisations are campaigning against pollutions as they bring deleterious effects to plants, lower animals and humans. The degree of damage is a function of the type of contaminant, the breed of livestock, species of plant and the prevalent environmental condition like ambient temperature and moisture availability.

Pollution tends to have jeopardizing effect on the environment and subsequently on the animate creatures. Pollution can be defined as the introduction of injurious contaminants into soil, water and air. These contaminants can have serious deleterious effects on plants, animals and humans as well (Ahmad et al 2013, Oksanen et al 2013). Expectedly, continuous exposure to pollutioncan have a cumulative negative effect on the body.Crops can be injured if and when exposed continually to pollutants. The negative effect varies and it includes: markings on the leaves, reduction in growth and yield and untimely death of plant. The degree of injury is a function of the concentration of pollutants, duration of exposure to the pollutant, specie of the plant, stage of growth and the treatments that the seeds or the crops have received before planting or after planting. Pollutants are said to be local if they are emitted from a specific stationery source and it leads to pollution of a defined area.

Examples of local pollutants are fluorides, ammonia and sulphur dioxide. A major part of the oxidants, ozone, is produced in the atmosphere in the course of interaction including nitrogen oxides and hydrocarbons, parts of automobile discharges and fossil fuel breakdown. In addition, because this process takes place in the presence of light, it is described as photo-chemical reaction (Maher et al 2009). Besides, it is possible to have vegetation injury as a result of accumulation of oxidants in the atmosphere and this may cover a large expanse of area or zone. Owing to industrial works and vehicular activities, a considerable number of contaminants are dispersed into the atmosphere and these are gaseous harmful substances: carbon monoxides, sulphur oxide, ozone and sulphur dioxide. In addition, there is possibility of having harmful or toxic elements and heavy metals which can as well cause pollution. Examples of such heavy metals are: cadmium (Cd), lead (Pb), mercury (Hg), cobalt (Co),chromium (Cr), nickel (Ni) and zinc (Zn) (White et al 2009).

HOW AGRICULTURAL ACTIVITIES CAUSE POLLUTION

Bids to improve on agricultural activities in order to meet up with the ever widening quests for food have led to the use of different chemicals, adoption of technologies which can elicit odours, dust, smokes and allergic pollens. The use of chemicals on farm for agricultural purpose must be done with caution and carefulness. Agriculture can also pollute soil, air and water through pesticides, odours, methane, smoke, dust, allergic pollens and wastes from agricultural activities.

USE OF PESTICIDES FOR AGRICULTURAL PURPOSES CAN CAUSE POLLUTION

Pesticides are toxic chemicals made to kill pests that are possibly affecting the growth and productivity of crops. However, they often get to places other than their targets; when sprayed on crops, some of it can be found in air, soil, water and even food! They can be found in both surface water (streams, rivers, lakes and oceans) and ground water as they are moved by the rain as part of the runoff water (Hillocks 2012, Lau et al 2012). When pesticides are applied by spraying or surface application, air is always the agent that transfers the chemical(s) to the intended and unintended places. Use of pesticides disrupts the ecosystem of the soil. Pesticides reduce quality of the soil and this reduces the activities of soil microflora, biofertilizers and plant strengtheners. Besides, nitrogen fixation which is very crucial for plant growth is hampered as the fixers cannot thrive when there are chemicals in the soil and this will lead to reduction in crop yield (Masiá et al 2013).

Pesticides are grouped into two: moderately persistent and permanent persistent. Examples of moderately persistent pesticides include: DDT, aldrin, dieldrin, endrin, heptachlor and toxaphene while examples of permanent persistent are: lead, mercury and arsenic. All things being equal, the less persistent ones should be embraced but those that degrade fast are extremely toxic and nonselective. Furthermore, application of pesticides to crops can kill pollinators and if there is no pollination, reproduction is reduced and this spells reduction in yield as well. There is tendency for poisoning of animals when residue of chemical is left on leaves after spraying and such leaves are consumed by animals. Notably, spraying of a particular area can eliminate or reduce the feed sources that some animals consume and this may make these animals to relocate, change their feed or starve (Mishra et al 2012, Sarigiannis et al 2013).

Poisoning by pesticides can as well affect the food chain. For instance, birds can become poisoned if and when they consume insects that have consumed pesticides. Some pesticides come in granular form and if birds mistaken them for grins, they can pick them up thereby losing their lives. The aquatic animals may also be affected by pesticides in that the pesticides may be washed into the stream, rivers and oceans. Also, herbicides may as well be poisonous as the pesticides. This is as a result of the fact that there is depletion of oxygen in the body of water this will make the fish and other aquatic animals to suffocate and die. If there is continuous exposure of fish to such polluted water by pesticides, this may change the physiological condition of such fish and hence behavioural changes like abandonment of nests, reduction in immunity to diseases and susceptibility to predators. All these have the potential of reducing the population of the aquatic beings (Wan et al 2013, Waterhouse et al 2012).

HOW ODOUR, POLLEN, DUST AND NOISE AFFECT AGRICULTURE

Over the years, there have been negative reactions from people that live in the environment where there is animal farm due to almost or absolutely unbearable odour that emanate from such farms. This is often aggravated if there is composting of animal manure in the vicinity. There is continuous move of farms from urban areas to rural areas because of unfavorable disposition of people to odour from farms (Cariñanos & Casares-Porcel 2011). To aggravate the situation, if there is disposal of dead animals indiscriminately, there is going to be a release of repelling odour which may be carried by wind to nearby and also distant places.

Although it bush burning has been discouraged from time to time but, it is still in practice by some farmers especially when they want to clear the farmland for agricultural purpose. There may be the desire to burn off weeds; all these will lead to pollution of air. There is tendency for pollution through the presence of allergenic pollen such as ragweed pollen and this can be blown to a considerable distance. Agricultural activities can also generate dusts. Dusts can be said to be particulate materials in the atmosphere which constitute contaminants and are inimical to environmental cleanliness (L. Smith & Lee 2003). These particulate materials can be grouped into three: particles whose diameter is more than 50 μm, they are referred to as lumps; particles whose diameters are between 2 and 50 μm referred to as dusts and those that are less than 2 μm are referred to as fumes.

Continuous removal of plants and grasses from the soil surface will definitely lead to generation of dusts from land and this aids wind erosion. There is the possibility of moving hulls of rice, pods of groundnuts, wheat offal and cassava sieviates from one place to the other by wind and this may be transferred or moved indiscriminately. Feed mills on farms can produce noise; grain drying and conditioning can elicit noise for the neighbours owing to noise and dusts it generates (Liaquat et al 2010).

Eutrophication

It occurs in the body of water when an increase of mineral and organic nutrients has depleted the available oxygen and encouraging an environment that favours the growth of plant to animal's survival. There is increase in mineral and organic nutrients deposits. This provides opportunity for the growth of algae and other water plants that choke fish and other aquatic animals in competition for oxygen. The main culprit to this is the movement of phosphorus and feedlots through erosion or surface water. The phosphorus may be from animal manure if not well managed (Eory et al 2013).

Salinity

Growth of crops in an irrigated environment depends largely on soil salt balance. The irrigated land is prone to high salt content due to the effect of evaporation. When the farmland is irrigated, some part of the water is evaporated and often, water contains some salts. When water is evaporated, residual salt is left on surface of the soil. This situation is worsened in semi arid or arid region because this region is already a salty area (Calheiros et al 2012). The accumulated salt must be removed and it is suggested that it be removed by leaching with excess water and this can also lead to erosion. Moreover, it is suggested that before water is used for irrigation, it can be desalinated for this process will give or release the purified part of the water and remove the salt fraction (Quinn 2011).

Emission of Methane and Wastes from Agricultural Processing

Human activities have been producing methane over the years and these activities could be industrial, agricultural and or domestic. Methane is largely produced and it is part of the greenhouse emissions. It accounts for 26% of the global warming. It is produced from leakages from gas fields, decay of rubbish on sites, emissions from livestock and degradation of vegetations. Methane is the basic part of natural gas and petroleum materials. It is often released into the atmosphere during production, processing, storage and distribution or sale of petroleum products and gas (Bhatia et al 2011).

Owing to the fact that gas is produced with petroleum, therefore, the production, refinement, storage and movement of crude oil is also implicated as one of the sources of methane emissions. In agriculture, livestock animals like sheep, goats, camels and cattle tend to produce a considerable amount of methane during the process of digestion. In other words, Methane is emitted from the animals owing to fermentation process carried out regularly in the gastro intestinal tract of the animal. Cattle are known to produce highest amount, especially from the dairy cows during lactation period. In addition, poultry is also known to produce methane but in a small quantity from their excreta. However, when the farm is into large production, like 40,000 capacities upwards, it must be stressed that the accumulative methane production from such farm becomes considerable (Eory et al 2013, Zhang et al 2012b).

Farmers are often implored to comply with the wastes removal, disposal or management policies to forestall or possibly minimize the methane production from agricultural farms. Besides, when manure is kept or managed in tanks or lagoons, methane is often produced. When wastes generated from homes are not properly managed, when such wastes are undergoing decomposition through the activities of bacteria in the absence of oxygen, methane is often generated. Other sources of methane production are volcanoes and wildfires (VanderZaag et al 2011). Wastes from agricultural activities can become pollution hazards. These wastes can gather from sugarcane pulp, tanning, fruits and vegetable canning, manufacturing of cornstarch and soya protein, sugar refineries and wool processing industries. If these are not well managed, they can become part of the runoffs and contaminants or pollutants to the environment (Hofmann 2013).

TYPES OF POLLUTION

Different types of pollution have been identified. But in this write up, air pollution, water pollution, soil pollution and noise pollution will be discussed.

AIR POLLUTION

Air pollutants contain some gases and solid particles and inhalation of these contaminants can lead to cancer and there is possibility of asthma and negative effect on reproductive system. Air pollution is not detrimental to air alone; it also damages the environment and the inhabitants. Crops and livestock animals are not spared. At times, the pollutants are the causes of the damage and sometimes, it may be the combination of the contaminants and negatively alter the quality of medium that aid existence of plants and the livestock animals and air is one of such resources (Kowalkowski et al 2012, Porter & Andersen 2013). Toxic air pollutants like mercury are not only injurious to human beings but they are deleterious to plants and they can as well settle on waters and when these are consumed by livestocks, the health of such animals is endangered.

Examples of air pollutants include: oxidants, sulphur dioxide, fluoride and ammonia. Air pollution can occur in outdoor and indoor situations. Outdoor air pollution can occur from road and off road automobiles, ships and aircrafts and from other sources like: power plants, manufacturing industries, volcanoes and agriculture). Indoor air pollution may arise from solid fuel heating and cooking, construction materials and consumer products (Menció et al 2011). Injuries arising from air pollution and its effects on agriculture are seen in many ways.

For instance, injury to plant is observable on the leaves as they exhibit or show necrotic lesions or chlorosis (yellowing of leaves). Plants may have stunted growth or may possibly die. Air has both chemical and physical components and these components are very crucial to both plants and animals. Quality of air is altered when pollutants come into it and both crops and livestock animals using such air are prone or susceptible to danger of survival (Olson et al 2009).

AIR POLLUTION AND ITS EFFECT ON AGRICULTURE

Undoubtedly, air pollution will have adverse effects on both agricultural crops and livestock animals for they are living things. Coal burning and incomplete combustion of petroleum products produce sulphur oxides. Glass and ceramic production as well as smelting releases fluorides, into atmosphere and other human activities, especially industrial activities from factories and developments of technologies have been implicated for the production of ammonia, chlorine, ethylene, mercaptans, carbon monoxide and nitrogen monoxide (Jayasingha et al., 2011, (Rinnan et al 2013). Reactions of contaminants increase or aggravate the varieties of pollutants in atmosphere and such pollutants in the air may also include: aldehydes, hydrocarbons, organic acids, ozone, peroxyacetyl nitrates, pesticides and radionuclides.

Effects on crops will most assuredly bring economic loss to farmers and this will also affects foreign exchange earning of nations, especially nations that have agriculture as the mainstay of their economies (Velthof et al 2009, Virgílio Cruz et al 2013). Negative influence of air pollution becomes noticeable in both plants and animals in the following areas: Influence on the enzymic nature, alteration of chemical and cellular nature, reduction in growth and production due to new poor metabolic ability and tissue degeneration. Contaminants that gain entrance into atmosphere other than the ones from agriculture are grouped as: products of combustion, products of reactions in the air, acid gases and multifarious effluents (Hansen et al 2010, Tang et al 2013).

OZONE AS A POLLUTANT AND ITS EFFECT ON AGRICULTURE

Ozone is the primary contaminant in the class of the oxidants. It is as a result of reaction among oxides of nitrogen, carbon monoxides and volatile organic compounds that arise from fossil-fuel combustion. The planet earth is prone to experience more warmth than it is expected due to increase in greenhouse gases that have conspired with other pollutants to contaminate the air. Air pollutants known as chlorofluorocarbons commonly called CFC depletes ozone layer in the stratosphere. This will leave holes in the layer which is very thin. These holes are termed ozone holes (Murphy & Mitchell 2013, Wang et al 2011). Ozone layer is very important because it protects the planet earth from the ultraviolet radiations that come from the sun. These radiations, if not checked, have the potential of causing skin cancer and destroylivestocks and plants. Of late, there is gradual reduction in CFC production owing to an accord among nations of the world and it is tagged "the Montreal Protocol".

How does ozone layer depletion harm animals and plants? Ozone particles in troposphere injure or destroy lung tissues of animals and blocks plant respiration by closing the stomata or openings on leaves (Bolaji & Huan 2013, Fares et al 2013). It follows that, when there is insufficient respiration, the plant can photosynthesize and the development will be hampered. To worsen the case, ozone is empowered to penetrate the stomata and rotten the plant cells. This leads to the formation of same in the atmosphere. The formed ozone penetrates plants through pores in the undersides of leaves. The effect of the injury on crops varies. Its radiation affects the growth of leaves in plants. The effects include reduction in leaf elongation and reduction in leaf area. Symptoms of ozone can be seen on the upper part of the affected leaves and it shows as a bronzing and bleaching of the leaf tissues. It can also be revealed in form of chlorosis, that is, loss of colour in the leaves. Increased ozone radiation will necessarily lead to a decrease in photosynthetic activity also known as photoinhibition.

Besides, it can be expressed in mottling, reddening and stunted growth. Undoubtedly, this will lead to reduction in yield. This is due to the fact that because the foliage has been affected, this has also affected photosynthesis and therefore the productivity. The effect of ozone on crops is a function of so many environmental factors (Launiainen et al 2013, Maione et al 2013, Toh et al 2013). Water availability, soil nitrogen and high relative humidity make the plants more prone to the effect of ozone. It has been reported that the bigger the leaf, the more susceptible the leaf becomes to the effect of ozone as the leaves are affected at middle and basal parts. In addition, it has been reported that ozone depletion causes polar ice melt and this alters the habitat for animals and plants living in this region. Ozone depletion has also led to ocean warming, increase in water runoff and less rainfall in the dry parts of the globe and hence limiting water availability for plants and animals.

SULPHUR DIOXIDE AS A POLLUTANT AND ITS EFFECT ON AGRICULTURE

Sulphur dioxide results from coal-burning activities as this is done for the generation of electricity and heating. In addition, it can also be as a result of incomplete combustion of petroleum products and the smelting of sulphur containing ores. Besides, it is one of the main components of acid rain. Effects of sulphur dioxide on crops are regulated by biological and the environmental factors such as plant type, sunlight intensity, humidity, temperature and the age of the plant (Chen et al 2013, Dai & Blanes-Vidal 2013). So, the environment plays a considerable role determining the effect and influence of sulphur dioxide. Just as the ozone, sulphur dioxide enters the plants through the stomata and this leads to negative effect on the plants which can be said to be either acute or chronic. Acute injury is as a result of absorption of high quantity of sulphur dioxide within a short time.

The effect is seen on leaves as appearance of bifacial lesion that is prominent along the margins of affected leaves. Appearance of the necrotic portion varies from a fair tan or close to white coloration; it can as well be as deep as orange-red (Fu et al 2013, Gibson et al 2013). Expanded leaves are the most prone to acute sulphur dioxide damage this is because the old and new leaves are more resistant. Contrary to acute injury, chronic injury is caused by long-term absorption of sulphur dioxide in sub-lethal quantity. The effects appear as yellowing of the leaves and plants differ in their susceptibility. The susceptibility is a function of geographical location, climate, stage of growth and maturation.

NITROUS OXIDE AS A POLLUTANT AND ITS EFFECT ON AGRICULTURE

There is increase in the nitrous oxide in the atmosphere through the agricultural and industrial activities. From agriculture, nitrous oxide arises from the use of inorganic nitrogen fertilizers. Increasing nitrogen (N) application on agricultural soil has heightened the emissions from lands. The production of N_2O is a function of the availability of mineral N as Nis the substrate for both nitrification and denitrification. In addition, the two processes also depend on soil temperature, soil water content and availability of labile organic compounds in the case of denitrification(Velthof et al 2009, Xia et al 2013). Nitrification is defined as aerobic process in which ammonium (NH_4^+)is oxidized to nitrate (NO_3^-).

Nitrification is effected by autotrophic organisms and some heterotrophic bacteria, fungi and algae. On the other hand, denitrification is the anaerobic reduction of NO_3^- to N_2O and N_2. Some bacteria have been identified as having the ability to effect denitrification. They are anaerobic and they can change to NO_3^- as the end electron acceptor if the amount of O_2 in the soil becomesreduced. The relationship between the two processes (nitrification and denitrification) and their contribution to N_2O production differ as it depends on climate, condition of the soil and management of the soil (Allen et al 2007, Bhatia et al 2011). Apart from these two conditions, increase in rainfall, bad drainage, fine soil texture and increased organic carbon materials heightens denitrification. Meanwhile, reduced rainfall, efficient drainage, good aeration and soil texture that are not fine increase nitrification and related N_2O emission.

FLUORIDE AS A POLLUTANT AND ITS EFFECT ON AGRICULTURE

Fluoridesare released into the atmosphere from activities like coal burning, production of brick, ceramics, glass, tiles, fertilizers, and hydrofluoric acid. During production of these materials, some compounds that contain fluorine are released into the air. Fluorides gain entrance into the leaves through the stomata of the plants. It is then permeates the leaves and move to the margins of broad leaves and to the tips of leaves of monocot plants. These parts of the affected leave accommodate and accumulate fluorides which will eventually harm the crops. Fluoride tends to cause yellow mottling or tan coloured damage on ends of leaves of the affected plants (Brougham et al 2013, Davison & Weinstein 2006). Young leaves are the most affected and this will subsequently affect or retard the growth of such plants. In some plants, leaves may not be affected but fruits because of the resistance that the leaves have. Example of such plants is peaches.

Susceptibility differs among different species of plants, locations and even varieties of plants of the same species. Examples of plants that are susceptible are grape, apricot and sweet corn. Tip burn that results from fluorides destroys the aesthetic and economic values of ornamental plants.

How does fluoride affect livestock animals? Eighty five percent of fluoride that animals consume is found in bones, teeth and calcified tissues of the animals as mineral (Ahmad et al 2013, Manoharan et al 2007). When fluoride is not utilized by body, it is, at times, excreted out as part of the urine. So, teeth and bones of the animals are the most susceptible to the negative influence of fluoride. Teeth are most susceptible especially when they are young or at the formative stage.

Animals that consumes more than 40 PPM fluoride will possibly be affected by lameness and experience easily worn out teeth. So, animals are not expected to consume more than 40 PPM annually. When developing teeth are exposed to fluorides, they may develop with colourvariation and this situation is described as mottling. If the concentration of fluoride increases, it may cause dental abnormalities like pitting of enamel and development of brittle, chalky and easily eroded teeth.At the extreme, a more deleterious effect is observed as it can lead to excruciating pain, wearing of teeth to the gum and it can prevent the animals from drinking cold water and chewing. When there is excessive fluoride ingestion, metacarpals, metatarsals parts of leg's bones and lower jaw of cattle may become enlarged. Exposure of cattle to hard ground can lead to fluorotic hoof and it can make the animal to become lame. When the fluorine consumption advances, it causes fluorosis characterized by mineralization of the ligaments, tendons and the structures surrounding the joints which eventually leads to lameness (Jonsson & Aoyama 2007, Niu et al 2009, Weinstein & Davison 2003).

Essentially, when water or air is polluted by fluoride and cattle ingest such at deleterious concentrations, it leads to tooth destruction, lameness and this prevents the animals from standing, eating or grazing; it reduces the milk production by the dam or dairy cattle and affects the weight of the beef cattle.Fluoride also affects man; it affects farmers who tend and look after the animals. They can suffer from skeletal fluorosis. Many nonskeletal symptoms have been reported and this includes gastrointestinal complaints and disorder, loss of desire for food, bad breath and rheumatism.Furthermore, x-ray revealed fluoride induced disease conditions which have caused structural alterations in bones, weakening of bones which induceosteoarthritis. Fluoride has also been implicated in bronchitis, pneumonia, tuberculosisand upper respiratory infections. When farmers are affected with these fluoride induced diseases, it will definitely hamper their activities, efficiency and effectiveness. This will reduce productivities from farms and it will also have economic effect (Ben Abdallah et al 2006, Franzaring et al 2007).

AMMONIA AS A POLLUTANT AND ITS EFFECT ON AGRICULTURE

Odour has become an issue of concern as it affects or influences the air quality and among other sources, bad management of agricultural activities, especially livestock production, has been implicated for production of ammonia. Ammonia is a by-product of animal waste and it results from poor usage of protein in feed by animals (Allen et al 2011, Carozzi et al 2013). Animals are fed good feeds that have the required nutritional qualities and good crude protein source is often one of the feed ingredients. Examples of crude protein ingredients are: soybean meal, groundnut cake, fish meal and meat meal. It arises if the proteinous content of ingredients is not well combusted or metabolized into products like milk, meat and eggs.

It is produced in form of urea (in mammals) or uric acids (poultry) in the urine of livestock and birds and in the form of urea, ammonia and organic nitrogen in animal faeces. Changing of urea or uric acid to ammonia needs enzyme (urease), and this is excreted in animal faeces (de Vries et al 2011, Eory et al 2013). Disintegration of complex organic nitrogen status in droppings or faeces happens not rapidly; it takes months or years. At any rate, nitrogen is changed to either ammonium (NH_4) when it is acidic or neutral pH conditions or ammonia (NH_3) at higher pH levels.

Ammonia is classified as one of the indoor sources of air pollution. This is because the gas does gather in non-well ventilated pens. Ammonia tends to have deleterious effects on animal health, activities and productivities. Animal that are reared in ammonia laden pens will have reduced body weight gain when the ammonia in the pen is 25 parts per million (ppm) or when it is higher than that. In the same corollary, when man is exposed to ammonia, his health may become jeopardized as it leads to irritation of his lungs and eyes (Hamaoui-Laguel et al, Ni et al 2012).

When there are many farms in an environment or location, and manure is poorly managed, then there will be outdoor ammonia challenges. There is likelihood of having deposition of ammonia in the atmosphere in the surface waters and if there is interaction with phosphorus, it can lead to eutrophication and support for the growth of deleterious algae. Eutrophication will reduce the growth fish and other aquatic livestocks animals. Dissolved ammonia in water bodies is not only dangerous to fish and aquatic animals, but it can also be changed to dangerous nitrates. Increased nitrate levels in drinking water are poses a threat to humans, causing dangerous depletion of oxygen levels in babies and this is known as "blue-baby syndrome" in some quarters.

It can also lead to abortions and cancer. Crops can be damaged by when grown in an overfertilized location possibly arising from ammonia deposition if the farm is situated close to ammonia sources. Accumulation of ammonia on soils with a poor buffering ability can lead to soil acidification and possibly, depletion of alkali cations (Philippe et al 2011, Rebolledo et al 2013). Moreover, apart from its effects on plants, water and edaphic materials, ammonia and its collusion with other compounds can form what is known as particulate matter (PM) and it can have a diameter of about 2.5 microns or possibly less and it is often called PM 2.5. The size of the PM allows them to penetrate into the lungs. Of course, when the lungs are affected, it is going to have a negative implication on respiratory and cardiovascular parts of the body.

This Pm 2.5 can also lead to untimely death and incessant hospitalization of children, women and people with health challenges that are related to lung such as asthma and emphysema. Farmers that work in ammonia accumulated farms or environment is susceptible to these and when farmers are affected, it will have its toll on agricultural activities and productivities (Theobald et al 2012, Velthof et al 2012, Vogt et al 2013).

AIR POLLUTION FROM COMBUSTION

Common products that result from combustion include the following: propylene, carbon monoxide, acetylene and ethylene. Apart from ethylene, it will take very high concentration before plants are seriously affected. For instance, flowers are adversely affected by ethylene. Its production has been observed in leaking pipelines, chemical industries and automobile industries (Magara- Gomez et al 2012, Seshadri et al 2013).

It has been reported that ozone, peroxyacetyl nitrate and ethylene result from interactions of chemical products in the air and they can cause plant injury. Ozone is primary contaminants influencing agricultural crops and livestocks. It has caused serious injuries in crops:tobacco, fruits, spinach and trees. The injuries inflicted by ozone are revealed as: tipburn, streaks, stipple and possibly yellowing of leaves. Symptoms revealed by peroxyacetyl nitrate are silver leaf and leaf banding (Williams et al 2012, Yu et al 2012).

ACID GASES AND ITS EFFECTS ON AGRICULTURE

Examples of acid gases are sulphur dioxide, chlorine and fluorides. Hydrogen fluoride has been reported to be very toxic to crops as it is possible to cause injuries to crops when exposed to concentrations less than one part per billion. At the beginning, the injury is done to chlorophyll, leading to chlorosis and then complete dam (Baek et al 2004, Brink et al 2005) age of the plant. The tolerance threshold of plant to hydrogen fluoride differs and plants that accommodate it are regarded as being tolerant. For example, maize is more prone to it than tomatoes. Admittedly, SO_2released into the air during the combustion of oil and coal stimulates the development of necrosis.

At particular level, depending on the crop, SO_2 will begin to have negative effect on plants when the stomata are not closed (Roumeliotis et al 2010, Tavares et al 2011). Necessarily, high relative humidity, availability of light, optimum temperature and availability of water are conditions that plants need to open their stomata. Besides, plants that do not open their stomata are much more tolerant to SO_2. However, the sulphur dioxide absorbed by the leaf reacts with water to form toxic sulphite. Meanwhile, this is oxidized and become harmless. So, it is convenient to say that the harm that sulphur dioxide does depends on the absorption rate by the crop as speedy absorption will quickly damage the plant life. Chlorine as pollutant will lead to bleaching and death of the leaves (Vetter & Bester 2006).

WATER POLLUTION

Soil and Water Pollution and Concomitant Effects on Agriculture

Indispensability of soil and water to agriculture cannot be overemphasized. They play key role in agriculture. Therefore because of their active and irreplaceable role, it is important to ensure that their sanctity is preserved and maintained. This becomes important because once they are polluted, agricultural activities become hampered and this will have a declining effect on the health of plants and livestock. Pollution of the same will lead to reduction in yield and economic loss to farmers. The following may have the negative on agriculture when they cause pollution. They include: plant nutrient, sediment, inorganic salt and minerals, infectious agents, organic wastes, industrial and agricultural chemicals and heat.

SEDIMENT AND PLANT NUTRIENTS

It is a valuable material that removes from land and moves to another place thereby reducing the quality of waters it joins. It disturbs free flow of water as the channels are blocked. It also reduces the irrigation canals, farm ponds and irrigation reservoir. Undoubtedly, this act does not only heighten the cost of water clarification but it also jeopardizes the dissolved-oxygen balance in water. The quality is reduced as its value becomes depleted (Bartoli et al 2012, Collins et al 2012). Nutrients are needed by plants for optimal growth and maximum production of fruits. But, it is likely that they become displaced when they become unavailable to plants as they are taken away by surface water and possibly located in the ground water. When that arises, as it does at times, then such nutrients have become pollutants.

In that case, aquatic weeds become nourished by such nutrients that are from agricultural wastes, manure, municipal and industrial wastes. Invariably, the weeds in the aquatic environment grow and become disturbances to free flow of water, irrigation and drainage channels and this will invariably increase the cost of maintenance (Vatn et al 2006).

ORGANIC WASTES AND AGRICULTURAL POLLUTION

Pollution by organic wastes is becoming a serious topical issue. It occurs when a substantial volume of organic materials from garbage, pulp mill, food processing industries, municipal sewage and animal farms provide substrates for microorganisms and they are discharged into water courses like lakes, rivers and even seas. Organic pollution has led to rise in organic content in aquatic ecosystems and subsequently to eutrophication. Worthy of note is the fact that polluted water can jeopardize water quality thus reducing use of such waters for many purposes. (Echols et al 2009) Moreover, these organic wastes may also encourage and provide conducive environment for disease causing (pathogenic) organisms.

Organic wastes become good substrates because they are often rich in carbohydrates, lipids, nucleic acids and protein. As the organic materials are undergoing decomposition, the available oxygen in the water will be depleted and this will have negative consequences on the water ecosystem. The reduction in oxygen availability in the water can lead to lowered fitness or even asphyxiation. In addition, the organic matter in the water course tend to contain solid materials which limit the availability or activities of photosynthetic organisms and it also affect the structure, positions, and locations of the water beds and this makes the ecosystem inhabitable for some organisms.This pollutionwill, among other things, lead to production of ammonia (Gonçalves et al 2011, Westerman & Bicudo 2005).

Moreover, when the organic matter accumulation increases, it leads to increase in turbidity of water and hence reduction of light availability to photosynthetic organisms. It is disturbing to note that pollution by these organic wastes makes the water unsuitable for recreational purpose, domestic use and irrigation.

ALGAE AND WATER POLLUTION

It is important to discuss the significant role that algae play in rivers, lakes and possibly seas. This is because waters algae are the primary producers in bodies of water. Notably, provision of the algal nutrients in water through organic wastes may promote the development of algal species leading to high surface growths that will consequently reduce the water quality and affect the use of such waters (Maestre-Valero et al 2013, Pell et al 2013). Algae can form thick mats on surface of waters and this is referred to as water bloom. Owing to the thickness of this bloom on water surface, penetration of light is hindered and this reduces breakdown of organic materials in the waters. Moreover, the death of these algae will further complicate the pollution because the dead algae may not decompose fast because of the turbidity of the waters. Whatever changes, the number and types of algae strongly influences all organisms in the chain including fish and other aquatic organisms.

Algae are also reported to be one of the primary determinants of tastes and odors in waters.Blue-green algae and coloured flagellates (particularly *Chrysophyta* and *Euglenophyta*) are the most reported algae that cause such challenges in water availability but green algae may also be necessarily involved. Some algae produce an attractive scent similar to that of flowersand vegetables.

POLLUTED WATER AND SOIL CARRYING INFECTIOUS BODIES AND CHEMICALS THAT ARE INIMICAL TO AGRICULTURE

Infectious organisms are often carried by water and soil if not carried by air. During agricultural practices, virus and bacterial diseases of crops are often being carried by equipment or tools that work on polluted soil. Weeds seeds can be carried during irrigation using polluted water. To mention but few, some of the animal diseases that water can carry are: salmonellosis, hog cholera, mastitis, tuberculosis, histoplasmosis, coccidiosis, anthrax and leptospirosis.

Crops and animals are often prone to diseases that are either water or soil borne (Oberholster et al 2013). Chemicals in waters and soil can have devastating effects on crops, and livestocks. Fish in rivers have been killed because of effects of insecticides or pesticides pollutants that got in contact with the river or streams. This can be the case when such chemicals enter drainage or ditches. Examples of such chemicals are: fungicides, herbicides, insecticides, detergents and nematocides. It is possible to experience the movement of herbicides and other chemicals to non targeted areas as the wind blows the chemicals when it is applied aerially or on ground.

So, the chemicals may affect even the roadside plants. Bad enough, detection of these chemicals by the public or the specific consumers of the agricultural producers may stimulate negative reactions from same and, of course, the economy of the concerned farmer will be affected (Collins & McGonigle 2008, Shi et al 2009).

CONTROL OF ENVIRONMENTAL POLLUTION

In order to control or reduce pollution and its effects on agriculture, it is important that some practical steps must be taken. Governments must set up regulatory bodies corporate bodies, farmers and non-governmental organisations must also be ready to cooperate with the regulatory bodies set up by government. There must also be sensitization towards the control of pollution. The entire populace must be educated and be informed about the detrimental effects of environmental pollution. The protection of environment is the duty of everybody. It must be borne in mind that pollutions can be stopped if there is genuine and sincere loyalty to this goal. Many approaches can be adopted in order to solve this problem.

USAGE OF FOSSIL FUEL EFFICIENTLY, REDUCTION OF HEAT LOSS AND USAGE OF ALTERNATIVE ENERGY SOURCES

It the fossil fuel will be used efficiently, and then there is possibility of reducing air pollution. Users of such fuels must regularly service the engines as this will reduce fuel usage by 5-17%. Farmers encouraged choosing appropriate tractors or machines on farm. They can use the ones that demand lowest power and still do the work effectively. If there is avoidance of unimportant journeys and cultivation practices that will use machines and therefore production of gases that will pollute the air, then, there will be reduction in pollutions (Dong et al 2012, Manfren et al 2011).

The fixed machines are to be maintained and serviced regularly. By that, the manufacturer's instructions should be followed religiously. Examples of such machines are: grain drier and bulk milk tanks.Usage and installation of thermal screens can be help in conservation of energy and retention of heat in buildings that need heat. Examples of such buildings are: Mushroom houses, polythene covered structures and heated glass houses. Such conservation will prevent energy dissipation through infra-red radiation, ventilation and convection. Besides, loss of heat can be maintained by proper servicing of boilers and burners and using walls, roofs and heating pipes that are insulated. It will be of help in prevention of pollution if people are encouraged to begin to use non-fossil sources of energy for such will minimize the release of pollutants. Such alternatives are: biogas from manure digestion, water power, heat pumps, straw-burning boilers, solar power and wind power (Ozyurt & Ekinci 2011, Zhang et al 2012a).

Efficient Utilization of Fertilizers and Protection of Natural Environment

Production and manufacturing of fertilizers consumes a considerable quantity of fossil fuel. Owing to this assertion, it is therefore suggested that the production and distribution must take into consideration the needs and the environmental condition. This will no doubt, help in ameliorating the environmental pollution. It is also important to borne in mind the soil analysis available soil nutrients before the application of the organic manure or any other fertilizers. Farmers are enjoined to ensure that the spreaders of fertilizers (machine) are well maintained (1990, Aguilera et al 2013, Qiao et al 2012).

Protection of natural environment helps in prevention of environment. In the process of converting the uncultivated land to arable land, agricultural practices like clearing, stumping, ploughing, harrowing, ridging, planting, weeding and harvesting involve the use of machines and this will no doubt, contribute to CO_2 and nitrous oxide production as these activities encourages soil bacteria to produce these gases via respiration. In addition, the machines also release pollutants into the environment.

Minimizing Methane and Nitrous Oxide Emission Production

Methane emission can be reduced by following the animal production policies strictly. When farmers are given specific or maximum number of livestock to be produced per year, they are encouraged to stick to that, otherwise, they should be penalized. Diets of animals are to be regulated and modified such that production of methane on the account of diets will be negligible (Adams et al 2012). Proper management of manure and slurry should be embraced adopting a regulated anaerobic digestion procedure as this will lead to production of needed biogas for farmstead use.

As per the reduction of nitrous oxide production, it is important to service the fertilizer spreader in order to ensure there is accurate application. It is also important to have good planning concerning crop nutrient management. Farmers will need to have updated nutrient profile of the farmland for this will help in determining how much fertilizer is needed and should be applied. It will also be proper and useful if the use of machinery is minimized. Another way to reduce the nitrous oxide production is to embrace the incorporation of manure or organic materials in place of inorganic fertilizers (Liang et al 2013).

Reduction of Ammonia Production from Farmland

In order to reduce the level of ammonia production, it is important to regulate and properly calculate the crude protein content of the formulated diets for the animals as this will help to ensure that animals are not fed more proteins than what is needed or necessary for the production of milk, egg or meat production. This has the possibility of minimizing the quantity of nitrogen produced as urea in urine and faeces or as uric acid in birds for these will be converted to ammonia (Carozzi et al 2013). Phase feeding has been recommended in poultry and pig farming for this will ensure that different nutritional demands by different animals and at different phases are met.

Another step that can be used in minimizing production of ammonia is to ensure that animal pens are kept clean. Good cleanliness will not only reduce the ammonia production, it will as well forestall production of odour which can come from unclean environment. This can be achieved by regularly scrapping, washing floor and flushing excreta or solid manure into designated place, possibly, the lagoon. Furthermore, in order to reduce the ammonia production from the birds, ensuring that droppings dry fast will be of help and this can be achieved that making sure that the droppings are dry and crumbly. In addition, water spillage should be avoided completely. Ammonia can escape from the slurry intended for biogas production. This can be reduced by using a tank with a lid, permitting a crust to form on the slurry or covering the slurry with straw and avoiding stirring. In addition to the above assertions, to reduce pollution by ammonia, farmers are enjoined to only apply quantity of manure or slurry that is needed to meet the crop nutrient requirement of the crop (Velthof et al 2009, Winiwarter & Klimont 2011).

It is important to take into consideration the nutrient requirement of the crop and the fertility of the soil. It may be necessary to dilute the slurry before application and method of application is equally very important. Three major methods of application have been identified and they are: injection, band spreading and splash plate spreading. Among these, the most efficient is injection method.Climatic parameters like: rainfall, wind speed and temperature do influence and affect the ammonia emissions from slurries.

The place of soil type and the degree of wetness of such soil on ammonia emission cannot be overemphasized. Time of application of slurry is also very important; it is suggested that slurry be applied in the morning or towards the evening time. When manure is applied beneath the soil, pollution by ammonia is minimized (Vaddella et al 2013).

Prevention of Burning Wood and Vegetation on Farm

Many farmers, especially in Sub saharan Africa are still fond of burning the vegetation as a way of clearing the farm land in preparation for next planting season. Farm wastes are not to be burnt as this will add to the greenhouse gases into the atmosphere. In addition to that, burning pollutes the air with poisonous gases, grit and dust. In addition, deleterious chemical residues can also pollute groundwater, surface water and the soil (Bari et al 2010). There are suggested better methods preferred to burning. They are: reusing and recycling materials, composting, burning in an authorized or designated incineration plants or furnace or outright disposal of wastes at authorized or designated areas. Farmers are not expected to burn cereal wastes or crop residues; rather they are to plough them back into the soil. These will provide good substrates for the microorganisms or the biofertilizers (Qin & Xie 2011, Zhang et al 2012c).

It is also possible to consider such crop residues as feed or feed ingredients for farm animals. Besides, management of animal carcasses can also influence the ammonia production. Poor management of animal carcasses will increase the ammonia production. It is good to follow the animal health environmental permit in the locality. Some will permit burial of the carcass while some will permit incineration of the carcass.

Reduction of Noise and Dusts Pollution

Noise and dusts can be prevented by using buildings, trees or hedges to prevent neighbours from dusts and noise that emanate from the farm. If the windows and doors are shut, it will also prevent the noise and dusts from spreading. If the equipment is thoroughly maintained, it will prevent it from making unnecessary noise. Insulation of the building with acoustic materials can be of help.

Use of Algae in Reduction of Pollution

Some algae are grown for sewage treatment together with bacteria. Examples of such algae are: *Chlorella, Chlamydomonas*and*Scendensmus*. Organic sewage wastes broken down by bacteria are utilized by algae for their growth. When such algae have grown abundantly, they are often removed and add them as part of animal feed as they serve as source of protein. Thus, contaminated water is cleaned via the activities of bacteria and algae. It is a good and positive "service" from bacteria and algae (El-Sikaily et al 2007,

Hoko & Makado 2011). In addition to this, water containing metals as contaminants can be cleaned through by the growth of algae like *Chlorella* on such waters.

The algae absorb and use such metals for their growth and from time to time, such algae can be weeded and destroyed. Notably, algae like *Duniellatertiolacta, Skeletonemacostatum, Cricosphaeracarterae* and *Amphidiumcarterae* can be used for the cleaning of waters that are polluted by oil. Especially in oil producing areas where is the likelihood of oil spillage. Therefore, growth of these algae in polluted water plays an important part in purification of such waters and by and large, algae play important role in food chain of aquatic ecosystem (Shen et al 2011).

LEGISLATION AGAINST POLLUTION

Pollution control isso important that there should be legislations and laws from arm(s) of governments prohibiting pollution of water, soil, air and any other media. There must be stiff penalty against anyone who contravenes the laws. It is a joint responsibility of everyone to cooperate with the regulating bodies in order to ensure that our environment is sincerely unpolluted. The laws need to be stated from the specific to the general, from the local municipalities to the states or provinces and then to the international organisations. Steps must be both reactive measures to foresight management; emissions fromcrude activities to emissions from technology driven systems must be prevented (Insa et al 2010, Papu-Zamxaka et al 2010).

The trends and styles that promote and increase pollution and contamination must be resisted. Undoubtedly, coalition among all tiers of governments in support of pollution legislation and regulation will go a long way in reinvigorating protocols and commitments that will be of help in fighting this battle. At the international level, enforcement will primarilybe shouldered by nations because countries differ in their readiness for acceptance of imposed air pollution legislation.

CONCLUSION

From the foregoing, it is evident that environmental pollution does affect the total wellbeing of agricultural crops and livestock. In effect, this threatens human livelihood, national revenue, food and feed availability-security, international trade, availability of raw materials for industrial use, transport, foreign exchange earnings and job opportunities. Hence, farmers, transporters, engineers, scientists, environmentalists, other professionals and indeed everyone is implored to take into cognizance the fact that our actions or inactions will affect the state of the environment.

Moreover, the issue of environmental protection is a global responsibility that deserves international attention for the promotion of total wellbeing of man. Governments at local or municipality level, state or provinces level and nations are enjoined to give this the attention that it requires so as to boost our agricultural productivities and foster better life on earth.

REFERENCES

Adams CA, Andrews JE, Jickells T. 2012. Nitrous Oxide and Methane Fluxes vs. Carbon, Nitrogen and Phosphorous Burial in New Intertidal and Saltmarsh Sediments. Science of The Total Environment 434: 240-51

Aguilera E, Lassaletta L, Sanz-Cobena A, Garnier J, Vallejo A. 2013. The Potential of Organic Fertilizers and Water Management to Reduce N2O Emissions in Mediterranean Climate Cropping Systems. A Review. Agriculture, Ecosystems and Environment 164: 32-52.

Ahmad MN, Büker P, Khalid S, Van Den Berg L, Shah HU, et al. 2013. Effects of Ozone on Crops in North-west Pakistan. Environmental Pollution 174: 244-49.

Allen DE, Dalal RC, Rennenberg H, Meyer RL, Reeves S, Schmidt S. 2007. Spatial and Temporal Variation of Nitrous Oxide and Methane Flux Between Subtropical Mangrove Sediments and the Atmosphere. Soil Biology and Biochemistry 39: 622-31.

Allen R, Myles L, Heuer MW. 2011. Ambient Ammonia in Terrestrial Ecosystems: A Comparative Study in the Tennessee Valley, USA. Science of The Total Environment 409: 2768-72.

Baek BH, Aneja VP, Tong Q. 2004. Chemical Coupling Between Ammonia, Acid Gases, and Fine Particles. Environmental Pollution 129: 89-98.

Bari MA, Baumbach G, Kuch B, Scheffknecht G. 2010. Temporal Variation and Impact of Wood Smoke Pollution on a Residential Area in Southern Germany. Atmospheric Environment 44: 3823-32.

Bartoli G, Papa S, Sagnella E, Fioretto A. 2012. Heavy Metal Content in Sediments Along the Calore River: Relationships with Physical–chemical Characteristics. Journal of Environmental Management 95, Supplement: S9-S14.

Ben Abdallah F, Elloumi N, Mezghani I, Boukhris M, Garrec J-P. 2006. Survival Strategies of Pomegranate and Almond Trees in a Fluoride Polluted Area. Comptes Rendus Biologies 329: 200-07.

Bhatia A, Ghosh A, Kumar V, Tomer R, Singh SD, Pathak H. 2011. Effect of Elevated Tropospheric Ozone on Methane and Nitrous Oxide Emission from Rice Soil in North India. Agriculture, Ecosystems & Environment 144: 21-28.

Bolaji BO, Huan Z. 2013. Ozone Depletion and Global Warming: Case for the Use of Natural Refrigerant – A Review. Renewable and Sustainable Energy Reviews 18: 49-54.

Brink C, van Ierland E, Hordijk L, Kroeze C. 2005. Cost_Effective Emission Abatement in Agriculture in the Presence of Interrelations: Cases for the Netherlands and Europe. Ecological Economics 53: 59-74.

Brougham KM, Roberts SR, Davison AW, Port GR. 2013. The Impact of Aluminium Smelter Shut-down on the Concentration of Fluoride in Vegetation and Soils. Environmental Pollution 178: 89-96.

Calheiros CSC, Quitério PVB, Silva G, Crispim LFC, Brix H, et al. 2012. Use of Constructed Wetland Systems with Arundo and Sarcocornia for Polishing High Salinity Tannery Wastewater. Journal of Environmental Management 95: 66-71.

Cariñanos P, Casares-Porcel M. 2011. Urban Green Zones and Related Pollen Allergy: A Review. Some Guidelines for Designing Spaces with Low Allergy Impact. Landscape and Urban Planning 101: 205-14.

Carozzi M, Loubet B, Acutis M, Rana G, Ferrara RM. 2013. Inverse Dispersion Modelling Highlights the Efficiency of Slurry Injection to Reduce Ammonia Losses by Agriculture in the Po Valley (Italy). Agricultural and Forest Meteorology 171-172: 306-18.

Chen W-H, Chen S-M, Hung C-I. 2013. A Theoretical Approach of Absorption Processes of Air Pollutants in Sprays Under Droplet–droplet Interaction. Science of The Total Environment 444: 336-46.

Collins AL, McGonigle DF. 2008. Monitoring and Modelling Diffuse Pollution from Agriculture for Policy Support: UK and European Experience. Environmental Science & Policy 11: 97-101.

Collins AL, Zhang Y, McChesney D, Walling DE, Haley SM, Smith P. 2012. Sediment Source Tracing in a Lowland Agricultural Catchment in Southern England Using a Modified Procedure Combining Statistical Analysis and Numerical Modelling. Science of The Total Environment 414: 301-17.

Dai XR, Blanes-Vidal V. 2013. Emissions of Ammonia, Carbon Dioxide, and Hydrogen Sulfide from Swine Wastewater during and After Acidification Treatment: Effect of pH, Mixing and Aeration. Journal of Environmental Management 115: 147-54.

Davison AW, Weinstein LH. 2006. Chapter 8: Some Problems Relating to Fluorides in the Environment: Effects on Plants and Animals in Advances in Fluorine Science, ed. T Alain, pp. 251-98: Elsevier.

de Vries W, Leip A, Reinds GJ, Kros J, Lesschen JP, Bouwman AF. 2011. Comparison of Land Nitrogen Budgets for European Agriculture by Various Modeling Approaches. Environmental Pollution 159: 3254-68.

Dong C, Huang GH, Cai YP, Liu Y. 2012. An Inexact Optimization Modeling Approach for Supporting Energy Systems Planning and Air Pollution Mitigation in Beijing City. Energy 37: 673-88.

Echols KR, Meadows JC, Orazio CE. 2009. Pollution of Aquatic Ecosystems II: Hydrocarbons, Synthetic Organics, Radionuclides, Heavy Metals, Acids, and Thermal Pollution In Encyclopedia of Inland Waters, ed. EL Editor-in-Chief: Gene, pp. 120-28. Oxford: Academic Press.

El-Sikaily A, Nemr AE, Khaled A, Abdelwehab O. 2007. Removal of Toxic Chromium from Wastewater Using Green Alga Ulva lactuca and its Activated Carbon. Journal of Hazardous Materials 148: 216-28.

Eory V, Topp CFE, Moran D. 2013. Multiple-pollutant Cost-effectiveness of Greenhouse Gas Mitigation Measures in the UK Agriculture. Environmental Science & Policy 27: 55-67.

Fares S, Matteucci G, Scarascia Mugnozza G, Morani A, Calfapietra C, et al. 2013. Testing of Models of Stomatal Ozone Fluxes with Field Measurements in a Mixed Mediterranean Forest. Atmospheric Environment 67: 242-51.

Franzaring J, Klumpp A, Fangmeier A. 2007. Active Biomonitoring of Airborne Fluoride Near an HF Producing Factory Using Standardised Grass Cultures. Atmospheric Environment 41: 4828-40.

Fu X, Wang S, Zhao B, Xing J, Cheng Z, et al. 2013. Emission Inventory of Primary Pollutants and Chemical Speciation in 2010 for the Yangtze River Delta Region, China. Atmospheric Environment 70: 39-50.

Gibson MD, Heal MR, Li Z, Kuchta J, King GH, et al. 2013. The Spatial and Seasonal Variation of Nitrogen Dioxide and Sulfur Dioxide in Cape Breton Highlands National Park, Canada, and the Association with Lichen Abundance. Atmospheric Environment 64: 303-11.

Gonçalves C, Evtyugina M, Alves C, Monteiro C, Pio C, Tomé M. 2011. Organic Particulate Emissions from Field Burning of Garden and Agriculture Residues. Atmospheric Research 101: 666-80.

Hamaoui-Laguel L, Meleux F, Beekmann M, Bessagnet B, Génermont S, et al. Improving Ammonia Emissions in Air Quality Modelling for France. Atmospheric Environment.

Hansen B, Thorling L, Dalgaard T, Erlandsen M. 2010. Trend Reversal of Nitrate in Danish Groundwater-a reflection of Agricultural Practices and Nitrogen Surpluses Since 1950. Environmental science & technology 45: 228-34.

Hillocks RJ. 2012. Farming with Fewer Pesticides: EU Pesticide Review and Resulting Challenges for UK Agriculture. Crop Protection 31: 85-93.

Hofmann P. 2013. Wasted Waste—Disappearing Reuse at the Peri-urban Interface. Environmental Science & Policy 31: 13-22.

Hoko Z, Makado PK. 2011. Optimization of Algal Removal Process at Morton Jaffray Water Works, Harare, Zimbabwe. Physics and Chemistry of the Earth, Parts A/B/C 36: 1141-50.

Insa E, Zamorano M, López R. 2010. Critical Review of Medical Waste Legislation in Spain. Resources, Conservation and Recycling 54: 1048-59.

Jonsson CM, Aoyama H. 2007. In vitro Effect of Agriculture Pollutants and Their Joint Action on Pseudokirchneriella Subcapitata Acid Phosphatase. Chemosphere 69: 849-55.

Kowalkowski T, Pastuszak M, Igras J, Buszewski B. 2012. Differences in Emission of Nitrogen and Phosphorus into the Vistula and Oder Basins in 1995–2008—Natural and Anthropogenic Causes (MONERIS model). Journal of Marine Systems 89: 48-60.

L. Smith J, Lee K. 2003. Soil as a Source of Dust and Implications for Human Health in Advances in Agronomy, pp. 1-32: Academic Press.

Lau MHY, Leung KMY, Wong SWY, Wang H, Yan Z-G. 2012. Environmental Policy, Legislation and Management of Persistent Organic Pollutants (POPs) in China. Environmental Pollution 165: 182-92.

Launiainen S, Katul GG, Grönholm T, Vesala T. 2013. Partitioning Ozone Fluxes Between Canopy and Forest Floor by Measurements and a Multi-layer Model. Agricultural and Forest Meteorology 173: 85-99.

Liang L, Lal R, Du Z, Wu W, Meng F. 2013. Estimation of Nitrous Oxide and Methane Emission from Livestock of Urban Agriculture in Beijing. Agriculture, Ecosystems & Environment 170: 28-35.

Liaquat AM, Kalam MA, Masjuki HH, Jayed MH. 2010. Potential Emissions Reduction in Road Transport Sector Using Biofuel in Developing Countries. Atmospheric Environment 44: 3869-77.

Maestre-Valero JF, Martínez-Alvarez V, Nicolas E. 2013. Physical, Chemical and Microbiological Effects of Suspended Shade Cloth Covers on Stored Water for Irrigation. Agricultural Water Management 118: 70-78.

Magara- Gomez KT, Olson MR, Okuda T, Walz KA, Schauer JJ. 2012. Sensitivity of Hazardous Air Pollutant Emissions to the Combustion of Blends of Petroleum Diesel and Biodiesel Fuel. Atmospheric Environment 50: 307-13.

Maher K, Steefel CI, White AF, Stonestrom DA. 2009. The Role of Reaction Affinity and Secondary Minerals in Regulating Chemical Weathering Rates at the Santa Cruz Soil Chronosequence, California. Geochimica et Cosmochimica Acta 73: 2804-31.

Maione M, Giostra U, Arduini J, Furlani F, Graziosi F, et al. 2013. Ten Years of Continuous Observations of Stratospheric Ozone Depleting Gases at Monte Cimone (Italy) — Comments on the Effectiveness of the Montreal Protocol from a Regional Perspective. Science of The Total Environment 445-446: 155-64.

Manfren M, Caputo P, Costa G. 2011. Paradigm Shift in Urban Energy Systems Through Distributed Generation: Methods and Models. Applied Energy 88: 1032-48.

Manoharan V, Loganathan P, Tillman RW, Parfitt RL. 2007. Interactive Effects of Soil Acidity and Fluoride on Soil Solution Aluminium Chemistry and Barley (Hordeum vulgare L.) Root Growth. Environmental Pollution 145: 778-86.

Masiá A, Ibáñez M, Blasco C, Sancho JV, Picó Y, Hernández F. 2013. Combined use of Liquid Chromatography Triple Quadrupole Mass Spectrometry and Liquid Chromatography Quadrupole Time-of-flight Mass Spectrometry in Systematic Screening of Pesticides and Other Contaminants in Water Samples. Analytica Chimica Acta 761: 117-27.

Menció A, Boy M, Mas-Pla J. 2011. Analysis of Vulnerability Factors that Control Nitrate Occurrence in Natural Springs (Osona Region, NE Spain). Science of the Total Environment 409: 3049-58.

Mishra K, Sharma RC, Kumar S. 2012. Contamination Levels and Spatial Distribution of Organochlorine Pesticides in Soils from India. Ecotoxicology and Environmental Safety 76: 215-25.

Murphy BR, Mitchell FJG. 2013. An Association Between Past Levels of Ozone Column Depletion and Abnormal Pollen Morphology in the Model Angiosperm Arabidopsis Thaliana L. Review of Palaeobotany and Palynology 194: 12-20.

Ni J-Q, Heber AJ, Cortus EL, Lim T-T, Bogan BW, et al. 2012. Assessment of Ammonia Emissions from Swine Facilities in the U.S.—Application of Knowledge from Experimental Research. Environmental Science & Policy 22: 25-35.

Niu R, Sun Z, Cheng Z, Li Z, Wang J. 2009. Decreased Learning Ability and Low Hippocampus Glutamate in Offspring Rats Exposed to Fluoride and Lead. Environmental Toxicology and Pharmacology 28: 254-58.

Oberholster PJ, Genthe B, Hobbs P, Cheng PH, de Klerk AR, Botha AM. 2013. An Ecotoxicological Screening Tool to Prioritise Acid Mine Drainage Impacted Streams for Future Restoration. Environmental Pollution 176: 244-53.

Oksanen E, Pandey V, Pandey AK, Keski-Saari S, Kontunen-Soppela S, Sharma C. 2013. Impacts of Increasing Ozone on Indian Plants. Environmental Pollution 177: 189-200.

Olson BM, Bennett DR, McKenzie RH, Ormann TD, Atkins RP. 2009. Nitrate Leaching in Two Irrigated Soils with Different Rates of Cattle Manure. Journal of Environmental Quality 38: 2218-28.

Ozyurt O, Ekinci DA. 2011. Experimental Study of Vertical Ground-source Heat Pump Performance Evaluation for Cold Climate in Turkey. Applied Energy 88: 1257-65.

Papu-Zamxaka V, Harpham T, Mathee A. 2010. Environmental Legislation and Contamination: The Gap Between Theory and Reality in South Africa. Journal of Environmental Management 91: 2275-80.

Pell A, Márquez A, López-Sánchez JF, Rubio R, Barbero M, et al. 2013. Occurrence of Arsenic Species in Algae and Freshwater Plants of an Extreme Arid Region in Northern Chile, the Loa River Basin. Chemosphere 90: 556-64.

Philippe FX, Laitat M, Wavreille J, Bartiaux-Thill N, Nicks B, Cabaraux JF. 2011. Ammonia and Greenhouse Gas Emission from Group-housed Gestating Sows Depends on Floor Type. Agriculture, Ecosystems & Environment 140: 498-505.

Porter IJ, Andersen SO. 2013. Chinese Political, Social and Economic Leadership in Protection of the Stratospheric Ozone Layer, Climate, and Biosecurity: A Montreal Protocol Case Study. Procedia - Social and Behavioural Sciences 77: 237-46.

Qiao J, Yang L, Yan T, Xue F, Zhao D. 2012. Nitrogen Fertilizer Reduction in Rice Production for Two Consecutive Years in the Taihu Lake Area. Agriculture, Ecosystems & Environment 146: 103-12.

Qin Y, Xie SD. 2011. Historical Estimation of Carbonaceous Aerosol Emissions from Biomass Open Burning in China for the Period 1990-2005. Environmental Pollution 159: 3316-23.

Quinn NWT. 2011. Adaptive Implementation of Information Technology for Real-time, Basin-scale Salinity Management in the San Joaquin Basin, USA and Hunter River Basin, Australia. Agricultural Water Management 98: 930-40.

Rebolledo B, Gil A, Pallarés J. 2013. A Spatial Ammonia Emission Inventory for Pig Farming. Atmospheric Environment 64: 125-31.

Rinnan R, Saarnio S, Haapala JK, Mörsky SK, Martikainen PJ, et al. 2013. Boreal Peatland Ecosystems Under Enhanced UV-B Radiation and Elevated Tropospheric Ozone Concentration. Environmental and Experimental Botany 90: 43-52.

Roumeliotis TS, Dixon BJ, Van Heyst BJ. 2010. Characterization of Gaseous Pollutant and Particulate Matter Emission Rates from a Commercial Broiler Operation Part I: Observed Trends in Emissions. Atmospheric Environment 44: 3770-77.

Sarigiannis DA, Kontoroupis P, Solomou ES, Nikolaki S, Karabelas AJ. 2013. Inventory of Pesticide Emissions into the Air in Europe. Atmospheric Environment 75: 6-14.

Seshadri B, Bolan NS, Naidu R, Wang H, Sajwan K. 2013. Chapter Six - Clean Coal Technology Combustion Products: Properties, Agricultural and Environmental Applications, and Risk Management In Advances in Agronomy, ed. LS Donald, pp. 309-70: Academic Press.

Shen Q, Zhu J, Cheng L, Zhang J, Zhang Z, Xu X. 2011. Enhanced Algae Removal by Drinking Water Treatment of Chlorination Coupled with Coagulation. Desalination 271: 236-40.

Shi G-T, Chen Z-L, Xu S-Y, Yao C-X, Bi C-J, Wang L. 2009. Salinity and Persistent Toxic Substances in Soils from Shanghai, China. Pedosphere 19: 779-89.

Tang H, Liu G, Zhu J, Han Y, Kobayashi K. 2013. Seasonal Variations in Surface Ozone as Influenced by Asian Summer Monsoon and Biomass Burning in Agricultural Fields of the Northern Yangtze River Delta. Atmospheric Research 122: 67-76.

Tavares JR, Sthel MS, Campos LS, Rocha MV, Lima GR, et al. 2011. Evaluation of Pollutant Gases Emitted by Ethanol and Gasoline Powered Vehicles. Procedia Environmental Sciences 4: 51-60.

Theobald MR, Løfstrøm P, Walker J, Andersen HV, Pedersen P, et al. 2012. An Intercomparison of Models Used to Simulate the Short-range Atmospheric Dispersion of Agricultural Ammonia Emissions. Environmental Modelling & Software 37: 90-102.

Toh YY, Lim SF, von Glasow R. 2013. The Influence of Meteorological Factors and Biomass Burning on Surface Ozone Concentrations at Tanah Rata, Malaysia. Atmospheric Environment 70: 435-46.

Vaddella VK, Ndegwa PM, Ullman JL, Jiang A. 2013. Mass Transfer Coefficients of Ammonia for Liquid Dairy Manure. Atmospheric Environment 66: 107-13.

VanderZaag AC, Wagner-Riddle C, Park KH, Gordon RJ. 2011. Methane Emissions from Stored Liquid Dairy Manure in a Cold Climate. Animal Feed Science and Technology 166-167: 581-89.

Vatn A, Bakken L, Bleken MA, Baadshaug OH, Fykse H, et al. 2006. A Methodology for Integrated Economic and Environmental Analysis of Pollution from Agriculture. Agricultural Systems 88: 270-93.

Velthof G, Oudendag D, Witzke H, Asman W, Klimont Z, Oenema O. 2009. Integrated Assessment of Nitrogen Losses from Agriculture in EU-27 Using MITERRA-EUROPE. Journal of Environmental Quality 38: 402-17.

Velthof GL, van Bruggen C, Groenestein CM, de Haan BJ, Hoogeveen MW, Huijsmans JFM. 2012. A Model for Inventory of Ammonia Emissions from Agriculture in the Netherlands. Atmospheric Environment 46: 248-55.

Vetter W, Bester K. 2006. Chapter 6 - Gas Chromatographic Enantioseparation of Chiral Pollutants—techniques and Results In Chiral Analysis, ed. WB Kenneth, AB Marianna, pp. 131-213. Amsterdam: Elsevier.

Virgílio Cruz J, Silva MO, Isabel Dias M, Isabel Prudêncio M. 2013. Groundwater Composition and Pollution due to Agricultural Practices at Sete Cidades Volcano (Azores, Portugal). Applied Geochemistry 29: 162-73.

Vogt E, Dragosits U, Braban CF, Theobald MR, Dore AJ, et al. 2013. Heterogeneity of Atmospheric Ammonia at the Landscape Scale and Consequences for Environmental Impact Assessment. Environmental Pollution 179: 120-31.

Wan N, Ji X, Jiang J, Qiao H, Huang K. 2013. A Methodological Approach to Assess the Combined Reduction of Chemical Pesticides and Chemical Fertilizers for Low-carbon Agriculture. Ecological Indicators 24: 344-52.

Wang W, Chen W-c, Wang K-r, Xie X-l, Yin C-m, Chen A-l. 2011. Effects of Long-Term Fertilization on the Distribution of Carbon, Nitrogen and Phosphorus in Water-Stable Aggregates in Paddy Soil. Agricultural Sciences in China 10: 1932-40.

Waterhouse J, Brodie J, Lewis S, Mitchell A. 2012. Quantifying the Sources of Pollutants in the Great Barrier Reef Catchments and the Relative Risk to Reef Ecosystems. Marine Pollution Bulletin 65: 394-406.

Weinstein LH, Davison AW. 2003. Native Plant Species Suitable as Bioindicators and Biomonitors for Airborne Fluoride. Environmental Pollution 125: 3-11.

Westerman PW, Bicudo JR. 2005. Management Considerations for Organic Waste Use in Agriculture. Bioresource Technology 96: 215-21.

White AF, Schulz MS, Stonestrom DA, Vivit DV, Fitzpatrick J, et al. 2009. Chemical Weathering of a Marine Terrace Chronosequence, Santa Cruz, California. Part II: Solute Profiles, Gradients and the Comparisons of Contemporary and Long-term Weathering Rates. Geochimica et Cosmochimica Acta 73: 2769-803.

Williams A, Jones JM, Ma L, Pourkashanian M. 2012. Pollutants from the Combustion of Solid Biomass Fuels. Progress in Energy and Combustion Science 38: 113-37.

Winiwarter W, Klimont Z. 2011. The Role of N-gases (N2O, NOx, NH3) in Cost-effective Strategies to Reduce Greenhouse Gas Emissions and Air Pollution in Europe. Current Opinion in Environmental Sustainability 3: 438-45.

Xia Y, Li Y, Li X, Guo M, She D, Yan X. 2013. Diurnal Pattern in Nitrous Oxide Emissions from a Sewage-enriched River. Chemosphere 92: 421-28.

Yu T-Y, Lin C-Y, Chang L-FW. 2012. Estimating Air Pollutant Emission Factors from Open Burning of Rice Straw by the Residual Mass Method. Atmospheric Environment 54: 428-38.

Zhang C, Chen J, Wen Z. 2012a. Assessment of Policy Alternatives and Key Technologies for Energy Conservation and Water Pollution Reduction in China's Synthetic Ammonia Industry. Journal of Cleaner Production 25: 96-105.

Zhang D-m, Chen Y-x, Jilani G, Wu W-x, Liu W-l, Han Z-y. 2012b. Optimization of Struvite Crystallization Protocol for Pretreating the Swine Wastewater and its Impact on Subsequent Anaerobic Biodegradation of Pollutants. Bioresource Technology 116: 386-95.

Zhang H, Wang S, Hao J, Wan L, Jiang J, et al. 2012c. Chemical and Size Characterization of Particles Emitted from the Burning of Coal and Wood in Rural Households in Guizhou, China. Atmospheric Environment 51: 94-99.

Grain Size Analysis of Beach Sediment Along the Barrier Bar Lagoon Coastal System, Lagos, South – West, Nigeria; Its Implication on Coastal Erosion

Rabiu Abdulkarim* and **Akinnigbagbe Edward Akintoye**

ABSTRACT

Beach sediments were collected from four selected beaches along the barrier bar lagoon coastal system namely Alpha, Takwa Bay, Eleko and Badagry beaches. The sediments were texturally analyzed in order to determine the statistical parameters of their grain size distribution. The result shows that Badagry and Alpha beach are medium grained sand with average mean values of (1.10 Φ and 1.14 Φ respectively). Eleko beach sediment is coarsely grained with an average mean value of (0.56 Φ) while Takwa Bay beach sediment is fine grained and very well sorted with an average mean value of (2.25 Φ.). This suggest that Eleko beach sediment being coarse grained is deposited in a high energy condition hence less vulnerable to erosion compared to Takwa bay beach sediment which is fine grained and deposited in low energy condition hence more vulnerable to erosion. Alpha and Badagry beach sediment are medium grain and deposited in a moderate energy condition hence more stable to erosional forces than Takwa bay beach sediment. Grain size characteristics are reliable in understanding the provenance, transport

Nigeria Institute for Oceanography and Marine Research, 3 Wilmot point road, Victoria Island Lagos Nigeria.

mechanism and depositional environment of sediments. The grain size and amount of sand on a beach depends on wave energy, erodibility of sea cliffs and size of particles they produce.

Key Words: Barrier Bar Lagoon, Beach Sediments, Grain Size Distribution, Coastal Erosion.

INTRODUCTION

Coastal erosion is a natural phenomenon which has always existed and has contributed to the shaping of coastal landscapes. Coastal erosion is the main process which provides sediment to the coastal system including beaches, dunes, reef, mud flat and marshes. In turn coastal system provides a wide range of functions including absorption of wave energy and silting for recreational activities. However migration of human population towards the coastal zone has turned coastal erosion into problem of growing concern. The problem of coastal erosion along the barrier lagoon coastal system is exemplified by the erosion problem along the Victoria beach in Lagos. The problems most commonly encountered include collapse of the dune system as a result of storm event which result in flooding of the hinterland, destabilization of socio-economic activities and degradation of the environment. Ibe et al., (1985) reported an annual erosion rate of 25 to 30m at Victoria beach in Lagos.

Among the natural causes of erosion along the barrier lagoon coastal system is vulnerable sediment characteristics. Beach sediments along the barrier lagoon coast range from fine to coarse sand. The sediment particles are transported by stress due to motion of fluid which are carried in suspension and eroded away by low energy wave, longshore or tidal current. The amount of sediment carried by longshore or tidal currents depends on the grain size and the velocity of the current. Beach sediments along the barrier complex show wide variation in textural characteristics. The sediment compositions are affected by wave/tidal action, littoral current and the petrographical compositions of the shore; hence the grain size distribution of beach sand is a function of the hydrodynamic conditions. The sediment distributions along the beaches are hence a result of complex interaction between sediment source, wave energy level and the general offshore slope on which the beach is constructed (Komar, 1988).

The intensity of the wave action in the littoral zone generally redeposits and sort materials of all grain sizes. Thus, the composition of beach sediment is not affected only by wave action but depends largely on the amount of clastic materials supplied to the coast. This study was carried out along the active beaches of the Barrier Bar complex. The aim is to determine the grain size distribution with a view to understanding the geological sensitivity of the sediment to the forces of erosion. Knowledge of these characteristics is important in understanding the fundamental principles of shoreline dynamics necessary for the management of coastal erosion.

THE STUDY AREA

The Barrier/Lagoon coastal system extends eastward for about 200 km from the Nigeria/Benin Republic border to the western limit of the transgressive mud coast (Map 2.1). Its general evolution and morphology has largely been determined by coastal dynamics and the deposition of fluvial sediments. The beaches of the barrier bar complex are erosive, probably due to lack of Exoreic Rivers, which would have compensated for the sand lost from the action of longshore current. The Barrier Lagoon complex is backed by the Badagry Creek, the Lagos Lagoon, Lekki Lagoon and numerous other creeks whose only connection to the sea is through the commodore channel in Lagos.

The Barrier Lagoon coastal system consists of narrow beach ridges, which are aligned parallel to the coast. The origin of the barrier bar complex has been postulated by several workers. Benard (1962) stated that movement of sand on the front of a notched sector of the coast lead to the evolution of the lagoon. He suggested that sands deposited at appropriate locations filled the notches, reducing and shortening the coastline and resulting in a straight barrier beach which continues to grow in length. (Allen 1965) viewed the formation of barrier islands in terms of coast wide progradation resulting from longshore drift. Webb (1958) and Hoyt (1967) suggested the submergence of a dune or beach ridge to form the barrier island Lagoon.

Ibe and Awosika (1984) and Ibe (1998) postulated that sediments constituting the barrier Islands are of terrigenous origin of Benin formation, laid down through the agent of Rivers during the late Wisconsin low stand of the sea level (2000Bp). These sediments were later reworked and swept landward, away from the River Mouths by wave action during the ensuring marine transgression to form offshore bar.

METHODOLOGY

Beach sediment samples were collected from four selected beaches, this includes: Badagry, Alpha, Takwa bay and Eleko beach. The samples were collected from shallow trenches at 100 meters interval; using a plastic jar to ensure a uniform sampling depth of 5cm. Coordinates of the various sampling stations were taken using the global position system (GPS). Two samples representing the berm and fore shore were collected per profile. Eight samples were collected from each beach making a total of thirty 32 samples. In the laboratory, 70 grams of each sample was oven dried at 50° C in order to remove their moisture content.

The dried and weighed sediments were transferred carefully to the uppermost (coarsest) of a stacked series of graded sand sieves, sieves were gently brushed of all material from the container using a fine sieve brush. A 62 µm sieve was placed at the bottom of the stack of sieves and care was taken by using a pan below the finest sieve to catch the last of any fine material which may still pass. The stacked column of sieves was now transferred to a Rotap sieve shaker for a period 10-15 minutes.

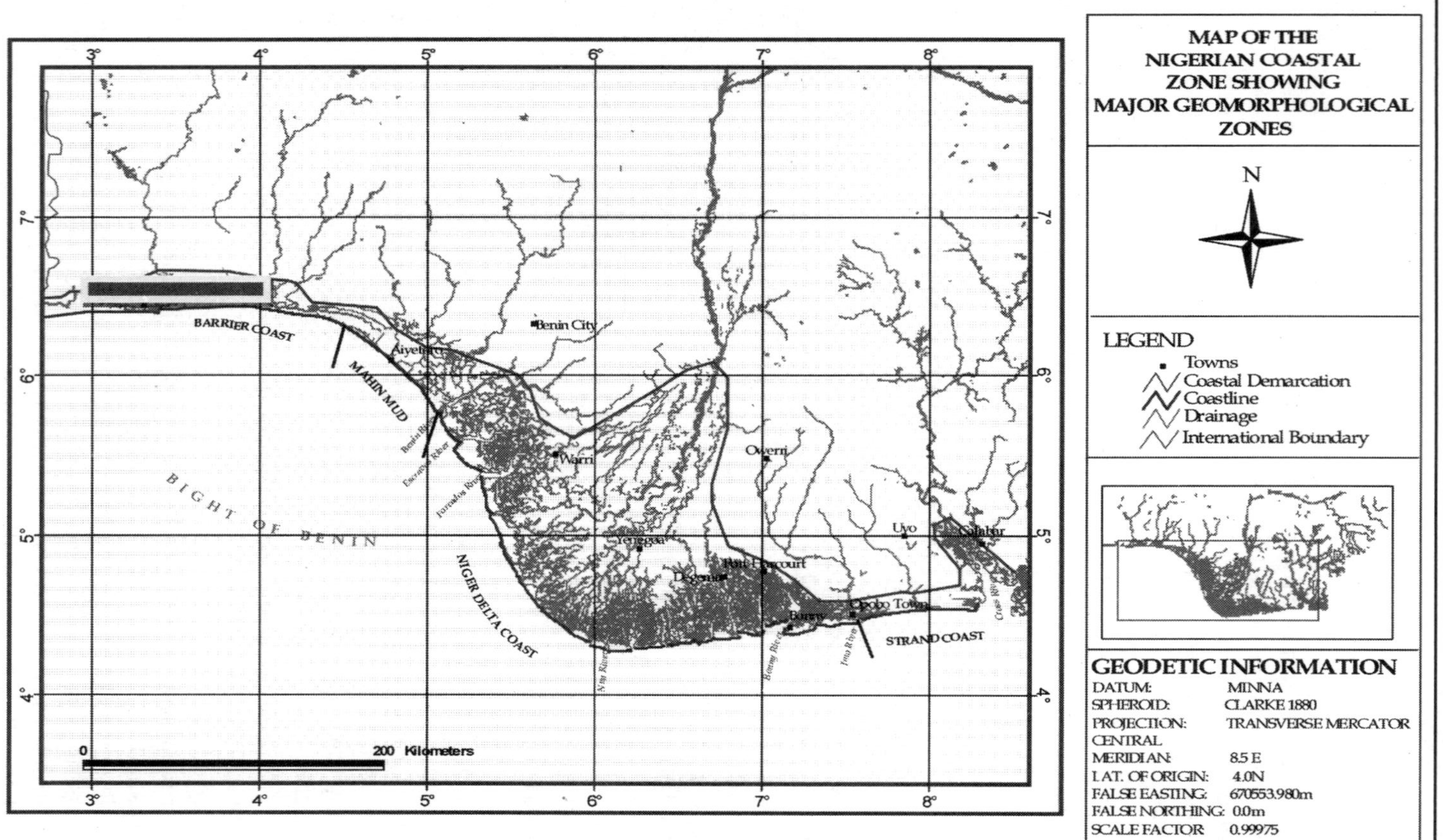

Map. 2.1: Map of the Nigeria Coastal Zone Showing the Major Geomorphic Zone (The Study Area Marked in Red)

The fraction of samples retained on each sieve was emptied on to a sheet of glazed paper and grains lodged in the sieve were removed with a sieve brush. The fractions were then transferred to a pre weighed dish for weighing. This was done for all the sieves till the material passing through the last (62 μm) sieve and that retained in the pan were also recorded. A graph of cumulative weight percent against sieve size was plotted. And from the cumulative frequency curve obtained grain size parameters such as average size (mean), spread of the sizes about the average (standard deviation) symmetry of preferential spread to one size of the average (skewness) and kurtosis or degree of concentration of the grains to the central size were determined.

RESULTS AND DISCUSSION

The statistical parameters of grain size distribution have been a major parameter in delineating the influence of deposional processes (Friedman, 1961; Folk, 1966). Generally, standard deviation and skewness are considered environmentally sensitive indicators while the mean is a reflection of the competence of the transport dynamic system. The results of the granulometric analysis of samples of Alpha, Badagry, Takwa bay and Eleko beaches have been presented in tables 2.1, 2.2, 2.3 and 2.4. Figures 2.1, 2.2, 2.3 and 2.4 shows the cumulauve curve and individual particle size of each sample from which the grain size parameters were calculated.

Table 2.1: Result of Granulometric Analysis of Alpha Beach Sediments

Sample No.	Mean	Standard Deviation	Skewness	Kurtosis	Description
AF 1A (BM)	1.54	0.53	0.19	1.09	Medium sand, Moderately well sorted, fine skewed, Mesokurtic.
AF2 B (WL)	1.39	0.59	0.09	1.03	Medium sand, Moderately well sorted, Near symmetrical, Mesokurtic
AF 2A (BM)	1.33	0.77	0.13	0.94	Medium sand, Moderately sorted, Fine skewed, Mesokurtic
AF 2B (WL)	0.93	0.66	0.10	0.93	Coarse sand, Moderately well sorted, Fine skewed, Mesokurtic.
AF 3A (BM)	1.11	0.66	0.12	0.89	Medium sand, Moderately well sorted, Fine skewed, Platykurtic
AF 3B (WL)	1.02	0.64	0.06	1.12	Medium sand, Moderately well sorted, Near symmetrical, Leptokurtic.
AF 4A (BM)	1.02	0.85	-0.10	0.76	Medium sand, Moderately sorted, Coarse skewed, Platykurtic.
AF 4B (WL)	0.83	0.80	-0.02	0.93	Coarse sand, Moderately sorted, Near symmetrical, Mesokurtic.

The sediment distribution range between medium to coarse sand, moderate to well sorted, finely skewed with mesokurtic distribution. The mean, which is a reflection of the overall size of the sediment, has values ranging from (0.83 Φ to 1.54 Φ) which represents medium-coarse grained sand while the standard deviation which is a measure of the sorting has values ranging from (0.53 Φ to 0.85 Φ) that represents moderate to well sorted. Skewness values range from (-0.02 Φ to 0.19 Φ) while kurtosis value lies between (0.76 Φ and 1.12 Φ). The plot of individual particle size against phi size for the various samples shows bi-modal peaks, which suggests more than one source of sediment supply to the Alpha beach sand.

Table 2.2: Result of Granulometric Analysis of Badagry Beach Sediment

Sample No.	Mean	Standard Deviation	Skewness	Kurtosis	Description
BD1A (BM)	1.28	0.57	0.17	1.29	Medium sand, Moderately well sorted, Fine skewed, Leptokurtic.
BD1B (WL)	1.17	0.51	0.10	1.009	Medium sand, Moderately well sorted, Fine skewed, Mesokurtic.
BD2A (BM)	1.10	0.57	0.18	1.06	Medium sand, Moderately well sorted, Fine skewed, Mesokurtic.
BD2B (WL)	1.15	0.67	0.27	1.39	Medium sand, Moderately well sorted, Fine skewed, Leptokurtic
BD3A (BM)	1.32	0.52	0.18	1.11	Medium sand, Moderately well sorted, Fine skewed, Leptokurtic.
BD3B (WL)	1.30	0.35	-0.10	1.21	Medium sand, Well sorted, Coarse skewed, Leptokurtic
BD4A (BM)	0.73	0.76	0.21	0.96	Coarse sand, Moderately sorted, Fine skewed, Mesokurtic
BD4B (WL)	0.77	0.72	0.19	0.98	Coarse sand, Moderately sorted, Fine skewed, Mesokurtic.

The result of grain size analysis of samples from Badagry beach is presented in table 2.2. The results show that the sediments are medium grained sand, moderately well sorted, finely skewed and mesokurtic. The mean which is a reflection of the overall size of the sediments has an average value of 1.10 Φ; (medium sand), the standard deviation has an average value of 0.51 Φ (moderately well sorted), skewness values ranged from – 0.10 Φ to 0.27 Φ (coarse to fine skewed) while kurtosis values lies between 0.96 Φ and 1.39 Φ (mesokurtic and leptokurtic). The plot of individual particle size against phi size showed uni-modal peaks and this suggests a single source of sediment supply to the Badagry beach.

Table 2.3: Result of Granulumetric Analysis of Takwa Bay Beach Sediment

Sample No.	Mean	Standard Deviation	Skewness	Kurtosis	Description
TK 1A (BM)	2.27	0.33	-0.001	1.05	Fine sand, Very well sorted, Near symmetrical, Mesokurtic.
TK1 B (WL)	2.11	0.44	0.003	1.09	Fine sand, Well sorted, Near symmetrical Mesokurtic.
TK2 A (BM)	2.29	0.29	-0.006	1.07	Fine sand, very well sorted, Near symmetrical Mesokurtic.
TK 2B (WL)	2.24	0.3	0.006	0.9	Fine sand, Well sorted, Near symmetrical, Mesokurtic.
TK 3A (BM)	2.38	0.27	-0.10	1.11	Fine sand, Very well sorted, Coarse skewed, Leptokurtic.
TK3 B (WL)	2.18	0.43	0.001	0.9	Fine sand, Well sorted, Near symmetrical, Mesokurtic.
TK4 A (BM)	2.42	0.29	-0.08	1.08	Fine sand Very well sorted Near symmetrical Mesokurtic.
TK 4B (WL)	2.1	0.41	-0.05	1.03	Fine sand, Well sorted, Near symmetrical, Mesokurtic.

The granulometric analysis results of sediments from Takwa bay is shown in table 2.3. The grain size is fine sand, very well sorted, near symmetrical and mesokurtic. The means has an average value of 2.25 Φ (fine sand), standard deviation has an average value of 0.34 Φ (very well sorted), skewness values ranged from -0.006 to 0.001 (near symmetrical to coarse skewed) while kurtosis value lies between 0.9 and 1.1 (Mesokurtic and Leptokurtic). The plot of phi size against the individual particle size showed uni-modal peaks. This suggests a single source of sediment to the Takwa bay beach sand.

Table 2.4: Result of Granulometric Analysis of Eleko Beach Sediment

Sample No.	Mean	Standard Deviation	Skewness	Kurtosis	Description
1	2	3	4	5	6
LK1A (BM)	0.55	0.74	0.03	0.91	Coarse sand, Moderately sorted, Near symmetrical, Mesokurtic
LK 1B (WL)	0.33	0.92	-0.105	0.72	Coarse sand, Moderately sorted, Coarse skewed, Platykurtic.
LK 2A (BM)	0.81	0.75	0.06	0.99	Coarse sand, Moderately sorted, Near symmetrical Mesokurtic.

(Contd...)

1	2	3	4	5	6
LK 2B (WL)	0.66	0.97	0.17	0.76	Coarse sand, Moderately sorted, Fine skewed, Platykurtic.
LK 3A (BM)	0.90	0.75	0.17	1.04	Coarse sand, Moderately sorted, Fine skewed, Mesokurtic.
LK 3B (WL)	0.01	0.89	-0.34	0.90	Coarse sand, Moderately sorted, Strongly coarse skewed, Mesokurtic.
LK 4A (BM)	1.18	0.64	0.1	1.23	Medium sand, Moderately well sorted, Fine skewed, Leptokurtic.
LK 4B (WL)	-0.05	1.02	-0.65	0.78	Coarse sand, Poorly sorted, Strongly coarse skewed, Platykurtic.

The granulometric analysis result of Eleko beach sediments is shown in table 2.4. The result show that the grain size distribution of Eleko beach sediments ranged from moderately sorted sands to coarse grained sands, fine skewed with Mesokurtic distribution. The mean has an average value of 0.56 Φ (coarse sand), while the average standard deviation is 0.83 Φ (moderately sorted). The plot of phi size against individual particle size for the various samples showed a uni-modal grain size composition and this suggests a possible single source of sediment supply to the beach.

CONCLUSION

The grain size distribution closely defines the energy level of the wave processes. Badagry and Alpha beaches are of medium grain size distribution with average mean value of (1.10 Φ to 1.14 Φ respectively); Eleko beach sediment is coarsely grained with an average mean value of (0.56 Φ) while Takwa Bay beach sediments are fine grained and very well sorted with average mean value of (2.25 Φ.) From this, we can deduce that Eleko beach sediments are deposited in a high energy condition and less vulnerable to erosion followed by Badagry and Alpha beaches which are deposited in a moderate energy condition and then Takwa Bay beach sediments which are deposited in a low energy condition and more vulnerable to erosion. For the effective management of erosion along the barrier bar coastal system, the grain size distributions of the sediments have to be appreciated. Hence the result of this study will be useful for the understanding of the sedimentary processes along the barrier bar coastal system. This study and other ocean dynamic studies will be needed to comprehend the regional sedimentary processes necessary for planning and decision making of the coastal projects along barrier bar coastal system.

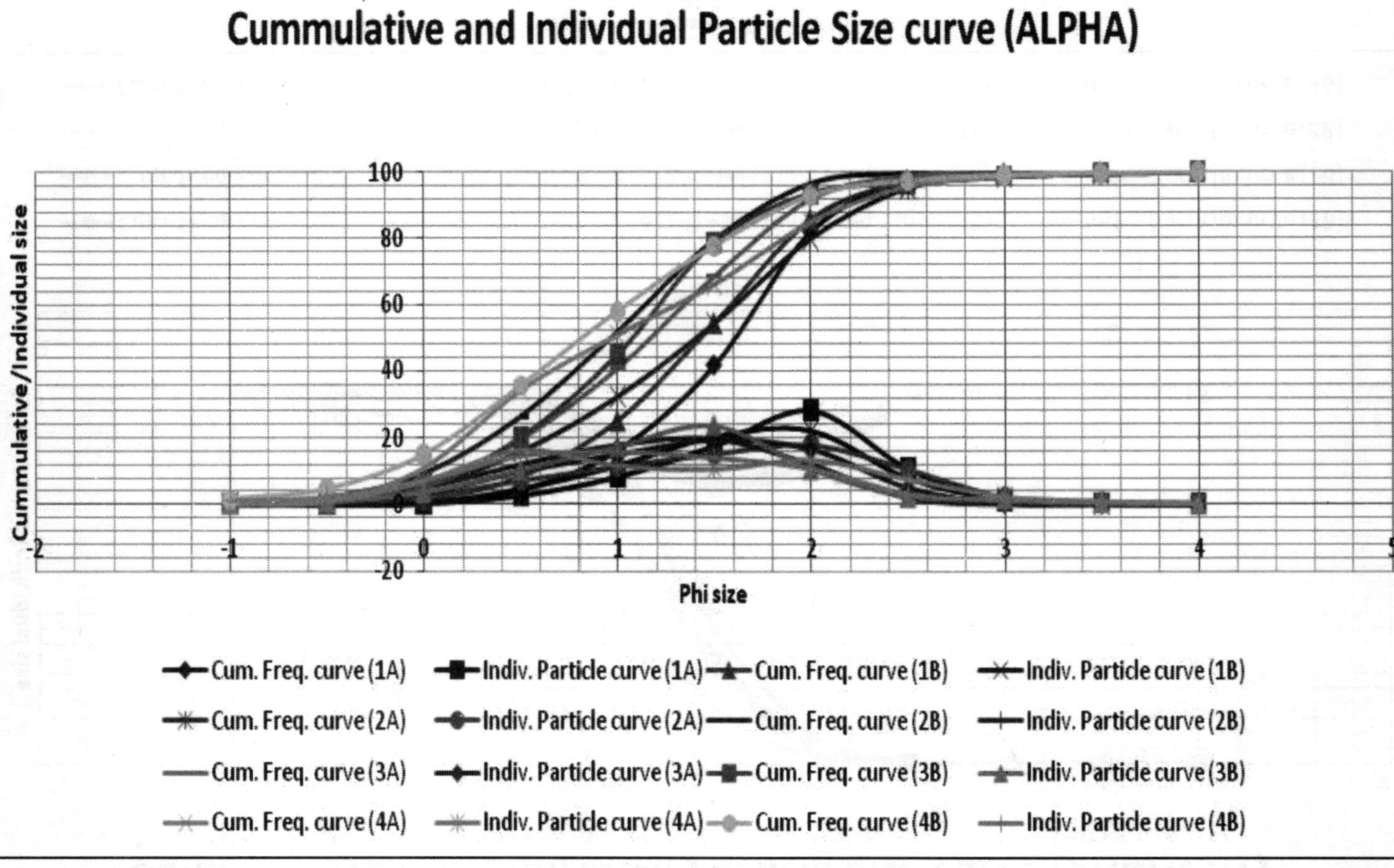
Cummulative and Individual Particle Size curve (ALPHA)
Cummulative/Individual size
100
80
60
40
20
0
-20
-2
-1
0
1
2
3
4
5
Phi size
Cum. Freq. curve (1A)
Indiv. Particle curve (1A)
Cum. Freq. curve (1B)
Indiv. Particle curve (1B)
Cum. Freq. curve (2A)
Indiv. Particle curve (2A)
Cum. Freq. curve (2B)
Indiv. Particle curve (2B)
Cum. Freq. curve (3A)
Indiv. Particle curve (3A)
Cum. Freq. curve (3B)
Indiv. Particle curve (3B)
Cum. Freq. curve (4A)
Indiv. Particle curve (4A)
Cum. Freq. curve (4B)
Indiv. Particle curve (4B)

Figure 2.1

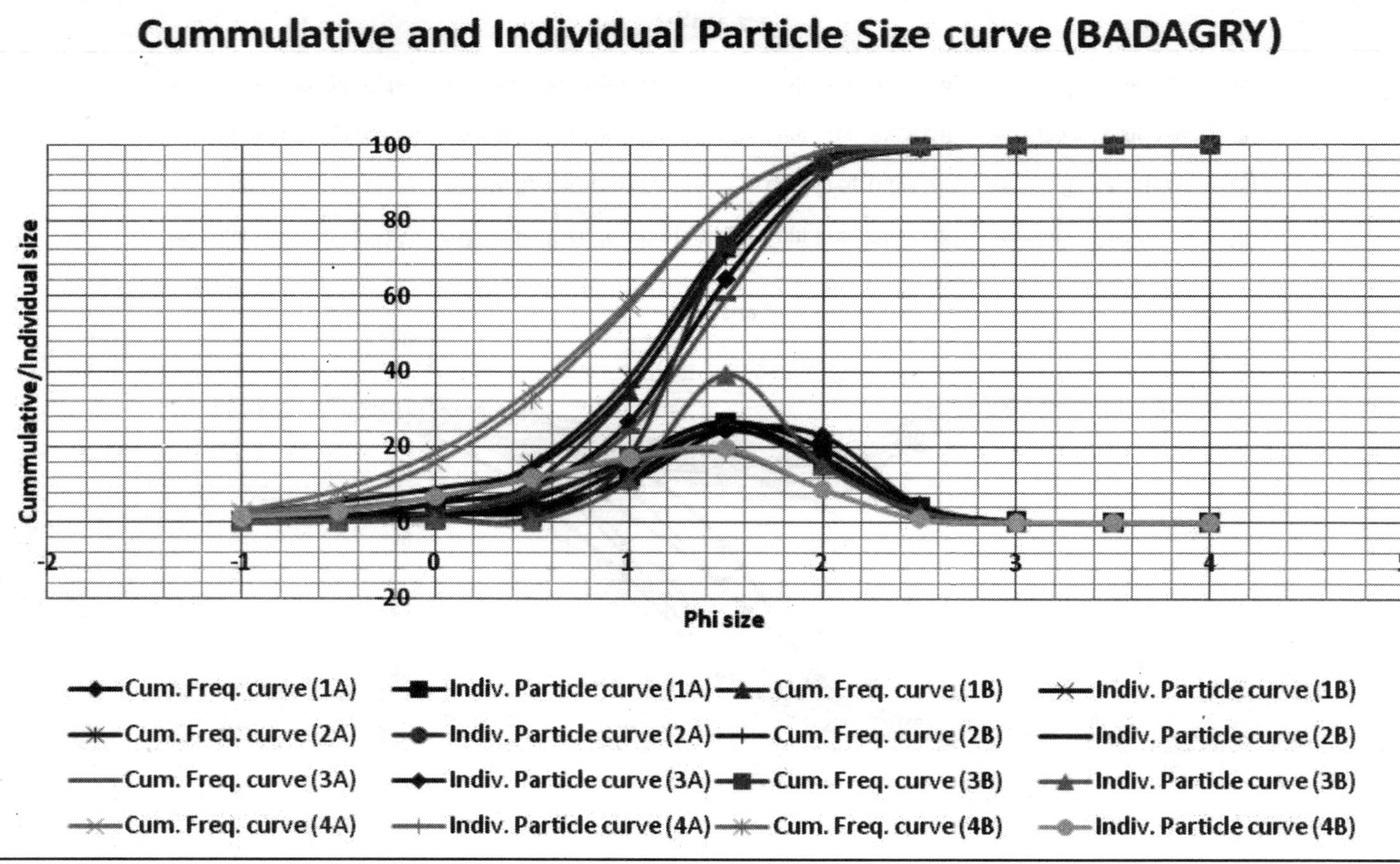
Cummulative and Individual Particle Size curve (BADAGRY)
Cummulative/Individual size
100
80
60
40
20
0
-20
-2
-1
0
1
2
3
4
5
Phi size
Cum. Freq. curve (1A)
Indiv. Particle curve (1A)
Cum. Freq. curve (1B)
Indiv. Particle curve (1B)
Cum. Freq. curve (2A)
Indiv. Particle curve (2A)
Cum. Freq. curve (2B)
Indiv. Particle curve (2B)
Cum. Freq. curve (3A)
Indiv. Particle curve (3A)
Cum. Freq. curve (3B)
Indiv. Particle curve (3B)
Cum. Freq. curve (4A)
Indiv. Particle curve (4A)
Cum. Freq. curve (4B)
Indiv. Particle curve (4B)

Figure 2.2

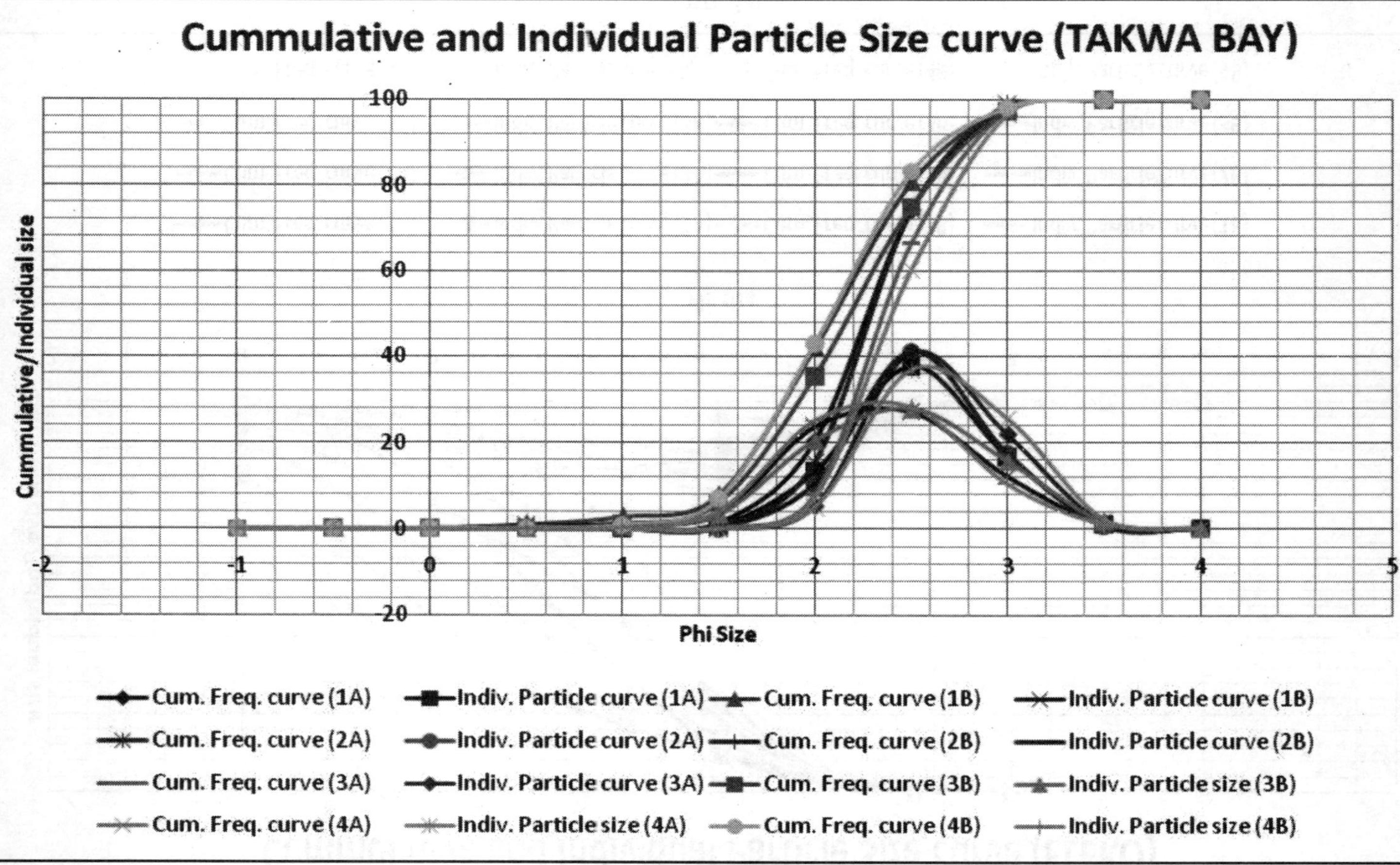

Cummulative and Individual Particle Size curve (TAKWA BAY)
Cummulative/Individual size
Phi Size
Cum. Freq. curve (1A)
Indiv. Particle curve (1A)
Cum. Freq. curve (1B)
Indiv. Particle curve (1B)
Cum. Freq. curve (2A)
Indiv. Particle curve (2A)
Cum. Freq. curve (2B)
Indiv. Particle curve (2B)
Cum. Freq. curve (3A)
Indiv. Particle curve (3A)
Cum. Freq. curve (3B)
Indiv. Particle size (3B)
Cum. Freq. curve (4A)
Indiv. Particle size (4A)
Cum. Freq. curve (4B)
Indiv. Particle size (4B)

Figure 2.3

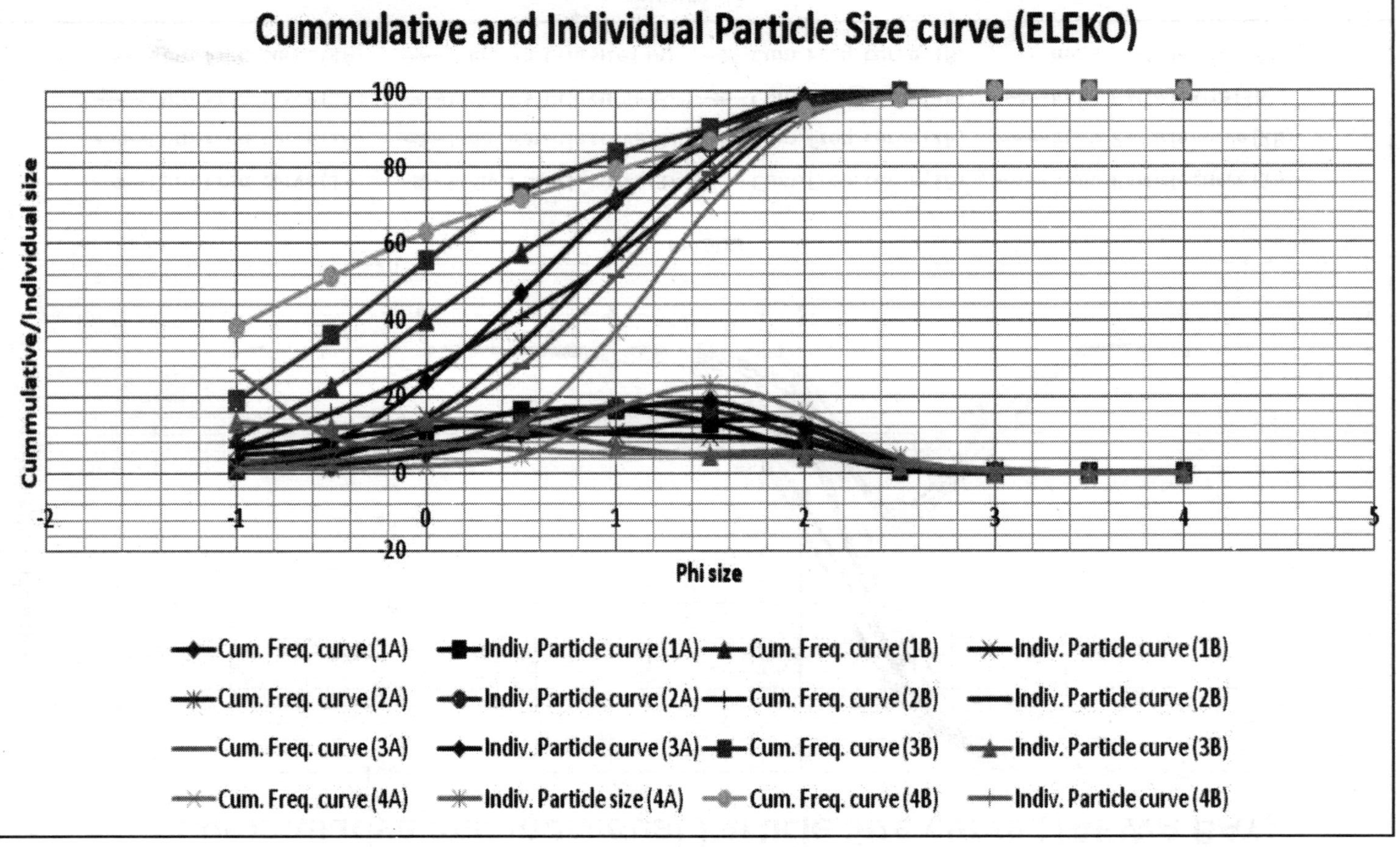
Cummulative and Individual Particle Size curve (ELEKO)
Cummulative/Individual size
100
80
60
40
20
0
-20
-2
-1
0
1
2
3
4
5
Phi size
Cum. Freq. curve (1A)
Indiv. Particle curve (1A)
Cum. Freq. curve (1B)
Indiv. Particle curve (1B)
Cum. Freq. curve (2A)
Indiv. Particle curve (2A)
Cum. Freq. curve (2B)
Indiv. Particle curve (2B)
Cum. Freq. curve (3A)
Indiv. Particle curve (3A)
Cum. Freq. curve (3B)
Indiv. Particle curve (3B)
Cum. Freq. curve (4A)
Indiv. Particle size (4A)
Cum. Freq. curve (4B)
Indiv. Particle curve (4B)

Figure 2.4

REFERENCES

Anita, E.E. (1993) Preliminary Assessment of the Impact of Erosion Along the Nigeria Shoreline NIOMR Tech paper No. 13, p. 17.

Awosika et'al (2007) Assessment of Ocean Surge and Erosion Threats and Mitigation Options to the Goshen estate Lekki. A Consultancy Report for Goshen Estate.

Folk, R.H (1966) A Review of Grain Size Parameters Sedimentology Vol. 6, pp. 73-93.

Freidman, G.M. (1961) Distinction Between Dune Beach and River Sand from Textural Characteristics. Journal of Sedimentary Petrology Vol. 31, pp. 514.

Ibe, A.C and Awosika, L.F (1988). Sedimentology of Beaches of Barrier Bar Complexes in Nigeria. NIOMR Tech Paper No. 28, p. 18.

Ibe, A.C., Awosika, L.F and Ibe, C.E. (1993) Factors Responsible for Varying Granulumetric Characteristics of Sediments from the Western Nigeria Coastline. Coastline of Western African Coastal Zone 93. Ed. Larry Awosika, Chidi Ibe and Peter schnoder. Pub American Association of Civil Engineers.

Li, Z. and Komar, P.D., 1992. Longshore Grain Sorting and Beach Placer Formation Journal of Sedimentary Petrology 62, 429-441.

Zdenek kukal (1971) Geology of Resent Sediment. Eds Jan Petranek Academic Press London and New York. pp. 209-221.

Impact of Water Quality on Zooplankton Biodiversity in River Betwa, Madhya Pradesh, India

SantoshVishwakarma; Archna Mishra; Bilal A Batt Imtiyaaz A Batt[1]; Alok Varma[2]; Geeta Saxena[3]

ABSTRACT

The present study deal with the role of biotic parameter especially zooplankton community and its trophic level to assess water quality of Betwa River Madhya Pradesh, India. The zooplankton of the river Betwa was studied from April 2012 to March 2013 at different sampling stations. Four sampling station were selected for the study, station -1 Jhirri, station-2 Nayapura, station-3 Mandideep and station-4 Bhojpur. During the study period various species of Rotifers, Copepods, Cladocerans were recorded, in all samples total 34 species of zooplankton identified, 14 species of Cladocerans, 12 species of Rotifers and 08 species of Copepods. The zooplankton community was dominated by *Cladocerans*, in all samples. The highest zooplankton densities were recorded in the month of February and March.

Physico-chemical parameters like Temperature, pH, Dissolve oxygen, Biological oxygen demand and Chemical oxygen demand were also measured and the correlation coefficient value of temperature, pH, Dissolve oxygen with zooplankton showed significant relation (0.432),

1. Department of Zoology, Govt. Science and Commerce College Benazeer, Bhopal (MP) India.
2. Department of Zoology, Govt. Raja Bhoj College, Mandideep Raisen (MP), India.
3. Department of Zoology, Institute of Excellence, Bhopal (MP), India.

(0.321), (0.185) and inverse relation with Biological oxygen demand and Chemical oxygen demand (-0.132), (-0.180)., it was found that they influence zooplankton abundance in river Betwa.

Keywords: Zooplankton, Betwariver, Mandideep, Rotifera, Physico-chemical parameter.

INTRODUCTION

In India there is a clear visible threat to quality and utilization of water sources. Among the limited freshwater resources, the rivers are the most dynamic and variable in their physico-chemical and biological composition due to regular and unidirectional flow of water. Aquatic pollution in India has now reached at a critical point. Almost every river system in India is now polluted to a considerable extent.In developing countries 1.8 million people, mostly children, die every year as a result of water-related diseases (WHO, 2004).According to an estimate, about 80% of the total population in India is deprived of pure and safe drinking water. A recent study revealed that there were 1, 53,000 village in India, which had infected water supply. 90% of total drinking water is severally polluted. Ganga is the most polluted river in the world. Other Indian rivers include Damoder, Hoogly, kulu, which have almost the same story to reveal.

The word plankton is derived from the Greek *planktos*, meaning wandering. It is used to describe the small, usually immotile, freely floating organisms living in aquatic habitats (Powell *et al.* 1975). Plankton drives energy cycling in aquatic ecosystems as they are the productive base of food webs, converting basic forms of energy into forms usable by higher trophic levels (Vilar*et al.* 2003). Due to their fundamental role in aquatic ecosystems, and their consumption of carbon dioxide, plankton determine the survival of all other aquatic organisms, and along with terrestrial primary producers, are drivers of global carbon cycles (Daly & Smith Jr 1993; Vilar*et al.* 2003). Plankton growth and dynamics depends on the characteristics of their environment – light and nutrient availability, temperature, salinity, pH, currents, turbulence, and predation intensity. Zooplankton mainly four groups i.e. Rotifera, Cladocera, Ostracoda and Copepoda.

Rotatoria (Rotifers) are the microscopic faunal component living mostly in fresh water, are characterized by the presence of an anterior wheel like rotating structure called "Corona". The rotifers are being considered as the most important soft bodied invertebrates (Hutchinson, 1967). As a group, the rotifers display an amazing range of morphological variations and adaptations. Yet the great majority has several fundamental features in common. Cladocerans popularly called as 'water flea' prefers to live in deep water and constitute a major item of food for fish. Thus they hold key position in food chain and energy transformation (Uttangi, 2001). Most members of the order cladocera are between 0.2 and 3.0 mm. long. Copepods constitute one of the major zooplankton communities occurring in all types of water bodies. They serve as food to several fishes and play a major role in ecological pyramids. Most species 2.0 mm. long, drab grayish or brownish in color, but others, especially littoral species in the spring of the year and at high altitudes, are brilliant orange, purple, or red. Qualitative and quantitative analysis of different groups of organisms have led to establishment of bio-indicators, indices and systems which can be used to assess the pollution and trophic status of water bodies.

The Betwa is a river in Northern India, and a tributary of the Yamuna. Originating in the Kumra (jhirri) village in Raisen district of Madhya Pradesh, it flows in a northeast direction through Madhya Pradesh and enter into Uttar Pradesh near village Bangawan of Jhansi district. The total length of the river from its origin to confluence with the Yamuna if 590 K.m, out of which 232 K.m lies in Madhya Pradesh and the balance 358 K.m in Uttar Pradesh. The river joins the Yamuna near Hamirpur in Uttar Pradesh at an elevation of about 106 meters. The river basin lies between the latitudes of 22* 54′ N and 26*00, N and the longitudes of 77*10′ E and 80*20′ E. The total catchment area of the basin in 43895 sq.Km. out of which 30217 sq.Km. lies in Madhya Pradesh and the remaining 13678 Km. lies in Uttar Pradesh, (KBLP,1995). The River Betwa plays a significant role in the human life of the villages villages located in Mandideep, Nayapura and Bhojpur areas. It has become polluted at some places of Mandideep due to industrial activities and the confluence of sewage, domestic wastes and industrial effluents of many big and small enterprises with various types of organic compounds and heavy metals deterioted to human health and aquatic organisms. Urban areas, farms, factories and individual households – all contribute to the contamination of this river. The present works is aimed at understanding various types of pollution in River Betwa at selected sites, and observe the impact of pollution on different sites of River Betwa, both biologically as well as chemically, bioassessment will be done by using zooplankton as bioindicators of pollutions.

MATERIALS AND METHODS

Study Area (Sampling Sites)

The river basin lies between the latitudes of 22* 54′ N and 26*00, N and the longitudes of 77*10′ E and 80*20′ E. The total catchments area of the basin in 43895 Km^2 out of which 30217 Km^2 lies in Madhya Pradesh and the remaining 13678 Km lies in Uttar Pradesh. On the basis of the survey conducted and literature available, five stations and ten monitoring sites were selected to sample water. The sites were selected mostly on the basis of various activities occurring on surrounding area of the river (Figure 3.1).

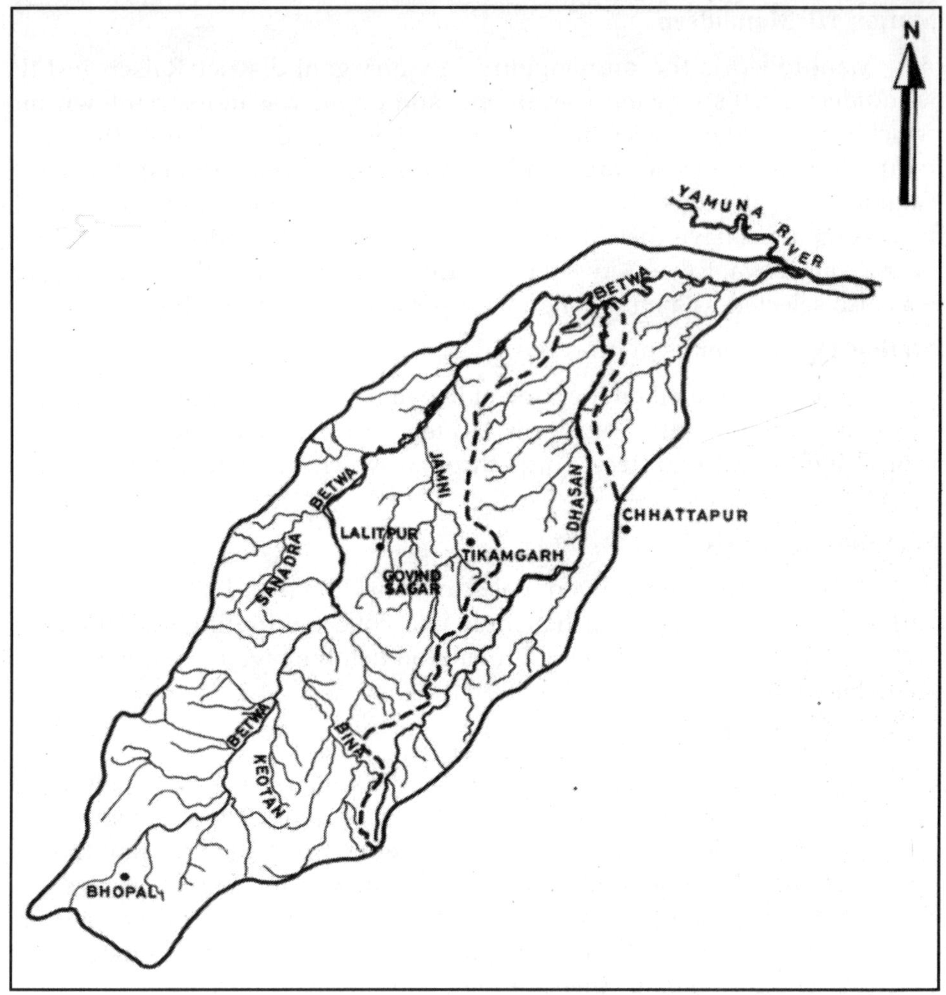

Fig. 3.1: Map of Betwa Basin

Samples were taken at the following points during alternate month:

Station I Jhirri

This station is located near village Jhirri. River Betwa originates from this point. It is fifteen kilometer away from Bhopal on Kolar Dam Road, touching the border of Ratapani sanctuary; home too many wildlife and birds (1 to 2 sites).

Station II Nayapura

It is a village near Mandideep, the Betwa touches the boundary of this village near Road Bridge where it confluences with the Kaliyasot tributaries (3 to 4 sites).

Station III Mandideep

Mandideep is the municipality in Goharganj district Raisen in MP. Mandideep is 20 km away from Bhopal and popular as industrial township which came in to existence in late 1970s. It has an industrial area, the major industries that are closer are Hindustan Electro Graphite (HEG), Procter & Gamble, Eicher tracters Ltd, Lupin laboratories, and national and international level companies have their manufacturing units at Mandideep. It is located near River Betwa. River Betwa encircle this industrial area, thus, Mandideep was also selected as a study site in the present research work (5 to 6).

Station IV Bhojpur

Bhojpur is situated on the bank of Betwa River 28 km away from Bhopal, the state capital of MP. The site is located on sandstone ridges, typical of central India, next to a deep gorge through which the Betwa River follows (7 to 8).

Sampling Methods

Zooplankton samples were collected from the (fixed site name 1 to 8) surface water of the river each sample was collected by filtering 50 liter of water through mesh size 60-65 μm plankton net, they were preserved in 4% formalin solution.

Laboratory Methods

In laboratory zooplankton samples were concentrated to a volume of 100 mL. 0.5 mL subsamples were used for the examined for its contents. A total of 100 individuals were measured alternate month. The quantitative enumeration of the zooplankton was carried out with the help of a Sedgwick-Rafter (S-R) counting cell which is 50 mm long, 20 mm wide and 1 mm deep. Before filling the SR cell with sample, the cover glasses were diagonally placed across the cell and then samples were transferred with a large bore pipette so that no air bubbles in the cell covers were formed. Number of plankton (Zooplankton) in the S-R cell was derived from the following formula (Gosh, *et.al.*, 2011).

$$\text{No./ml} = \frac{C \times 1000\ \text{mm}^3}{L \times D \times W \times S}$$

Where,

C = Number of Organisms Counted; L = length of each strip (S-R cell length) in mm; D = depth of a strip (whipped grid image width) in mm; S = number of strips counted.

The number of cells per mm was multiplied by a correction factor to adjust the number of organisms per liter (APHA 1976). Zooplankton was identified with the help of standard books and monographs, Nedhaam and Nedhaam (1962), Pennak (1953), Edomondson (1965), Dhanpati (2000). The physico-chemical parameters such as temperature, pH, dissolved oxygen, biological oxygen demand and chemical oxygen demand and were measured as according to APHA (1976). The correlation between abiotic (physico-chemical) parameters was done by using coefficient of correlation Karl Pearson's formula:

$$r = \frac{\Sigma d_x d_y}{\sqrt{\Sigma d_{x^2} \; \Sigma d_{y^2}}}$$

RESULTS

During the study period total 34 species of zooplankton identified 14 species of Cladocerans, 12 species of Rotifers and 08 species of Copepods. The zooplankton community was dominated by *Cladocerans* 14 species, in all samples. In all zooplanktonic group 14 species and 07 genera of Cladocerans, namely *Daphnia carinata, Daphnia longis. Daphnia magna, Daphnia pulex, Ceriodaphnia dubia, Ceriodaphnia megalops,Cariodaphnia recticulata, Diaphanosoma sarsi, Diaphanosoma excisum, Alona intermedia, Moina brachiata, Moina macrocopa, Scapholeberis mucronata, Simocephalus vetulus* (Table 3.1). 12 species and 04 genera of Rotifers zooplankton namely *Brachionus bidentata, Brachionus calyciflorus, Brachionus caudatus, Brachionus rubens, Branchionus urceolaris, Brachionus variabilis , Brachionus plicatilis, Euchlanis dialatata, Keratella cochlearis, Keratella quadrata, Keratella tropica, Asplanchna priodonta* (Table 3.2).

08 species and 05 genera of Copepods zooplankton namely *Cyclops strenus, Cyclops vernalis, Cyclops virdis, Acanthocyclops robustus, Diacyclops nanus, Mesocyclops americanus, Mesocyclops edax, Macrocyclops fuscus* (Table 3.3). In the present study the peak period of zooplankton occurrence during February and March, and in all samples of zooplankton Cladocerans species were dominated than other Rotifers and copepods groups. The species composition of Cladocera was 34% at station-1, 13% at station-2, 15% at station-3 and 38% at station-4 respectively. Rotifer species composition was 22% at station-1, 24% at station-2, 25% at station-3 and 29% at station-4. Copepoda species composition at station-1 was 33%, 18% at station-2, 19% at station-3 and 30% at station-4 (Graph 3.1, 3.2, 3.3).

Various Physic-chemical parameters recorded in different ranges, temperature was recorded 23.5 at station-1, 28.3 at station-2, 27.6 at station-3 and 19.5 °C at station-4 respectively. pH was recorded 7.9 at station-1, 5.9 at station-2, 6.1 at station-3, 8.2 at station-3. Dissolve oxygen recorded 6.4 at station-1, 2.5 at station-2, 2.8 at staion-3, and 5.7 mg/l at station-4. Biological oxygen demand was found 4.3 at station-1, 8.6 at station-2, 6.4 at station-3, 4.5 mg/l at station-4. Chemical oxygen demand was found 5.3 at station-1, 10.4 at station-2, 8.7 at station-3, 5.2 mg/l at station-4 respectively (Table 3.4). The correlation coefficient value of temperature, pH, Dissolve oxygen with zooplankton showed significant relation (0.432), (0.321), (0.185) and inverse relation with Biological oxygen demand and Chemical oxygen demand (-0.132), (-0.180) (Table. 3.5).

Table 3.1: Total Number of Cladocerans Individual at Different Stations

Species Composition	St.-1 Jhirri	St.-2 Nayapura	St.-3 Mandideep	St.-4 Bhojpur
Daphnia carinata	335	112	100	250
Daphnia longis.	224	109	110	290
Daphnia magna	334	124	116	324
Daphnia pulex	124	113	120	320
Ceriodaphnia dubia	332	134	125	412
Ceriodaphnia megalops	387	123	142	432
Ceriodaphnia recticulata	290	122	134	324
Diaphanosoma sarsi	339	125	123	324
Diaphanosoma excisum	338	132	121	354
Alona intermedia	220	114	132	357
Moina brachiata	342	116	154	342
Moina macrocopa	410	121	124	356
Scapholeberis mucronata	234	124	115	321
Simocephalus vetulus	365	132	130	435

Table 3.2: Total Number of Rotifers Individual at Different Stations

Species Composition	St.-1 Jhirri	St. -2 Nayapura	St.-3 Mandideep	St.-4 Bhojpur
Brachionus bidentata	180	220	178	221
Brachionus calyciflorus	176	210	157	223
Brachionus caudatus	187	190	189	243
Brachionus rubens	157	169	167	231
Keratella cochlearis	198	135	198	120
Keratella quadrata	180	156	198	232
Keratella tropica	163	176	170	134
Asplanchna priodonta	189	168	194	321
Branchionus urceolaris	194	123	190	235
Brachionus variabilis	160	187	165	256
Brachionus plicatilis	150	169	145	286
Euchlanis dialatata	160	176	198	243

Table 3.3: Total Number of Copepods Individual at Different Stations

Species Composition	St.-1 Jhirri	St.-2 Nayapura	St.-3 Mandideep	St.-4 Bhojpur
Cyclops strenus	223	123	119	189
Cyclops vernalis	127	112	118	150
Cyclops virdis	226	120	115	220
Acanthocyclops robustus	250	156	113	210
Diacyclops nanus	185	89	123	198
Mesocyclops americanus	229	187	143	202
Mesocyclops edax	324	113	221	289
Macrocyclops fuscus	290	101	112	249

Table 3.4: Water Quality Parameter at Different Stations

Parameter	St.-1 Jhirri Mean Value	St.-2 Nayapura Mean Value	St.-3Mandideep Mean Value	St.-4 Bhojpur Mean Value
Temperature	23.5	28.3	27.6	19.5
pH	7.9	5.9	6.1	8.2
D.O	6.4	2.5	2.8	5.7
B.O.D	4.3	8.6	6.4	4.5
C.O.D	5.3	10.4	8.7	5.2

Table 3.5: Correlation of Coeffi. of Water Quality Parameter with Zooplankton

Parameters	Zooplankton	Co-eff. correlation	Comment
Temperature	Zooplankton	0.432	Significant Relation
pH	Zooplankton	0.321	Significant relation
D.O	Zooplankton	0.185	Significant relation
B.O.D	Zooplankton	-0.132	Inverse relation
C.O.D	Zooplankton	-0.180	Inverse relation

DISCUSSION

Zooplankton organisms occupy central position in the food webs of aquatic ecosystem. They do not only form an integral part of the lentic community but also contribute the biological productivity of the fresh water ecosystem (Wetzel, 2001). Due to short life cycle, zooplankton communities often respond quickly to environmental changes Sharma *et. al.*, (2007). In ecologically, zooplankton are one of the most important biotic components influencing all the functional aspects of an aquatic ecosystem , such as food chain , food webs, energy flow and cycling of matter, The zooplankton plays an integral role and serves bioindicators and it is well- suited tool for understanding water pollution status, Murugan *et. al.*, 1998; Dadhick and Saxena, 1999; Sinha and islam, 2002.

Biodiversity of Zooplankton

Zooplankton population was composed of the numbers of Cladocera, Rotifera, Copepoda. In the present study 34 species of zooplankton have been identified from the samples collected at four major stations (08 sites. A total of 16 genera were recorded from the study area in river Betwa. Among them 07 belonged to cladocera, 05 belonged to copepoda, 04 to rotifer. All identified zooplanktons belong to four groups, Cladocera (14 taxa), Copepoda (08 taxa), Rotifer (12).

Rotifera

Rotifera are the most important soft bodied metazoans among the plankton. There name comes from the apparently rotating wheel of cilia known as corona used for locomotion and sweeping food particles toward the mouth. Species diversity was highest at station – II and III in river Betwa at Nayapura and Mandideep (Graph 3.1). Species composition was lowest at station- I due to the purity of water. Among the Rotifers, Brachionus genus was abundant at station- II and III. The genus Brachionus is considered as a biological indicator for the eutrophication, Nogueira (2001). In the present study station- II and III are the polluted sites. Similar observation was also noticed by various workers Arora, (1996) and Patil *et. al.*, (2006).

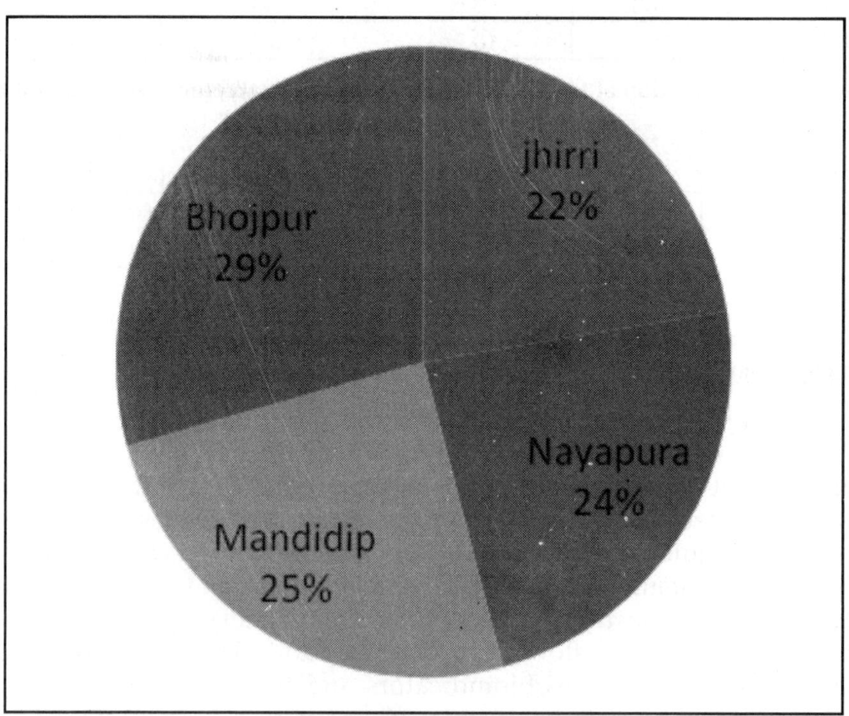

Graph.3.1: Species Composition of Rotifer at different Station

Cladocera

Cladocera popularly called as water flea prefers to live in deep water and constitute a major item of food for fish. Thus, they hold key position in food chain and energy transformation (Uttangi, 2001). During the present study of river Betwa in all stations total number of cladocera (14) Fourteen recorded, belong to (07) Seven genera and 14 taxa (Table 3.1 & Graph 3.2). Zooplankton diversity was dominant by *Daphnia* and *Ceriodaphnia* at all sampling stations of river Betwa. Among the total zooplankton population cladocera species was reported as first in order of abundance in Betwa river where river water very clean. In the present study species Daphnia found rarely at station - II Nayapura and station- III Mandideep, but maximum abundant at station- I, IV. According to Pennak (1978) cladocera such as Daphnia pulex are also found to rare in rapid stream and grossly polluted water.

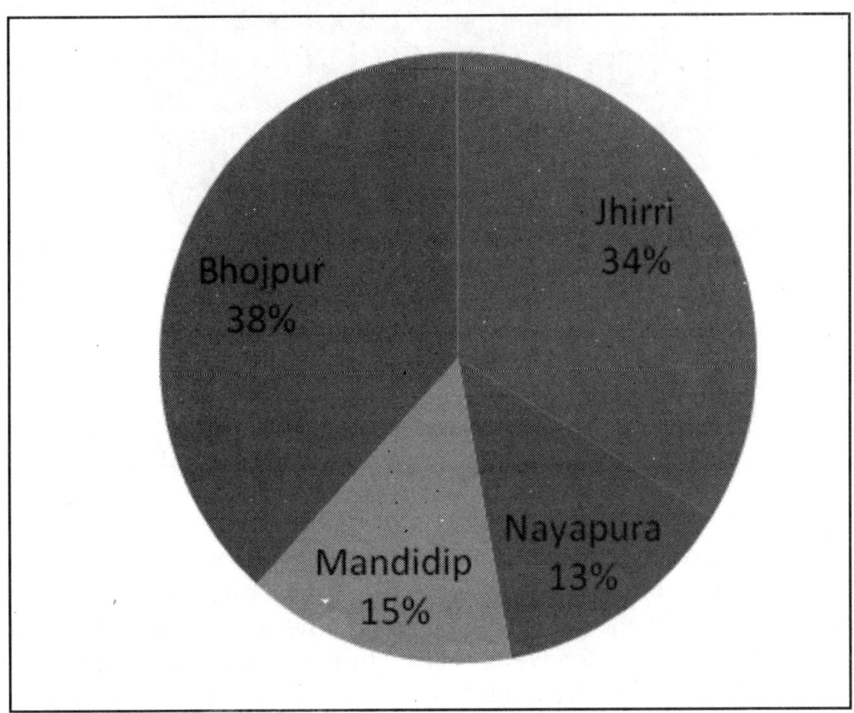

Graph 3.2: Species Composition of Cladoceran at Different Station

Copepoda

Fresh water copepods constitute one of the major zooplankton communities occurring in all types of water bodies. Copepods are the primary consumer of phytoplankton and are the main prey item of larval juvenile fishes that link pelagic food webs. In the present study, 08 species of

05 genera (Table.3.3 & Graph 3.3) of copepods were identified in river Betwa. Low diversity of copepods was found in winter while higher population was found in March and April. Pennak (1955) opined that cyclops was found to indicate oligotrophic condition. Copepods were high instable environmental condition and they disappear as pollution level increased, Das *et. al.,* (1996).

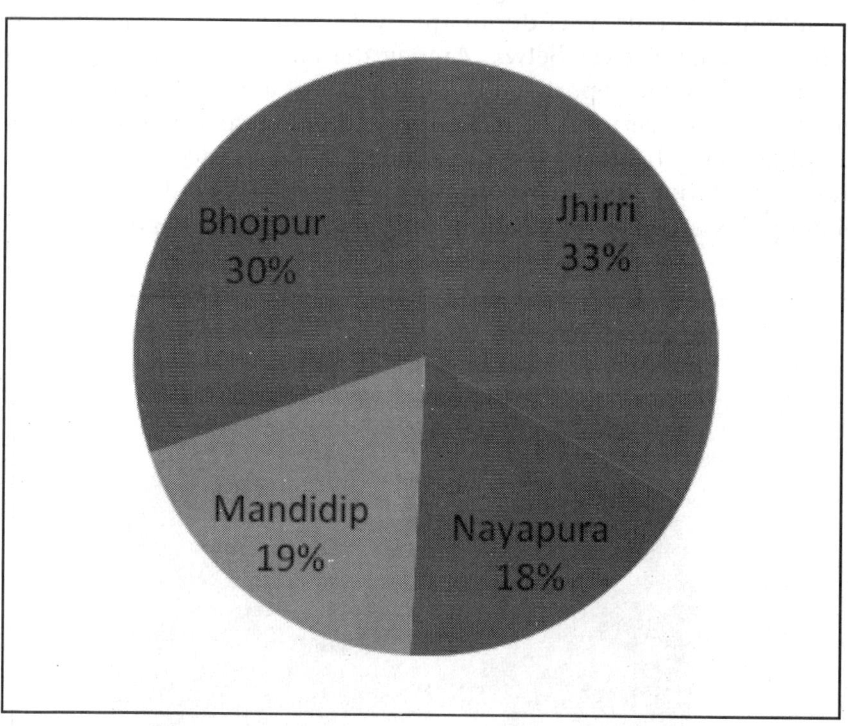

Graph 3.3: Species Composition of Copepods at Different Station

Temperature influences the life of all biological organisms. It affects many physical and chemical characteristics of water such as viscosity, density, solubility of salts and gases. The surface of water directly receives solar radiation, suitable for the growth of plankton. The seasonal variation in the temperature of river water were observation all sampling stations. The seasonal variation showed a similar trend at all the stations. The temperature at station No. III was slightly higher because of mixing of sewage and industrial effluents (Graph. 3.4). During the study period of investigation, due to shallowness of river Betwa at Mandideep, the water temperature has show a tendency to follow closely the atmospheric temperature. The findings were common with the observations of Malhotra *et. al.,* 1986; and Das *et. el.;* (2003).

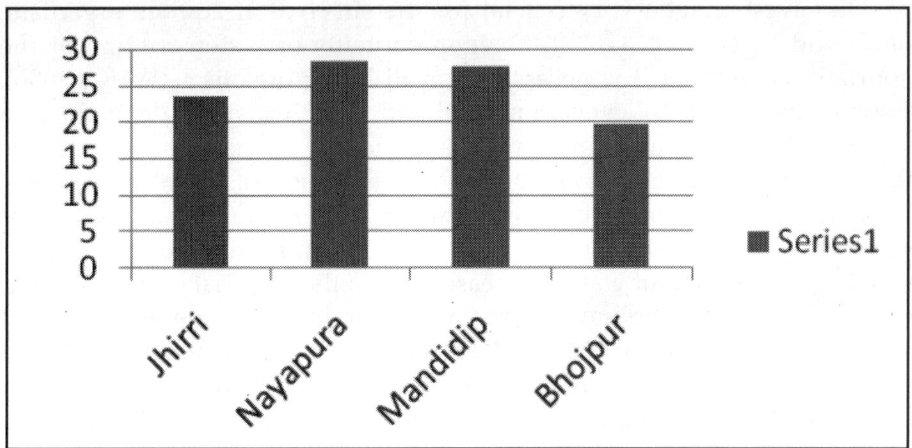

Graph 3.4: Level of Temperature at Different Stations

The pH of a solution refers to its hydrogen ion activity and is expressed as the logarithm of the reciprocal of the hydrogen activity in moles per liter at a given temperature (APHA.1992). The pH expresses the intensity of acidity or alkalinity of an aquatic environment. The present finding reveal that in river Betwa pH fluctuate in station II Nayapura and station III Mandideep, while in other stations pH was uniform ranged recorded (Table 3.4). In the present study low pH value were found may be due to industrial effluent of nearby industries. Effect of low pH on zooplankton was studied by Zhaung Dehvi (1995) he observed that the species of zooplankton were found to decline gradually with a reduction of pH value. The change in pH values of station II and III. It was observed that pH decreased. The reduction in the pH of river Betwa could have been due to the discharged industrial effluents.

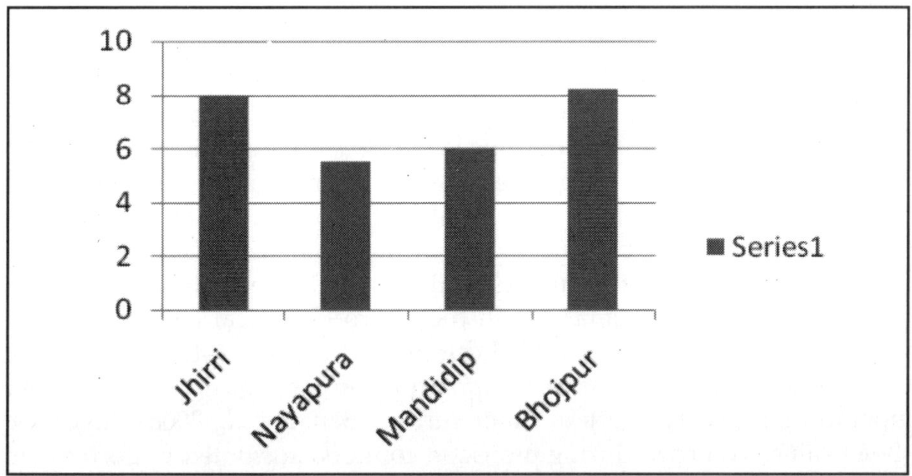

Graph 3.5: Level of pH at Different Stations

Dissolved oxygen very crucial for the survival of aquatic organism, Yakub and Ugwvmba, (2009). Oxygen contents of water are one of the important factors and it is necessary for all living organism (WHO, 2006). Dissolved oxygen (DO) levels in natural and waste water are dependent on the physical, chemical and biochemical activities prevailing in the water body. Running water contain relatively high concentration of dissolved oxygen. The high content during winter was due to higher solubility of oxygen at lower temperature favoring retention of oxygen. During summer, the volume as well as rate of flow of water decreases, while the disposal of waste water, industrial effluents and sewage remain virtually the same at station- II Nayapura and station- III Mandideep showed lowest value of dissolved oxygen. The same results were reported by Verma and Mathur (1971), Baruah *et.al.*, 1996. Minimum dissolved oxygen due to effluents discharge, Emongor *et. al.*, 2005.

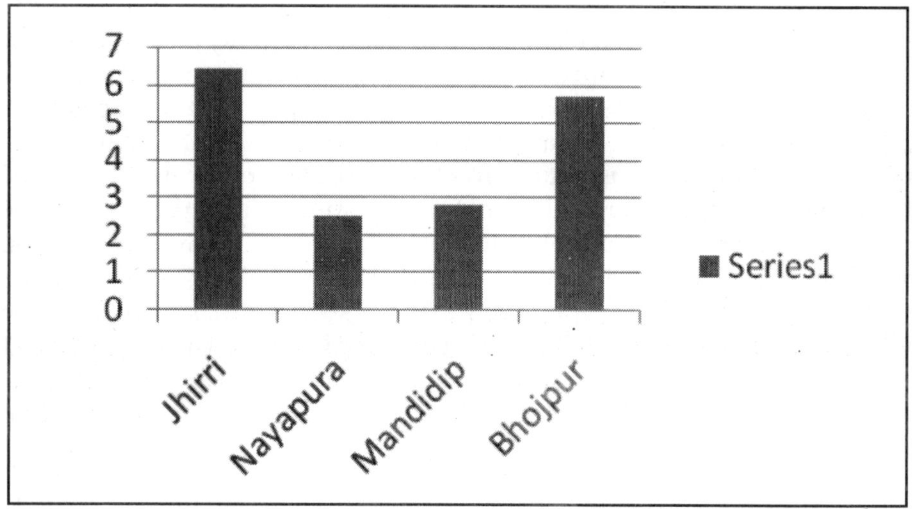

Graph 3.6: Level of Dissolve Oxygen at Different Stations

Biological oxygen demand (BOD) is an important parameter which is widely used to determine the pollution load of waste water. Biological oxygen demand is the amount of oxygen required by microorganism for stabilizing biologically decomposable organic matter (carbonaceous) in water under aerobic condition. In the present finding the lowest BOD value was recorded station –I Jhirri, while the highest value of BOD recorded station –III Mandideep. Seasonal fluctuations in the hydro biological factors revealed higher value of BOD were observed during late summer (May-June). These were due to higher rate of decomposition of organic matter at higher temperature, turbidity and less water current (Sanap *et.al.*, 2006) . Decrease in BOD values recorded during monsoon could be attributed to decrease in temperature and dilution in the concentration of dissolved organic matter due to heavy rains. Minimum value of BOD was observed during winter. Low BOD contents indicated that the riverine stretch was free from organic pollution. Similar observation recorded Sachidanandamurthy and Yajurvedi, (2004), and Pratima (2008).

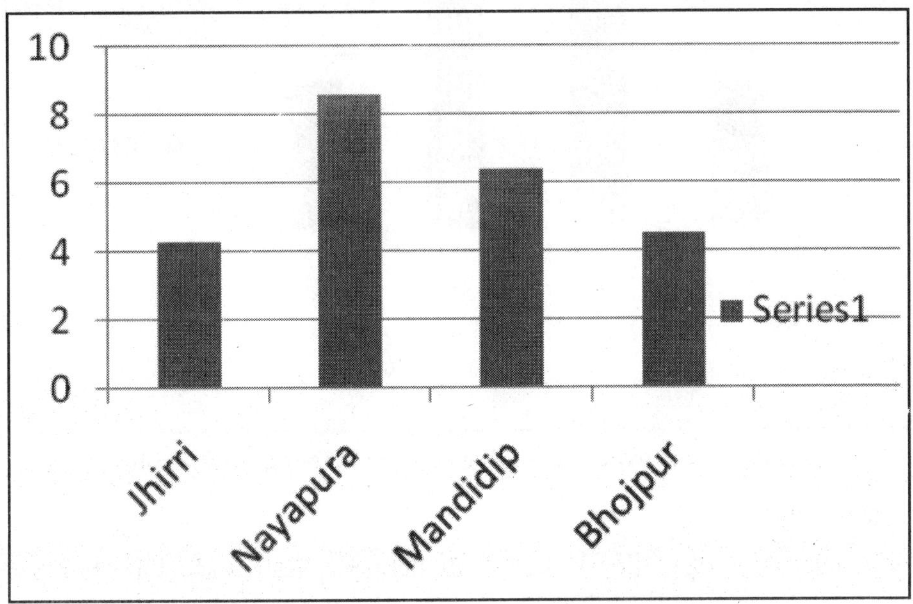

Graph 3.7: Level of Dissolve Oxygen at Different Stations

Chemical oxygen demand is a test which is used to measure pollution of domestic and industrial waste. COD gives us reliable parameter for judging the extent of pollution in water (Shrivastava and Patil 2002). The measure of COD determines the quantities of organic matter found in water. This makes COD useful as indicators of organic pollution in surface water (King *et. al.*, 2003). The chemical oxygen demand (COD) was higher than the NESREA (2011) and WHO (1993) values recommended for good water quality. This also provides direct measures of state of pollution in water bodies. High COD value at the discharge point could be due to high organic load of total solid and total suspended solid from industries. This could probably explain the linear relationship between solid and COD (Osibanjo and Adie, 2007). Highest value of COD indicates that most of pollution in study zone in Betwa river in caused by industrial effluents discharged by industrial units. Similar results were also reported by Pande and Sharma (1998).

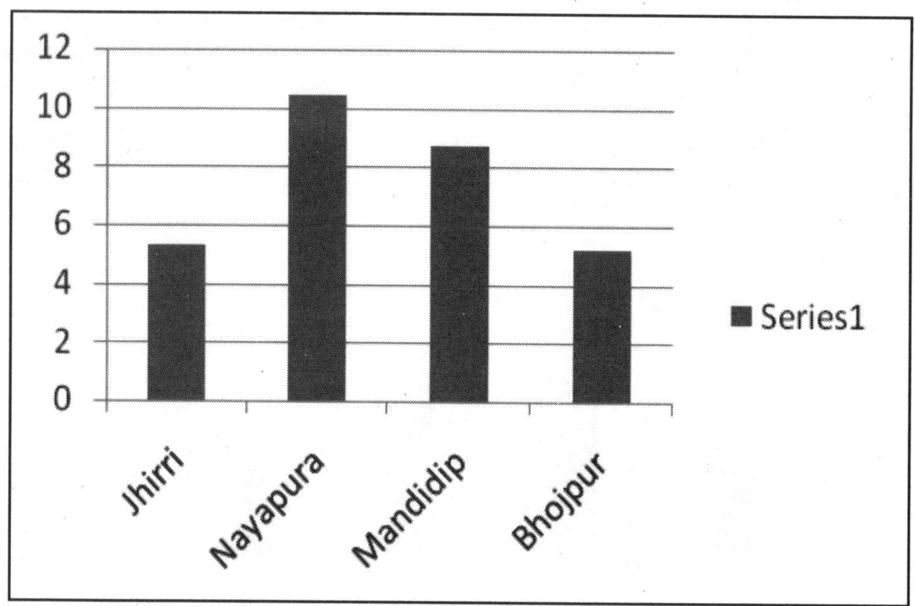

Graph 3.8: Level of Dissolve Oxygen at Different Stations

CONCLUSION

Increasing population is a great challenge in India. India has often been describing a rich land with poor people. The nexus between poverty and environmental degradation can be hardly be over emphasized. Zooplankton are free floating animals which play a vital role in aquatic food web, zooplankton are highly sensitive to environmental variation, as a result change in their abundance, species diversity or community composition can provide important indication of environmental change or disturbance. The present study was undertaken to understand the water quality and zooplankton biodiversity of river Betwa.

On account of its portability, the water of river is being used for various purposes such as irrigation, industries, fishing, drinking and recreational uses. After independence, the river are badly exploited and polluted due to industrial development and human activities. Lastly, it is estimated that the ecological conditions of river Betwa is being deteriorating gradually. If positive steps are not taken to improve it, the self purification power of the river will be affected severely. Thus, these observations have made clear, the need for integrated studies involving both abiotic parameters and community studies.

REFERENCES

A.P.H.A, (1992): Standrad Methods for the Examination of Water and Waste Water. American Public Health Associations, New York.

Arora, H.C.(1996): Rotifera as Indicators of Trophic Nature of Environment. Hydrobiologia.27, 146-149.

Baruah, B.K. Baruah, D. and Das, M. (1996): Study of the Effect of Paper Mill Effluent on the Water Quality of Receiving Wetland. Poll. Res,15 (14): 389-393.

Dadhick, N. and M.M. Saxena. (1999): Zooplankton as Indicators of Trophical Status of Some Desert Waters Near Bikaner. J. Environ. Pollut., 6, 251-254.

Das, A.C. Baryagm B.K., Baruha, D. and Sengupta, S. (2003): Study on Wetlands of Guwahati City: 2, Water Quality of Fiver and Drains; Poll. Res. 22(1): 117-119.

Dhanapathi, M.V.S.S.S (2000): Taxonomic Notes on the Rotifers from India. Indian Association of Aquatic Biologists (IAAB) Hyderabad.

Edmondson, W.T. (1959): Freshwater Biology, Edward and Whipple, 2nd Ed^{n}. John Willey Sons Inc. New York, 95-189.

Emonger V., Kealotswe E., Koorapetse I., SanKwasa S. and Keikanestswe S., (2005): Pollution Indicators in Gaberone Effluents. J. Appl. Sci., 5, 147-150.

Hutchionson, G.E. (1967): A Treatise on Limnology, Volume II. Introduction to Lake Biology and the Limnoplankton. Wiley, New York. 1115 pp.

KBLP, 1995. Ken Betwa Link Project Report.

King, J.M., Scheepers, A.C.T., Fisher, R.C., Reinecke, M.K. and Smith, L.B. (2003): River Rehabilitation: Literature Review, Case Studies and Emergin Principles. WRC Report No. 1161/1/03.

Malhotra, Y.R., S.P.S. Dutta, and S.N. Suri (1986): Limnology of Fish Pond in Regional Research Laboratory. *Jamu. Matsya*, (12-13): 174-177.

Murugan, N., P. Murugavel and M.S. Koderkar. (1998): Freshwater Cladocera; Indian Associ. of Aqua. Biologists (IAAB), Hyderabad. pp. 1-47.

Needham, J G. Needham, P.R. (1962): A Guide to the Fresh Water Biology, Holdend-day inc. Sanfrancisco, California: 108.

Nogueira, M.G. (2001): Zooplankton Composition Dominance and Abundance as Indicators Environmental Compartmentalization in Jurumirim Reservoir (Paranapanema river), Sao Paulo, Brazil. Hydrobiologia, 455, 1-18.

Osibanjo, O. and G.U. Adie, (2007): Impact of Effluents from Bodijia Abatter on the Physicochemical Parameter of Oshunkaye Stream in Ibadan City, Nigeria. Afr. J. Biotechno., 6:

Pande, K.S. and S.D. Sharma, (1998): Studies of Toxic Pollutants in Ramganga River at Moradabad India. Envtal Geo., 1(2): 93-96.

Patil, S.U., M.B. Mule and S.S. Kharade, (2006): Zooplankton Study of Krishna River from Walwa Taluka, District Sangli, Maharashtra. Research Hunt.1, 31-35.

Pennak, A (1955): Comprative Limnology of Eight Colorado Mountain Lakes. *Univ.Colorado Stud., Ser. Biol.*, 2: 1-75.

Pennak, R.W .(1978): *Freshwater Invertebrates of the United State*. 2nd Ed., John Willy and Sons, New York, U.S.A., p. 803.

Pratima M. Shiddamallayya N. (2008): Impact of Domestic Sewage on Fresh Water Body. Journal of Environmental Biology 29(3): 303-308.

Sachidanandamurthy K.L. and Yajurvedi H.N. (2006): A Study of an Physicochemical Parameters of an Aquaculture Body in Mysore City, Karnataka, India. Journal of Environmental Biology 27(4): 615-618.

Sanap, R.R. Mohite, A.K. Pingle, S.D. and Gunale, V.R (2006): Evaluation of Water Qualities of Godawari river with Reference to Physicochemical Parameters, dist. Nasik (M.S.), India. Poll. Res., 25(4), pp. 775-778.

Sharma, M.S., V. Sharma and H. Malara, (2007): *Biodiversity of Zooplankton in Relation to Different Types of Aquatic Pollution.* C.P. 46. NSL 2007. pp. 300-302.

Shrivastava, V.S. and P.R. Patil: (2002): Tapti River Water Pollution by Industrial Wastes: A Statistical Approach. Nat. Environ. Pollut. Tech., 1, 279-283.

Sinha, B. and M.R. Islam. (2002): Seasonal Variation in Zooplankton Population of Two Lentic Bodies and Assam State Zoo cum Botanical Garden, Guwahati, Assam. Eco. Environ. Cons., 8, 273-278.

Uttangi, J.C. (2001): Conservation and Management Strategy for the Water Flow of Minor Irrigation Tanks Habitats and Their Importance as Stopover Site in the Dharwad District, 179-221.

Varma, S.R. and Mathur, R.P. (1971): Characterictics and Pollution Effect of Paper Mills Wastes on the Hindon River: Seminar on Water Supply and Sanitation.

W.H.O., (2004): World Health Organisation.

Wetzell, R.G. (2001): Limnology: Lake and River Ecosystem, 3rd ed. Academic Press. ISBN –12-744760-1.

Zhaung, J. Yan J. Zhang ZF. (1995): National River Chemistry Trends in China: Huanghe and Chanjiang, Ambio- AJ. Hum. Enviro., 24 (5): 275-279.

Adverse Impacts of Oil Pollution on Environment

Navneet Rai*[1]; Kamal Joshi[2]

ABSTRACT

Oil keeps the factors of the industrialized countries working and provides the revenues, which enable oil exporters to execute ambitious national and economic development plans. The march of progress would be retarded and life itself would be unbearable if the world is deprived of oil. The oil and gas history in India dates back to 1867, with the discovery of oil deposits in Makum, near Margherita, Assam. The oil and gas sector in India has since witnessed the birth of numerous oil and gas companies. Since the discovery of oil in India in 1867, the country has been suffering the negative environmental consequences of oil exploration and exploitation.

In last 30-40 years a number of oil spills have occurred in Indian waters and the damage caused to the marine environment on such occasions was alarming in some cases. When oil is spilled or leaked into in waterways and the ocean, it spreads very quickly with the help of wind and currents. A single gallon of oil can create an oil slick up to a couple of acres in size. There's really no aspect of a marine and coastal environment

1. Department of Chemistry, DIT University, Dehradun (UK), India.
2. Department of Environmental Studies, Graphic Era Hill University, Dehradun (UK), India.

that is not in some way adversely affected by an oil spill. The closer the spill occurs to the shoreline, the more pronounced the damage will be due to coastal zones being home to more concentrated and diverse populations of marine bird and animal life than far out to sea. It threatens the extinction of several plants, and has already harmed many land, air, and sea animal and plant species.

In the present study we have studied some recent oil spills in India and an attempt has been made to assess the impacts of these oil spills on the environment.

Keywords: Oil Pollution, Oil Spill, Offshore drilling, Coast, Impact.

INTRODUCTION

Organisation of the Petroleum Exporting Countries (OPEC) forecasts that oil demand will continue to grow strongly and oil will remain the world's single most important source of energy for the foreseeable future. OPEC forecasts that oil's share of the worldwide energy market will fall from almost 40 per cent in 2010 to less than 37 per cent in 2020. But oil will still be the world's single largest source of energy. The reduction in oil's market share is largely due to the stronger growth enjoyed by other forms of energy, particularly gas. The amount of oil demanded worldwide is actually expected to rise, from around 88 million barrels per day in 2010 to about 100 million barrels per day in 2020 (OPEC Annual Statistical Bulletin: 2010-11).

The origin of oil & gas industry in India can be traced back to 1867 when oil was struck at Makum near Margherita in Assam. At the time of Independence in 1947, the Oil & Gas industry was controlled by international companies. India's domestic oil production was nearly 5,000 barrels per day and the entire production was from one state - Assam. The oil and gas sector in India has since witnessed the birth of numerous oil and gas companies. The present consumption of petroleum products in India is around 3.2 million barrels per day (OPEC Annual Statistical Bulletin: 2010-11). The demand for petroleum is expected to be 10.5 million barrels per day by the year 2024-25. To meet its growing petroleum demand, India is investing heavily in oil fields abroad. India's state-owned oil firms already have stakes in oil and gas fields in Russia, Sudan, Iraq, Libya, Egypt, Qatar, Ivory Coast, Australia, Vietnam and Myanmar. Oil and Gas Industry has a vital role to play in India's energy security and if India has to sustain its high economic growth rate.

Along with the fast economic growth of the nations surrounding the Indian Ocean comes a tremendous increase in maritime activities mainly transport of oil products through ships in the seas around our country. This causes the ever presence of the danger of oil spills which can occur anywhere on land or at sea which knows no respect for national boundaries. The density of marine traffic, especially oil tankers, in close proximity of the Indian coast and offshore petroleum exploration and production platforms, make our region a high risk area (DOS-DCP, 2009). The pollution from blow out, collision, stranding, and other marine accidents can threaten marine life in the inter-tidal zones, fisheries, sea birds, harbors, wildlife, human health, recreational beaches, tourism and industrial plants with subsequent loss of revenue. Hence such incidents warrant an advanced preparedness or contingency planning making it desirable to coordinate activities amongst a number of agencies.

Nowadays, in the world, oil spill in the ocean is one of the serious sea pollution issues which is concerned by international community. The US National Research Council (NRC) has estimated the amount of oil entering the sea from different sources - a total 3.2 million tones worldwide annually. The biggest source of oil into the sea is from urban and industrial inputs. The NRC estimates a total from this source of 960,000 tonnes - or 30% of the total tanker. Tanker operations are the next biggest source (22%), followed by tanker accidents (13%). Offshore production is the smallest source - contributing less than 2% of the oil entering the sea worldwide. A surprising amount of oil in the oceans occurs naturally - seeping through cracks in the earth's crust. The US NRC estimates that about 8% of oil comes from these natural seeps - four times the amount arising from exploration and production (Van *et al*, 2009).

RECENT OIL SPILLS IN INDIAN MARINE ENVIRONMENT

For a country like India with a long coastline, surrounded by busy shipping lanes together with growing number of offshore oil fields, pollution from oil is a continuous threat. About 80 per cent of India's demand for oil is met from the sea, 46 per cent is carried aboard ships and 34 per cent is extracted from offshore areas (Chaudhury, 1997). Two main oil tanker routes which originate in the Gulf countries cross the Northern Indian Ocean. One of them goes via Mozambique Channel, round South Africa to the western hemisphere. The other one is along the Exclusive Economic Zone (EEZ) of India, round Sri Lanka across the southern Bay of Bengal through the Malacca strait to Far East and Japan. Nearly 500 million tones of crude oil are carried by about 3500 tankers along this route (NOS-DCP, 2008). Any major oil spill occurring in the Arabian Sea and Bay of Bengal will lead to large scale damage to marine environment. This, coupled with increasing emphasis on offshore oil exploration in many countries in the area, makes the northern Indian Ocean very vulnerable to oil pollution. Besides tanker accidents, offshore drilling and discharge of the refinery waste, the major source of oil pollution is the intentional dumping of bilge and bunker washings from the tankers. The presence of about 75% of oil in the marine environment is due to operational discharges. Fortunately, only a few tanker disasters have occurred along these routes so far.

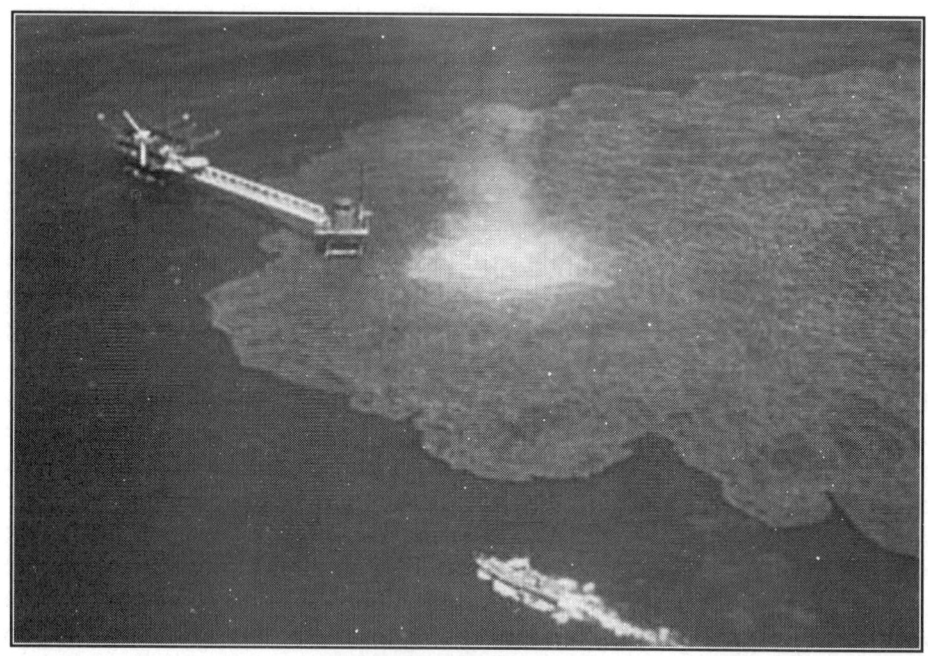

Oil Spill at Arabian Sea

Oil spill incidents have occurred in various parts and at different times along our coast. A few ships sink in Indian coastal waters every year; in 2007, as many as five vessels with a total of 658 tonnes of oil went down. *M. V. Malavika*, an Essar-owned vessel was hit by a barge at Gopalpur port (Ganjam District, Orissa) on 12 April 2010. A crack developed in the ship's fuel tank leading to leakage of fuel oil that soon covered the coast ranging from Arjipalli beach (which is adjacent to Gopalpur port) to Rushikulya River mouth, about 20 km from the port. Oil rapidly spread to a stretch of 20-30 km towards the river mouth and over a 7 sq. km area off the beach, 200 m away from the river mouth where the olive ridleys turtles had laid eggs. Some of the oil also reached the sands of the nesting grounds at Gokharkuda and Kantigada beaches (Reddy, 2010). On 13th June' 2011, a wreckage was found of a Chinese ship off Orissa's Gahirmatha coast in close proximity to DRDO's Wheeler Island test range. Since there was no threat of an oil spill, it was unlikely to damage marine ecology and forest officials were worried about the possible threat to Olive Ridley turtles. (Tribune, New Delhi, Date: 17/06/2011).

There are a number of factors which can cause oil spills. It may happen during the transport of oil across oceans. Oil is commonly transported by barges, tankers, pipelines, and trucks, each of which has its own imperfections that can lead to an oil accident. Tankers and barges can crash or run into unexpected land that causes a crack or hole which allows oil to escape. Oil shipping trucks can also instigate an oil spill in the event of an accident. For example, recently in August 2010, when the MSC Chitra collided with the Khalijia, it had a cargo of 1,219 containers holding 2662 tonnes of fuel, 283 tonnes of diesel and 88040 litres of lubricant oil. Thirty-one containers had pesticide in them. The Chitra tilted sharply under the impact of the collision, resulting in the 800 tonnes of oil spill (Rai, 2011).

Likewise, pipelines which transport oil can develop leaks or cracks that allow oil to seep into the environment e.g. a leakage in the Mumbai Uran Trunk (MUT) pipeline operated by India's Oil & Natural Gas Corporation (ONGC) caused a 1.6 kilometre spill off the coast of India on 21 January, 2011, resulting in about 30,000 barrels of crude leaking into the ocean (Business Line, 2011).

Some oil can escape while it is being moved from one vessel to another, a process called lightering. Uncontrollable factors such as hurricanes and other violent weather can cause tankers or barges to wreck or can damage offshore drilling facilities, incidents that can lead to oil spills. For example, Around one lakh litres of diesel spilled off Mundra coast in Kutch district of Gujarat from the oil jetty of a private port on 21st June' 2011, when a consignment of Hindustan Petroleum Corporation Limited (HPCL) was being off-loaded from a ship. The incident took place when a diesel consignment of HPCL was being transferred from the ship to tanks. The valve of one of the tanks was tightened so much that due to the back pressure, the pipeline ruptured for 3-4 minutes, resulting in a leakage of about one lakh litres of diesel (Times Of India, 22/06/2011).

Oil spills can occur during other phases of production, such as when oil is being extracted from an oil well or being converted into other products at a refinery. Human mistakes as well as equipment failure are common causes of accidents in such situations. Sometimes oil is even spilled intentionally as an act of war or vandalism (Pearce, 1991). Illegal dumping of oil is another deliberate act that causes harm to the environment.

EFFECT OF OIL SPILL ON ENVIRONMENT

The potential threat from operational or accidental oil spills from tankers and other oil related activities could lead to large scale destruction of marine life and property of the coastal region. While the size of a spill is obviously important, the amount of damage done can depend even more on other factors like the type of oil spilled and the location of the spill - as well as temperature, wind and weather. Oil spills in marine waters can damage social and economic systems as well as the natural environment of surrounding seas which support valuable fishing grounds, coastal ecosystems, Protected Marine National Park areas, long recreational and tourist beaches. India has several ecologically sensitive areas like Coral Reefs, mangroves and areas of unique biodiversity like turtle nesting grounds, etc.

When oil is spilled or leaked into in waterways and the ocean, it spreads very quickly with the help of wind and currents. A single gallon of oil can create an oil slick up to a couple of acres in size for example in Mumbai oil spill' 2010, the oil slick spread over an area of 25 square kilometers within few hours (Rai, 2011). Oil spills involve the release of dangerous hydrocarbons such as benzene and polynuclear aromatic hydrocarbons into the soil and water sources. After the Mumbai oil spill' 2010, samples revealed that the soil at Awas beach contained 60,000 mg/kg of total petroleum hydrocarbon, while the international permissible limit is 1000 mg/kg. On the other hand, at INS Kunjali in Navy Nagar, the oil contamination was 3,81,000 mg/kg. Petroleum hydrocarbons can accumulate in the tissues of some organisms like bivalves, prawns and fishes (Chandra *et al.*, 1998; Mehta *et al.*, 1994). The gaseous and liquid components of oil evaporate, some get dissolved in water and even oxidize, and yet some undergo bacterial changes and eventually sink to the bottom by gravitational action. The soil is then contaminated with a gross effect upon the terrestrial life. As the evaporation of the volatile lower molecular weight components affect aerial life, so the dissolution of the less volatile components with the resulting emulsified water, affects aquatic life (Michel *et. al.*, 1999). Spilled oil, its water soluble fractions and certain clean up operations are threat to different types of marine habitats and species in different ways (Mohammed, 2005 and Teruhisa *et al.*, 2003). Phytoplankton, due to lack of self-mobility are more vulnerable to oil toxicity. Bioassays conducted on phytoplankton communities have shown inhibition of growth by water soluble fraction of a crude oil (Ansari *et al.*, 1998).

Oil pollution harms sea birds when the oil touches their feathers making them unable to fly. The birds cannot remove the oil from their own bodies which makes them vulnerable to hypothermia because the oil prevents the feathers from helping to insulate them from extreme cold. Marine mammals like polar bears have similar problems with extreme cold whenever oil gets into their fur. Oil pollution also destroys smaller organisms in the water that birds, fish and marine animals eat. Even when the oil does not kill, it can have more subtle and long lasting negative effects. For example, it can damage fish eggs, larva and young - wiping out generations. It also can bio-accumulate up through the food chain as predators (including humans) eat numbers of fish (or other wildlife) that have sub-lethal amounts of oil stored in their bodies.

The formation of a thick layer of poisonous oil in the seawaters inflicts a distressing blow to the bionomical equilibrium by rendering fishes, turtles and other species immobile due to its high viscosity. In Gopalpur port oil spill, April 2010, some of the oil reached the sands of the nesting grounds at Gokharkuda and Kantigada beaches. This stretch is one of the three mass nesting sites of olive ridleys turtles and nearly 25, dead turtles were found floating on the water between Arjipalli and Prayagi. The spill also led to death of fishes and may have affected the fish breeding sites, which is likely to affect the turtles feeding on live fish (Reddy, 2010). After Mumbai oil spill' 2010, as well, various marine species died after coming in contact with the oil. Further, that was the breeding season for marine animals, and environmentalists feared that the spill may impact not only the breeding cycle, but also much more in the future if the oil contaminates the sediments and the sea bed (Rai, 2011).

Dead Olive Ridley Turtles After Oil Spill at Gopalpur Port

The coastal and offshore environment of India supports rich biodiversity. Bacteria, fungi, and zooplankton species are abundant. Over 630 species of marine algae have been reported. The annual production of seaweed is estimated at 70,000 tonnes. The total standing crop is estimated at 7000-8000 tonnes. Mangrove cover in India has been estimated at approximately 3,15,000 hectares confined mainly along the east (Orissa and West Bengal) coast and Andaman and Nicobar islands. The Sunderbans in West Bengal have one of the largest mangrove forests in the world. The mangrove flora of India is comprised of 50 exclusive species belonging to 20 genera (Rao *et al.*, 1999). A total of 50 genera and 13 sub-genera of reef-building corals are known to occur in Indian reefs representing more than half of those recorded from all over the world. Fisheries in the Indian marine environment comprise 15 pelagic and the same number of demersal fisheries. The oil spill affects these ecosystems in many ways. Oil kills plants and animals in the estuarine zone. Oil settles on beaches and kills organisms that live there; it also settles on ocean floor and kills benthic organisms such as crabs. For example, after the

Mumbai oil spill, the impact was felt along the Mumbai coastline, with fish and other marine creatures found covered with oil. The oil slick was entered the sensitive mangrove belt and damaged the environment there. The shores along the green mangroves were coated with slick black oil. Containers of pesticide were also thought to have spilled over and this was causing alarm to environmentalists (Rai, 2011).

Oil spills can also take place on the land as a result of leakage from terrestrial pipelines and pilferage activities. Oil spills on land pose a three-fold menace: fire hazards, groundwater pollution due to percolation, and air pollution due to evaporation. In one such accident, tonnes of heavy furnace oil spilt into the Ghanauli drain, which falls into Satluj river, following a burst in a pipeline of the Guru Gobind Singh Super Thermal Power Plant in Ropar on 24 April, 2009. The oil spill damaged the nearby wetlands that were home to migratory birds. And various samples collected from the river showed that it was highly polluted (Tribune, Dated: 25/04/2009).

A Bird Covered with Oil After Mumbai Oil Spill

Besides a deadly impact on marine ecology and the lives of fishermen, oil spills cause operational problems to several coastal industries as well as shipping. For example, in atomic and thermal power plants, there is a possibility that oil contaminated seawater enters the cooling water system, thereby somewhat reducing the heat transfer in steam condensers and heat exchangers causing reduction in power generation during the period. That's why after Mumbai Oil spill' 2010, Bhabha Atomic Research Centre (BARC) was alerted by the Coastguard to stop using sea water for cooling down purposes as the slick had reached Sewree area where BARC is located

(ZEENEWS, 09 August, 2010). Ships and tankers also experience the similar difficulties due to which fresh water generation has to be stopped when navigating in oil-polluted waters. If the oil spill does not clear away, stationary rigs may face fresh water problems. All ballasting operations have to be stopped, otherwise a clean ballast tank may be contaminated, with the risk of oil pollution during deballasting operations. On all vessels, sea water is used as a cooling and fire extinguishing medium. An oil spill combined with a fire caused by the gases emanating from the oil spill, cannot be effectively controlled or extinguished. Thus, the hazards to life and property at sea are increased in geometric proportions.

Any kind of oil pollution in the sea tends to endanger the vital drinking water sources, i.e. desalination plants, at the first instance. The presence of oil close to the plant intake system may affect the plant either by possible suction of oil constituents into the plant equipments decreasing their performance efficiencies or adversely affecting the quality of the product water making it aesthetically unpleasant and unsafe for drinking purposes. Apart from that, as oil, dead fish and birds all get washed up on the shores and the oil slick interferes in activities such as fishing, sailing, swimming etc. The local tourist industry suffers as aesthetic beauty of sea shore is lost due to oil slick.

CONCLUSION

Oil spills are one of the worst cases of environmental pollution. Oil pollution can have a serious economic impact on coastal activities and on those who exploit the resources of the sea. In most cases such damage is temporary and is caused primarily by the physical properties of oil creating nuisance and hazardous conditions. The impact on marine life is compounded by toxicity and tainting effects resulting from the chemical composition of oil, as well as by the diversity and variability of biological systems and their sensitivity to oil pollution. The impact of oil spills can be far-reaching, from an environmental as well as a socio-economic perspective. Marine and coastal habitats, wildlife species, recreational activities, local industry, and fisheries, are among the resources and sectors that can be negatively affected by oil spills. It affects seabirds, marine mammals, fish and shellfish, and bottom-living animals. It destroys beaches, destroys aquaculture, fisheries and deteriorates health effects from cleanup operations.

Once oil has been spilled, a rapid and well-resourced response is vitally important for clean-up, so that environmental and socioeconomic impacts are kept to the minimum. Response options need to be reviewed when a spill occurs, and such review should be an ongoing process in cases of large scale lengthy clean-up operations. The advantages and disadvantages of different responses need to be weighed up and compared both with each other and with the advantages and disadvantages of natural clean-up. The process will require taking into account the circumstances of the spill, the practicalities of clean-up response, scientific understanding of the relative impacts of oil and clean-up options, and some kind of value judgement of the relative importance of social, economic and environmental factors.

Mumbai Coast After Uran Oil Spill

Computer simulation models, Geographical Information System and Decision Support System tools are very useful in oil spill modelling and management. The effectiveness of response system depends on knowledge based on various aspects such as physical oceanographic processes and resources. Hence, a substantial knowledge base incorporating all parameters should be generated and made available to the organisations/institutes that are responsible for Oil Spill Management. To minimize the harmful effect of oil spill, there is need for a comprehensive contingency GIS based plan for oil spill management.

Countries around the world are actively exploring the best way to solve oil pollution. Bioremediation technique has been gradually accepted and become a new direction in cleaning and controlling oil pollution (Erdogan *et al.*, 2011and Lü *et al.*, 2011). Bioremediation is the use of organisms to break down and thereby detoxify dangerous chemicals in the environment. Due to the advancement in technology, micro-organisms and safe chemicals are used in the cleaning process, but the best way to deal with oil pollution is to reduce the use of fossil fuels and to enhance green technologies. Efficiency and renewable energy can help us reduce our dependence on oil - the only real way to stop oil spills.

REFERENCES

Ansari, Z.A., Saldanha, M.C. and Rajkumar, R., (1997). Effects of Petroleum Hydrocarbons on the Growth of a Microalga, Isochysis sp. (Chysophyta), *Indian J. Mar. Sci.*, 26: 372-376.

Business Line (2011), Minor Oil Leak in ONGC Pipeline Plugged, Available at: http://www.thehindubusinessline.com/companies/article1109204.ece, Posted on Jan. 21, 2011.

Chandra Mohan, P. and Raghu Prakash, R., (1998), Concentration of Petroleum Hydrocarbons in Bivalve Mytilopsis Sallei and in the Harbor Waters of Visakhapatnam, East Coast of India, *Indian J. Mar. Sci.*, 27: 496-498.

Chaudhury, Rahul Roy (1997), Ocean/Marine Management in India, Paper Presented at the Third Meeting of the Maritime Cooperation Working Group of the Council for Security Cooperation in the Asia-Pacific (CSCAP), on May 30-June 1, 1997, at Bangkok, Thailand.

DOS-DCP (2009), District Oil Spill Disaster Contingency Plan (Karnataka), Ministry of Defence, Government of India, pp. 14.

Erdogan, E.E. and Karaca, A. (2011). Bioremediation of Crude Oil Polluted Soils. *Asian J. Biotechnol.*, 3: 206-213.

Lü, J.C., Li, Z.T., Hussain, K. and. Yang, G.K, (2011), Bioremediation: The New Directions of Oil Spill Cleanup, *Middle-East Journal of Scientific Research* 7 (5): 738-740.

Mehta, P., Kadam, A.N., Gajbhiye, S.N. and Desai, B.N., (1994). Petroleum Hydrocarbon Concentration in Selected Species of Fish and Prawn from Northwest Coast of India, *Indian J. Mar. Sci.*, 23: 123-125.

Michel, J. and Hayes, M.O, (1999). Weathering Patterns of Oil Residues Eight Years After the Exxon Valdez Oil Spill. *Marine Pollution Bull.*, 38, 855-863.

Mohammed, A., (2005). Toxicity of Water Soluble Fractions of Four Fuels for Metamysidopsis Insularis, an Indigenous Tropical Mysid Species, *Environ. Monit. Assess*, 104: 37-44.

NOS-DCP, (2008) Proceedings of the Eleventh National Oil Spill Disaster Contingency Plan (NOS-DCP) and Preparedness Meeting held at Chennai Port Trust, Chennai on 24th April, 2008.

OPEC Annual Statistical Bulletin: 2010-11.

Pearce, Fred (1991). "Gulf War Could Mean Largest Oil Spill Ever." *New Scientist*, Vol. 129 (19 January 1991): (18).

Rai, Navneet (2011), Effect of Oil Pollution on Environment- Role of Emulsifiers & Demulsifiers in Various Emulsions, Microemulsions & Nanoemulsions with Their Applications, Ph.D. Thesis, H.N.B. Garhwal University, Srinagar, Garhwal, Uttarakhand, India.

Rao T.A, Molur, S. and Walker, S. (1999). Mangroves of India: Report Summary 1998 *Publ. Zoo Outreach Organisation* ISSN 0971-6378, XIV (2). pp. 1-49.

Reddy, M. Vikram, (2010). Threat of Gopalpur Port Oil Spill to Olive Ridley Turtles and Their Hatchlings, *Current Science*, Vol. 99, No. 3, 267-268.

Teruhisa, K., Masahiro, N., Hiroshi, K., Tomoko, Y. and Kouichi, O., (2003). Marine Life Research Group of Takeno, Impacts of the Nakhodka Heavy Oil Spill on an Intertidal Ecosystem: An Approach to Impact Evaluation Using Geographical Information System, *Mar. Poll. Bull.*, 47: 99-104.

Times of India, Dated: 22/06/2011, 1 Lakh Litres Diesel Spills at Mundra Port. Available at: http://www.indiaenvironmentportal.org.in/taxonomy/term/8151.

Tribune (Bathinda Edition) Dated: 25/04/2009, Furnace Oil Spills into Sutlej. Available at: http://www.tribuneindia.com/2009/20090425/bathinda.htm.

Tribune (New Delhi), Date: 17/06/2011, Shipwreck may Endanger Olive Ridleys. Available at: http://www.indiaenvironmentportal.org.in/taxonomy/term/8152.

Van, Anh Le, Duong Nguyen Dinh, Thu Ho Le, (2009). Sources of Oil Pollution in Vietnam Sea and East Sea, 7th FIG Regional Conference Spatial Data Serving People: Land Governance and the Environment – Building the Capacity, Hanoi, Vietnam, 19-22 October 2009.

Zee News, (09 August, 2010). Mumbai oil spill: BARC advised against using seawater. Available at: http://zeenews.india.com/news/state-news/mumbai-oil-spill-barc-advised-against-using-seawater_647025.html.

Chloride Ion Content from Nine Selected Undetermined Areas of Coastal Guyana

R.C. Jagessar[1]*; L. Sooknundun[2]

ABSTRACT

The chloride ion concentration from nine selected area of coastal Guyana was determined using Mohr's titrimetric method. High chloride content has a corrosive effect on metal pipes and structures and is harmful to most trees and plants. Chlorides can also react with humic substances present in water to form trihalomethanes (THMs) which are very carcinogenic and can induce cancer during consumption. Organochlorine such as CFCs (chlorofluorocarbons), PCBs (Polychlorobiphenyls), Dioxin and others can also be formed. These compounds are harmful to both aquatic life and humans. Fish and aquatic communities cannot survive in high levels of chlorides. Selected coastal areas investigated were Skeldon, Guysuco Estate, number 58 village, Rosehall Town in Berbice. Good hope, Ogle and Stabroek in Demerara and Parika, Supernaam and Spring Garden in the region of Essequibo.

The concentration of chloride was found to be 30.72mg/L ± 4.09, 233.970mg/L ± 0.00, 472.67mg/L ± 19.57, 246.02mg/L ± 0.00, 179.85mg/

1. Senior Lecturer, Department of Chemistry, University of Guyana, Georgetown, Guyana, South America.
2. Final Year Chemistry graduate, 2010-2011, University of Guyana, Turkeyen campus, Georgetown, Guyana, South America.

L ± 8.19, 411.45mg/L ± 4.09, 583.74mg/L ± 10.16, 1214.75mg/L ± 4.09 and 1318.74mg/L ± 12.28 at # 58. Village, Rose Hall, Skeldon Guysuco Estate, Hope, Ogle, Stabroek, Parika, Supernaam and Spring Garden waste water respectively. The Permissible concentration of Chloride is 250 mg/L, and it imparts an alteration in taste. Thus, it seems that the Cl^- concentration is higher than the 250mg/L threshold limit at Rosehall town, Skeldon Guysuco estate, Good Hope, Stabroek, Parika Supernaam and Spring Garden and appropriate environmental procedures should be taken to prevent chloride ion concentration beyond the threshold limit.

Keywords: Chloride ion content, Mohr's titrimetric method, trihalomethanes, organochlorine, threshold limit.

INTRODUCTION

Waste water is one that has been used for washing, flushing, or that which is released from manufacturing processes[1-3]. In Guyana, groundwater provides 90 percent of the potable water supply and is extracted mainly from the coastal artisan basin[4-5]. However, potable water can be contaminated with elements such as mercury, anions: cyanide, phosphates, nitrates, chlorides and cation in calcium and other wastes from mining etc. However, their level of concentration needs to be determined to avoid pollution and their negative effects on human lives in Guyana. Other contaminants include untreated human and animal wastes in water supplies and wastes from many industries in water tables[6].

Providing sufficient quantities of high quality water to satisfy our domestic, industrial and Agricultural needs is an on going global problem. Increasing population size, climate change and pollution will only exacerbate the situation. There is no physical shortage of water on the planet earth as it covers 70% of the globe. However, 97% of the world water is saline and is thus non-drinkable, 2% is locked in glaciers and polar ice caps, resulting in 1% to meet humanity needs[6].

Chloride is one of the major inorganic anions in water and waste water. The salty taste produced by chloride ion concentrations in potable water is variable and is dependent on the chemical compositions. Chloride ion concentration from the nine selected areas of coastal Guyana was determined using Mohr's titrimetric method. This method is applicable to drinking, surface and saline waters, domestic and industrial wastes[1]. Chloride (Cl^-) ion is linear in shape and is one of the major inorganic anion in water and wastewater. Chloride anion has both positive and negative impact on human lives[7-8].

Biologically, chloride is the major intra and extra cellular anion found in the body. Its concentration in plasma appears to be regulated by the requirement to maintain electrical neutrality[9]. It is also responsible for maintaining acid/base balance, transmitting nerve impulses and regulating fluid in and out of cells. The amount of chloride in the blood is carefully controlled by the kidneys[9]. It is commonly measured in serum as part of the electrolyte profile but its utility in this fluid is restricted to calculation of the anion gap. Measurement of chloride in urine is useful to assist in determining the cause of a metabolic alkalosis. A low urine chloride (< 20 mmol/L) is consistent with metabolic alkalosis caused by vomiting, gastric suction or chloride diarrhoea.

Chloride anion is also an important component of the chloride-bicarbonate exchanger also known as the anion exchange (AE) protein. This carrier increases the permeability of the erythrocyte membrane to HCO_3^- more than a million fold. This protein is responsible for the movement of two anions: HCO_3^- and Cl^-. For each HCO_3^- that moves in one direction, one Cl^- moves in the opposite direction. In the absence of Cl^- ion, bicarbonate transport stops. Cl^- ion is also implicated in the genetic disease cystic fibrosis in that Cl^- ion is responsible for the function of the chloride ion channel[9]. Chloride is an essential micronutrient for higher plants. Rainwater, dust and air pollution are natural inputs of chloride to soils. Human practices such as irrigation and fertilization contribute significantly to chloride deposition[10].

On the positive sides, chlorides are associated with other ions to give a salty taste. With sodium ions the taste is detectable at about 250 mg l^{-1} Cl^-, but with calcium or magnesium as the predominant ion, the taste may be undetectable at 1,000 mg l^{-1}. The chloride concentration is higher in wastewater than in raw water because NaCl is a common component of diets and passes unchanged through the digestive system. Small amounts of chlorides are required for normal cell functions in plant and animal life.

On the negative side high chloride content has a corrosive effect on metal pipes, metals such as stainless steel, high alloyed materials and structures and is harmful to most trees and plants. Chlorides can also react with humic substances present in water to form trihalomethanes (THMs) which are very carcinogenic and can cause cancer during consumption. Organo chlorine can also be formed such as CFCs (chlorofluorocarbons), PCBs (Polychlorobiphenyls), Dioxin and others. These compounds are harmful to aquatic life and also humans. Chlorides can contaminate freshwater streams and lakes. Fish and aquatic communities cannot survive in high levels of chlorides. Sources of Chlorides includes rocks containing chlorides, agricultural runoff, wastewater from industries, oil well waste, effluent wastewater from waste water treatment plants etc. Chloride is an essential micronutrient[1-3].

The Mohr's method determines the chloride ion concentration of a solution via titration with silver nitrate solution[10-12]. As a solution of silver nitrate is slowly added to the submitted sample, a precipitate of AgCl is formed before the end point equation since the K_{sp} for AgCl is 1.8×10^{-10} and that for Ag_2CrO_4 is 1.2×10^{-2}.

$$Ag^+ (aq) + Cl^- (aq) \longrightarrow AgCl (s) \text{ (White Precipitate)}$$

$$2 Ag^+ (aq) + CrO_4^{2-} (aq) \longrightarrow Ag_2CrO_4 (s) \text{ (Brick red precipitate)}$$

The end point of the titration occurs when all of the chloride anions have been precipitated. Further addition or excess silver nitrate will react with the with the chromate ions of the potassium chromate indicator to form a brick-red silver chromate precipitate in the equivalence point region. This reaction signals the end point of the titration. It's important that the pH of the sample solutions be between 6.5 and 10. Mohr's method is applicable for the analysis of chloride ions concentration in seawater, stream water, river water, estuary water and waste water.

Substances that are present in potable water at normal amounts will not cause any interference. Sulphide, Thiosulphates and Sulphite ions interference can be removed by treatment with Hydrogen peroxide (H_2O_2). Orthophosphate in excess of 25 mg/L interferes by precipitating as Silver phosphate. Iron in excess of 10mg/L interferes by masking the end-point. All silver compounds and solutions are sensitive to light. Therefore these reagents must be stored in dark bottles in a dark place. The Mohr's titration is sensitive to the presence of both chloride and bromide ions in solution and will not be too accurate when there is a significant concentration of bromide present as well as chloride. However, in many cases, the concentration of bromide seems to be negligible[10-12].

Coastal water monitored were those at:

No.58 Village (Berbice)	1a
Rose Hall (Berbice)	1b
Skeldon Estate (Berbice)	1c
Good Hope (Demerara)	2a
Ogle (Demerara)	2b
Stabroek (Demerara)	2c
Parika (Essequibo)	3a
Supenaam (Essequibo)	3b
Spring Garden (Essequibo)	3c

Procedure

(a) Preparation of reagents: The following reagents were prepared:

Potassium chromate (K_2CrO_4) indicator, 5%

5.0g of Potassium chromate was dissolved in distilled water and diluted to 100ml in a 100ml volumetric flask. It was closed, shaken vigorously and labeled.

Standard Sodium chloride (NaCl) reference solution, 0.1M

7.090g of Sodium chloride previously dried at 105^{0}C was dissolved in distilled water then diluted to 1000ml in a one mark volumetric flask.It was closed, shaken vigorously and labelled.

Standard Silver nitrate ($AgNO_3$) titrant, 0.1M

8.494g of Silver nitrate previously dried at 105^{0}C was dissolved in 500ml distilled water. It was then diluted to 1000ml in a one mark 1L volumetric flask. It was closed, shaken vigorously and labeled. The solution was transferred to a clean dark glass bottle with a glass stopper. This solution can be stable for several months. It was then standardized against Sodium chloride of 0.1 M according to Mohr's method.

Sodium hydroxide solution (NaOH), 10%

10g of acetic acid was dissolved in distilled water and made up to mark in 100ml volumetric flask. It was closed, shaken vigorously and labelled.

Acetic acid (H_2SO_4) solution, 10%

10g of acetic acid was dissolved in distilled water and made up to mark in 100ml volumetric flask. It was closed, shaken vigorously and labeled.

Reagent for improvement of buffer capacity

Calcium carbonate ($CaCO_3$) or Sodium hydrogen carbonate ($NaHCO_3$) in powdered form was used.

(b) Preparation of sample

The minimum sample requirement is 50ml. Waste water samples were collected in plastic bottles, no preservation was required. Samples were later stored in the refrigerator. The waste water was filtered to remove traces of solid matter such as sand, seaweed or any other solid particle. 50 ml of the waste water sample was pipette into a 100 ml conical flask. The pH of the sample water was read using a pH meter. It is important that the pH of the sample solutions be kept between 6.5 and 10.0. When the pH of the sample was found to be outside the range of 6.5 to 10.0, it was adjusted using acetic acid (6 drops). When the pH is less than 5, it was adjusted using 3 drops of NaOH. Records of the volume required to adjust the pH were taken. If the pH is less than 6.5, pH adjustments with $CaCO_3$ and sodium hydrogen carbonate is preferred. The amount added is choosen so that a carbonate residue is left in the sample even after titration. Six drops of 5% potassium chromate indicator were added to the sample in the conical flask. The water sample was then titrated via the dropwise addition of $AgNO_3$ solution until the colour of the solution just changes to the reddish brown which is due to the formation of silver chromate. The above procedure is then repeated against a standard or Blank. For the standard, 50ml of distilled water was used. It is advisable that the Blank value shoudn't exceed the use of 0.2 ml of silver nitrate as the titrant, otherwise the purity of the H_2O needs to be checked.

RESULTS

Table 5.1: The Titre Values for the Standardization of Silver Nitrate, $AgNO_3$ which was Used to Calculate the Concentration of Cl^-

Standardization of Silver Nitrate, $AgNO_3$			
Initial Volume, ml	Final Volume, ml	Titre Value, ml	Average titre (ml)
1.30	26.50	25.20	
1.00	26.30	25.30	
4.50	29.70	25.20	25.23

Nb: 25.00ml of NaCl was used for the Standardization.

Table 5.2: The Titre Values of the Blank which was Used to Calculate the Corrected Titre in the Region of Berbice

BLANK			
Initial Volume, ml	Final Volume, ml	Titre Value, ml	Average titre value (ml)
33.00	33.60	0.60	
34.00	34.60	0.60	
35.00	35.60	0.60	0.60

Nb: 50ml of distilled water was used as the blank.

Table 5.3: The Titre Values of the Blank which was Used to Calculate the Corrected Titre in the Region of Demerara

BLANK			
Initial Volume, ml	Final Volume, ml	Titre Value, ml	Average titre value (ml)
43.50	44.00	0.50	
44.00	45.10	1.10	
45.10	45.70	0.60	0.73

Nb: 50ml of distilled water was used as the blank.

Table 5.4: The Titre Values of the Blank which was Used to Calculate the Corrected Titre in the Region of Essequibo

BLANK			
Initial Volume, ml	Final Volume, ml	Titre Value, ml	Average titre value (ml)
40.00	40.40	0.40	
40.40	40.80	0.40	
40.80	41.20	0.40	0.40

NB: 50ml of distilled water was used as the blank.

Table 5.5: Titre Value, Corrected Titre Value and the Volume of Sample Used to Calculate the Concentrations of Chloride (Cl^-)

CHLORIDE				
No.	Corrected Titre, ml	Titreml	Volume of Sample (ml)	
			BLANK	0.60
1a	0.40	1.00		50.00
	0.40	1.00		50.00
	0.50	1.10		50.00
1b	3.30	3.90		50.00
	3.30	3.90		50.00
	3.30	3.90		50.00
1c	6.00	6.60		50.00
	4.30	4.90		50.00
	9.70	10.30		50.00
			BLANK	0.73
2a	3.47	4.20		50.00
	3.47	4.20		50.00
	3.47	4.20		50.00
2b	2.67	3.40		50.00
	2.47	3.20		50.00
	2.47	3.20		50.00
2c	5.77	6.50		50.00
	5.87	6.60		50.00
	5.77	6.50		50.00

(Contd...)

No.	Corrected Titre, ml	Titreml	Volume of Sample (ml)	
			BLANK	0.40
3a	8.30	8.70		50.00
	8.20	8.60		50.00
	8.20	8.60		50.00
3b	17.10	17.50		50.00
	17.10	17.50		50.00
	17.20	17.60		50.00
3c	18.20	18.80		50.00
	18.70	19.10		50.00
	18.70	19.10		50.00

CALCULATIONS

The following formula were used for calculations:

- Normality of Silver Nitrate, $AgNO_3$ = Normality of NaCl × Volume of NaCl/Volume of $AgNO_3$

  Mg/L Cl = (A-B) × N x 35.450/Ml of sample used

  Where:

  A = titre of sample

  B = titre of blank

  N = Normality of the silver nitrate titrant (0.1M)

- The corrected titre is calculated from:(titre of sample - titre of blank) = (A-B)
- The standard deviation and variance were calculated in accordance with literature[13-15]
- Confidence interval at 95% was calculated using the formula below:

  Confidence interval at 95% = $\pm ts/\sqrt{N}$

  t = degrees of freedom = N -1

  S = standard deviation

  N = number of sample

DISCUSSION

Chloride anion concentration for the nine selected areas of coastal Guyana was determined using the Mohr's titrimetric method. This method determines the chloride ion concentration of a solution via titration with silver nitrate solution[10-12] using potassium chromate solution as the indicator. Distilled, deionised water was used as the blank in all cases.

Table 5.6: The Results Obtained for the Analysis of Chloride, where the Concentration of Chloride was Determined Using the Same Formula above. It Also Include the Average, Standard Deviation, Variants and Confidence at 95%

CHLORIDE					
No.	Concentration (mg/L)	Average	Standard Deviation	Variants	Confidence at 95% Level
1a	28.360				
	28.360	30.723	4.093	16.753	30.723 ± 10.161
	35.450				
1b	233.970				
	233.970	233.970	0.000	0.000	233.970 ± 0.00
	233.970				
1c	425.40				
	304.87	472.670	19.5760	38321.978	472.67 ± 485.995
	687.73				
2a	246.02				
	246.02	246.020	0.000	0.000	246.02 ± 0.00
	246.02				
2b	189.30				
	175.12	179.850	8.190	67.076	179.85 ± 20.333
	175.12				
2c	409.09				
	416.18	411.450	4.093	16.753	411.45 ± 10.161
	409.09				
3a	588.47				
	581.38	583.740	4.093	16.753	583.74 ± 10.161
	581.38				
3b	1212.39				
	1212.39	1214.75	4.093	16.753	1214.75 ± 10.161
	1219.48				
3c	1304.56				
	1325.83	1318.74	12.280	150.798	1318.74 ± 30.486
	1325.83				

Note: Figure in ml of sample column is the actual amount of sample used.
1c: samples diluted 25ml of samples in 25ml Distilled water, 1ml actual volume of sample used.
2a-2c: samples diluted 5ml in 50ml distilled water, 0.1ml actual volume of sample used.
3a-3c:samples diluted 25ml in 50ml distilled water, 0.5ml actual volume of sample used.

ND: (Not Detected) is assigned to a parameter when the value is below the detection limit or the product of the formula is negative.

GRAPHS

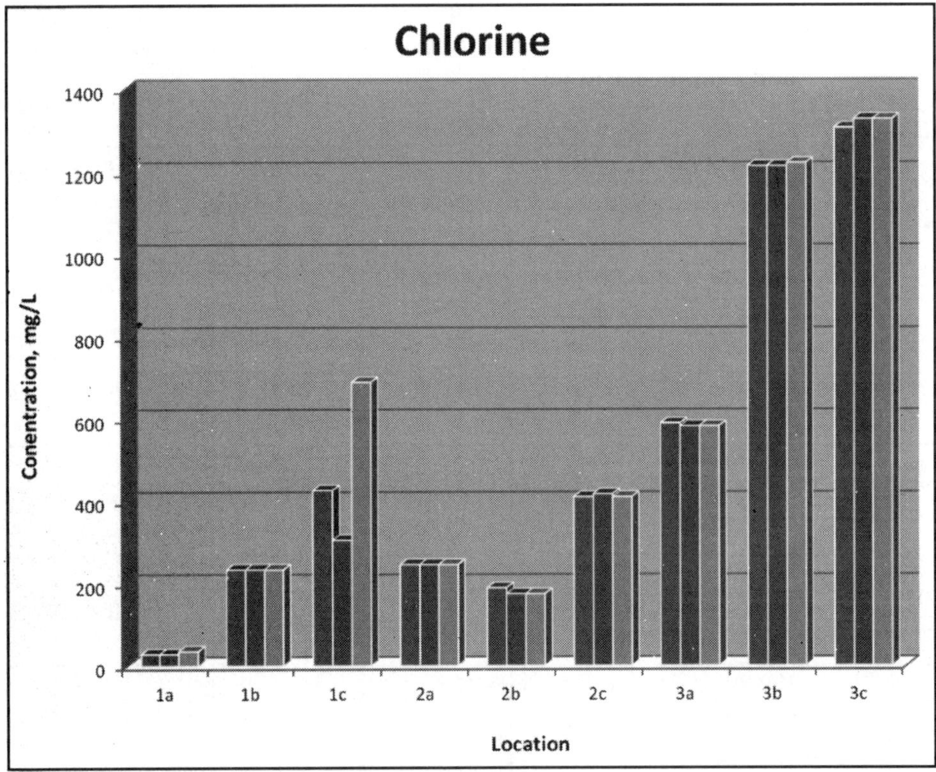

Fig. 5.1.: The Graph Shows the Results Obtained for the Analysis of Chlorides

KEY

1a..............No. 58 Village	2c.............. Stabroek
1b..............Rose Hall Town	3a.............. Parika
1c..............Skeldon GUYSUCO Estate	3b............ .Supenaam
2a..............Good Hope	3c.............. Spring Garden
2b..............Ogle	

The concentration of standardised $AgNO_3$ was found to be 0.1M. The permissible concentration also the threshold limit of chloride is 250mg/L. Along the sea coast, chloride may be present in higher concentrations due to leakage of salt water into the sewerage system. Its also intensified by industrial processes.Thus, its noticeable that the five of the selected areas demonstrated contamination of Cl^- beyond the threshold limit. These areas are: Skeldon Guysuco Estate, Stabroek, Parika, Supernaam and Spring Garden waters. Values registered were 472.67 mg/L ± 19.57, 411.45 mg/L ± 4.09 mg/L, 583.740 mg/L ± 4.09, 1214.75mg/L ± 4.09 mg/L, 1318.74 ± 12.28, 30.72 ± 4.09 for these areas. The highest value of 1318.74 ± 30.49 was noticeable for area 3C, Spring Garden, whereas the lowest value of 30.723 mg/L was observed for 1a, number 58 Livelihood village. Four areas registered less than the 250 mg/L permissible value. These were number 58 village, Rosehall Town, Good Hope, Ogle. These values been 30.72 mg/L ± 4.09 mg/L, 233.97 mg/L ± 0.00, 246 mg/L ± 0.00mg/L and 179.85 mg/L ± 20.33 mg/L respectively. These results are shown graphically in Figure 1.0. Thus, it seems that the chloride ion concentration is higher than the 250mg/L threshold limit at Rosehall town, Skeldon Guysuco Estate, Good Hope, Stabroek, Parika Supernaam and Spring Garden waste water and appropriate environmental procedures, both at the national and local level should be taken to prevent chloride ion concentration beyond the threshold limit.

CONCLUSION

The concentration of chloride was found to be 30.72mg/L ± 4.09, 233.970mg/L ± 0.00, 472.67mg/L ± 19.57, 246.02mg/L ± 0.00, 179.85mg/L ± 8.19, 411.45mg/L ± 4.09, 583.74mg/L ± 10.16, 1214.75mg/L ± 4.09 and 1318.74mg/L ± 12.28 at # 58. Village, Rose Hall, Skeldon Guysuco Estate, Hope, Ogle, Stabroek, Parika, Supernaam and Spring Garden waste water respectively.

REFERENCES

1. Eaton AD, Clessicens SL, Greenberg, EA (1995). Standard Methods for the Examination of Water and Wastewater, 19th ed. United Book Press Inc. Baltimore, Maryland USA; p. 4-48.
2. Booth RL (1983). Methods for the Chemical analysis of Water and Wastes, 2nd ed. Environmental Monitoring and Support Laboratory, Office of Research and Development, U.S. Environmental Protection Agency, Cincinnati: Ohio 45268; p. 352.
3. Hach Company, Water Analyses Handbook, 3rd ed. Loveland Colorado, USA; 1997, pp. 304-307.
4. Jagdeo B. National Development Strategy, Environmental Policy, Guyana Government News Letter, 40-45(2006).
5. Williams N (2010). Guyana Times, a News Magazine, (11).
6. Elliot S (2008). Testing the Water, Royal Society of Chemistry, RSC, News Magazine, 12 (5), 12-13.
7. Daintith J (2004). The Facts on File Dictionary of Inorganic Chemistry, Market House Books Ltd. 1st Edition, p. 51.
8. Bell CF, Lott KAK, (1966): Modern Approach to Inorganic Chemistry, 2nd ed, Butterworths, London; p. 260.,
9. Nelson DL, Cox MM. Lehninger Principles of Biochemistry, 4th ed. W.H. Freeman and Company, New York; p. 395 and 403.
10. Babatunde OA, Ajibola VO (2009). Determination of Some Anions Along the Profile of Irrigated Farm Soils, Environmental Research Journal 3(3): 101-106.
11. Allen SE, Grimshaw MH, Parkinson JA, Quarmby C (1974): Chemical Analysis of Ecological Materials. In: Allen SE (Ed). Blackwell Scientific Publications, Oxford London, Edinburgh, Melbourne, p. 386.

12. Kraemer EO, Stamm AJ (1924): Mohr's Method for the Determination of Silver and Halogens in Other than Neutral Solutions, J. Am. Chem. Soc., 46 (12) 2707-2709.
13. Daniel HC (2003): Quantitative Chemical Analysis, 6th ed. W.H. Freeman and Company, New York; pp. 61-79.
14. Skoog AD, Holler JF, Nieman AT(1998): Principles of Instrumental Analysis, 5th ed, Thomson Learning, Inc; pp. 329-353.
15. Skoog DA, West DM, Holler FJ (1996): Fundamentals of Analytical Chemistry, 7th ed. Thomson Learning, Inc; USA.

The Harmful Chemical Change of Asian Dust Particles during Their Transport Toward Receptor Areas

Chang-Jin Ma

ABSTRACT

This study is focused on the comprehensive and detailed interpretation for the chemical transformation of individual Asian dust (hereafter called "AD") particles during long-range transport from source regions to receptor area. A multi-stage particle sampler was operated at a ground-based site in Taean, Korea directly exposed to the outflow of air masses from China during AD period in April 2003. Both quantitative and qualitative analyses for size-classified individual particles were carried out by a microbeam X-ray fluorescence (XRF) method and a microbeam Particle Induced X-ray Emission (micro-PIXE), respectively. Among major characteristic elements, the elemental masses of soil derived components, sulfur, and chloride varied as a function of particle size showing the monomodal maximum with a steeply increasing at 3.3 - 4.7 μm particle size. Although the details on chemical composition of AD particle collected on a straight line from source area to our ground-based site are needed, a large amount of Cl coexisted in and/or on AD particles suggests that AD particles collected in the present study might be actively engaged in

Department of Environmental Science, Fukuoka Women's University, Higashiku, Fukuoka 813-8529, Japan.

chemical transformation by sea-salt and other Cl containing pollutants emitted from the China's domestic sources. Through the statistical analyses it was possible to classify individual AD particles into six distinct groups. The internally mixed AD particles with Cl, which has various sources (e.g., sea-salt, coal combustion origin HCl, gaseous HCl derived from the adsorption of acids to sea-salt, and Cl containing man-made particles) were thoroughly fractionated by the elemental spectra drivened by the double detector system of micro-PIXE.

INTRODUCTION

During long-range transport of air masses containing AD particles over China continent, Yellow Sea, and Korea Peninsula, AD particles can encounter gaseous or particulate matters and react with each other, leading to a chemical transformation (Hwang *et al.*, 2008; Roth and Okada, 1998; Iwasaka *et al.*, 1988). As suggested by Li and Okada (1999), the artificial fine particles emitted at the industrial areas in China may be incorporated into AD particles before getting out of China. The AD particles mixed with various anthropogenic pollutants can then be subject to long-distance transport to the receptor areas in East Asia as well as the Pacific Ocean.

During the past few decades, a good few researches have been carried out to the study of the processes of chemical alteration of AD particles like gas-to-particle transformation, coagulation, and growth processes of particles during long-rage transport (Zhang *et al.*, 2001; Zhang and Iwasaka, 1999; Duce *et al.*, 1980).

Coal-fired plants produce about 80 percent of China's national electricity output (China's Development Research Center of the State Council). Coal-fired power stations produce large quantities of waste ash and fly ash. These coal plants worsen air quality and create acid rain which then hurts soil quality and food safety. The harmful by-products of coal combustion of China should be a grave pollution problem in East Asia. When one assesses the chemical transformation of AD particles he must therefore consider these various by-products of coal combustion.

AD particles would also be expected to be affected by the local sources such as of coal-fired power station operating at receptor area. Even though sulfur dioxide (SO_2) can be removed and recovered in the flues of the power station, small amounts of SO_2 is still emitted from coal fired power station. This locally exhausted SO_2 can cause additional change in chemical properties of AD particles.

A study of HCl emissions from the seven coal-fired power plants in Maryland indicates that HCl emissions in 1991 totaled between 4,500 and 6,700 tons per year (Griffin, 2010). Therefore, the actual impact of HCl emitted from coal-fired thermal power plants should also be carefully considered on the chemical transformation of AD particles. Hence, as mentioned above, in consideration of the HCl drived from coal combustion, a thorough assessment is crucial for the diagnosis of an aging process of AD particles.

The main objective of this study was assessing the aging processes of individual AD particles collected on the western coast of Korean Peninsula through both quantitative and qualitative X-ray microbeam techniques.

MATERIALS AND METHODS

Collection of Size-segregated Ambient Particles

Aerosol sampling was performed at a ground-based site (N36.7; E126.2) with a height of 15 m above ground in Taean (see Fig. 6.1), Korea during AD period in April 2003. Because of its closeness to China, this sampling site marked as an empty circle in Fig. 6.1 can be directly exposed to the outflow of air masses from China during springtime (see Fig. 6.1). Thus, this site is one of the well suited areas to measure AD in Korean Peninsula.

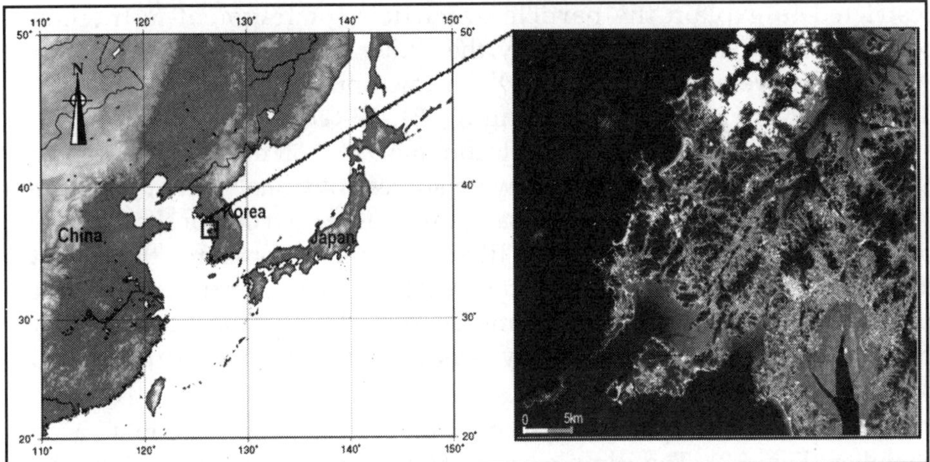

Fig. 6.1: Maps Showing Particle Collection Site on the Western Coast of Korean Peninsula

As one of local emission sources, the Taean thermal power generation station is located in the nothernest site about 20 km far away from our ground based particle sampling site. This power generation plant is operated with the bituminous coal that was mined at Guizhou Province located in southwest China. More details on this power generation station was already described in early study (Ma *et al.*, 2010).

For the purpose of segregating particles as a function of their size, an Andersen impactor sampler (AV-100, Tokyo Dylec Co.) was operated with 28.3 liter per minute flow rate on April 12, 2003. The file up of particles caused a long sampling duration time obscures the chemical determination of particle-to-particle variations. Therefore, the duration of sampling was adjusted to 50 minutes and 40 minutes at stage 1 to 3 and stage 4 to 5, respectively. This short sampling duration time is also a great way to estimate the particle composition because the long collection process can cause condensation or evaporation of volatile compounds, or chemical reactions. The heavy particle build-up under each nozzle often prevents sharp cut-size characteristics. A short sampling duration time also parcially partially reduces particle bounce and blow-off that may otherwise occur.

During sampling period the range of wind speed was 3.1 - 4.5 m s^{-1}, and it was generally blowing from west. The temperature was around 6.8 - 7.4 °C and average relative humidity in sampling period was 69%.

Chemical Analysis of Individual AD Particles

Quantitative Analysis

As bulk analytical methods are generally done by collecting samples of many fragments and particles on a sample holder, such techniques are often restricted to explain the particle-to-particle (or fragment-to-fragment) composition variations. In this study, the ultra trace elements in the individual AD particles were identified by an X-ray microprobe system equipped at the Super Photon ring 8 GeV (SPring-8), BL-37XU (Fig. 6.2). Through an application of this micro-analytical technique based on the X-ray fluorescence (XRF) method, multiple elements were successfully analyzed at femtogram level sensitivity. Although particle sampling was carried out for short duration time, particles were filed up on a filter. This file up obscures the chemical determination of particle-to-particle variations. Since particles passing the nozzles of Andersen impactor sampler formed a spot on filer, the single particle analysis of current study was restricted to individual particles deposited at the edge of the spot.

The particle sample was placed on the XY scanning stage in a vacuum chamber (Fig. 6.2). The sample areas (500-1000 μm^2 each time) were then selected randomly and scanned by the microbeam. The takeoff angle of 10° was used for the measurement of X-ray fluorescence, and the intensity of the incident X-rays was monitored by an ionization chamber. The XRF elemental image of sample can be obtained via the scanning processes. The point analysis for individual particles was carried out subsequently. The fluorescence X-rays were recorded with a Si(Li) detector placed in the electron orbit plane of the storage ring. The detector was mounted at 90° to the incident X-rays to minimize the the scattering background. Details of the calibration of the X-ray microprobe system to yield quantitative measures of elemental mass in individual particles including the effects of the self-absorption are described elsewhere (Hayakawa et al., 2001). Through the instrumentality of this XRF analytical technique, a total of 150 individual AD particles at each stage of Andersen air sampler were analyzed.

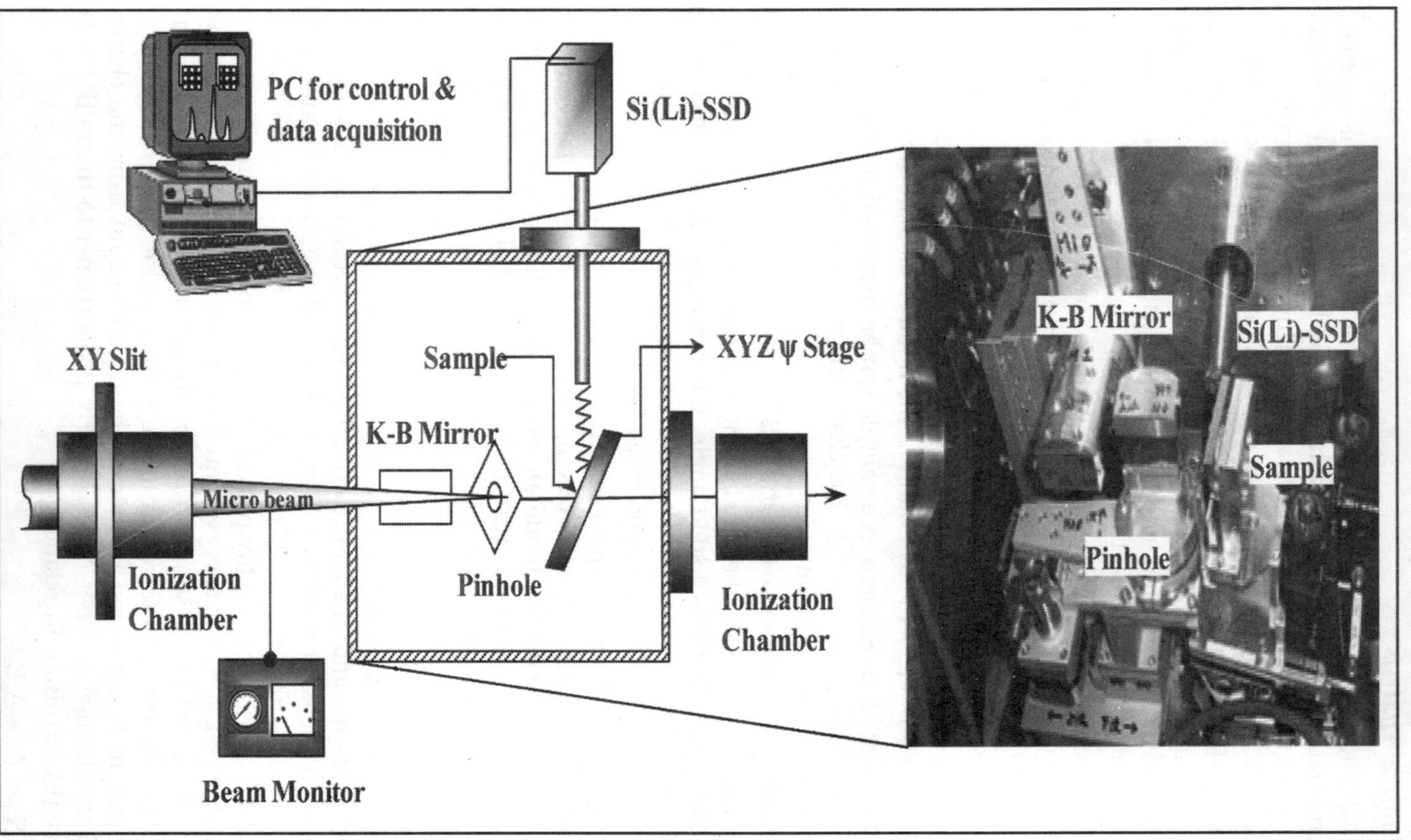

Fig. 6.2: Schematic Illustration of the Experimental Setup for XRF Microprobe at SPring-8, BL37XU

Qualitative Analysis

Although the excellent sensitivity is one of better traits, the restriction of elemental composition (Z>12) is the greatest flaw in the XRF method of present situation for proper understanding of the chemical transformation of AD particles by sea-salt and trace elements derived from local sources.

Micro-PIXE analytical measurements in the present work performed with the facilities of the Takasaki Ion Accelerators for Advanced Radiation Application in Japan atomic energy research institute. The followings are common principle of micro-PIXE analysis:

1. An electron in inner shell jumps with the interaction with a particle beam (in this study, a 2.5 MeV H^+ microbeam accelerated by a 3 MV single-end accelerator).
2. Another electron in outer shell moves to an inner orbit.
3. A characteristic X-ray that has particular energy is emitted.
4. Quantity of elements by counting the number of characteristic X-rays

Quantity of an element in a sample can be measured by counting the number of characteristic X-rays. The characteristic X-ray of element A can be calculated by following equation:

$$Y_A = N_A \times Q \times d\Omega \times E \times R_a \times \sigma^x \times 4\pi S^{-1}$$

where N_A is the number of element A in sample, Q is the total number of incident particle, $d\Omega$ is a solid angle, E is detecting rate of detector, R_a is the absorption rate of characteristic X-ray, σ^x is a section area of characteristic X-ray generation, S is beam spot, respectively.

Fig. 6.3 shows a schematic diagram of the beam scanning and data acquisition system of micro-PIXE employing double X-ray detectors. The HP-Ge X-ray detector has moderate energy resolution and poor detection efficiency below 2 keV because of its Ge L-shell absorption edge and backscattering proton absorber (60 ìm thick polypropylene). The Si(Li) X-ray detector was set at a symmetrical position with the HP-Ge X-ray detector with respect to the beam axis. The energy resolution of the Si(Li) detector is excellent, and this higher energy resolution results in a better signal-to-background ratio and smaller peak overlapping, especially in the low-energy regions. The detector window is 8 ìm-thick Be and attached with an annular type absorber (100 μm-thick Mylar) with a center hole (3 mm in diameter). This Si(Li) detector can finally provide a fairly good detection efficiency for X-rays below 2 keV. The energy of an X-ray is converted during the process of charge creation in semiconductor diode to the charge pulse and subsequently after amplification to the voltage pulse. The analog voltage pulse height is converted further to the digital output from the channel number. Channel number N_{ch} is linearly proportional to the initial X-ray energy (E) according to relation:

$$N_{ch} = A_1 + A_2E$$

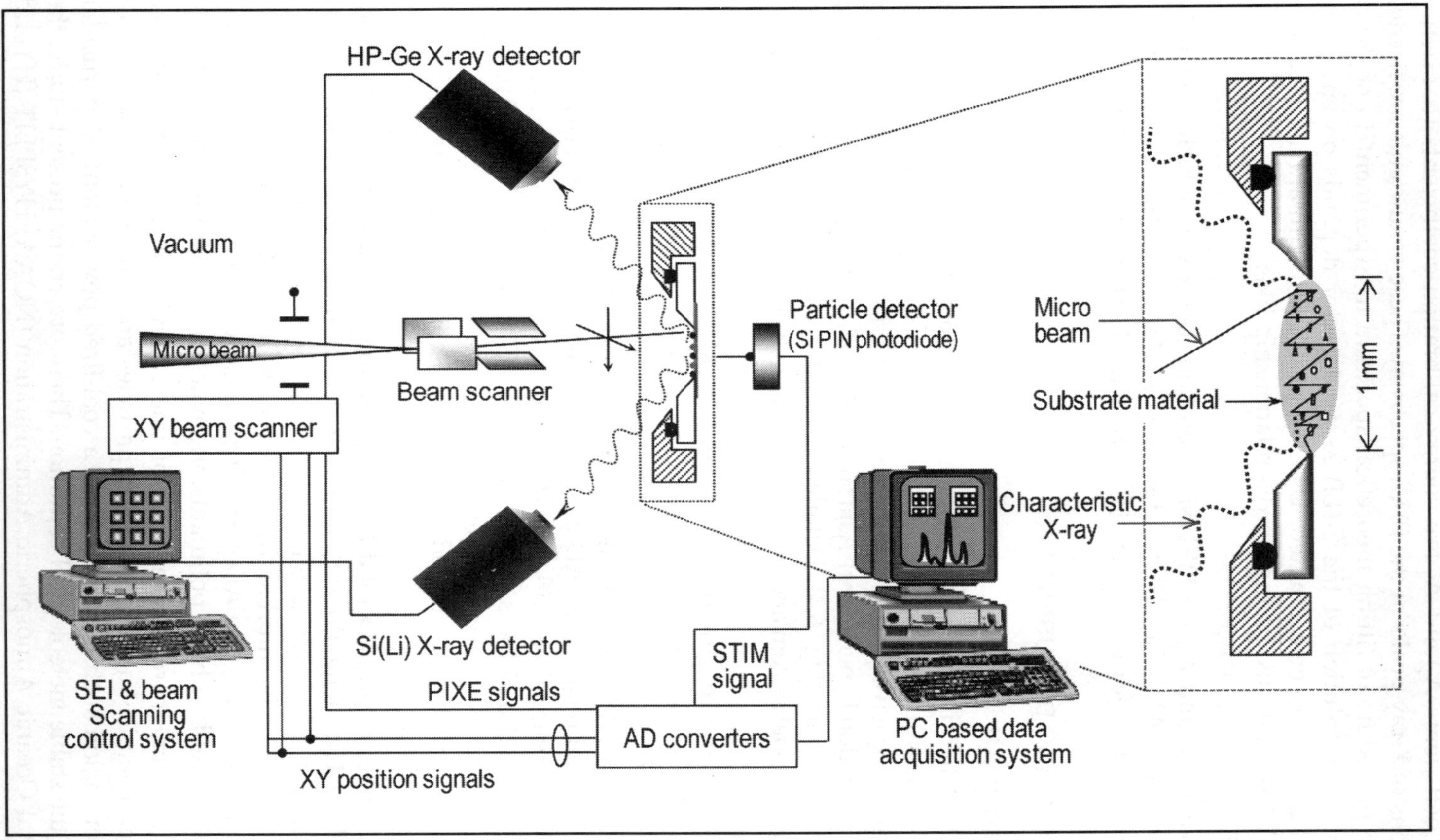

Fig. 6.3: A Schematic Diagram of the Beam Scanning and Data Acquisition System for Micro-PIXE System Consisting of the Advanced HP-Ge : Si (Li) X-ray Detectors

Coefficients A_1 and A_2 are energy calibration coefficients that define positions of X-ray peaks at the PIXE spectrum. These coefficients are needed for the procedure of fitting theoretical spectrum to experimental one. Since the energy resolution of the Si(Li) X-ray detector depends on energy as well, it also has to be calibrated. Usually, peak's full with at half maximum (FWHM) is calibrated, using simple relationship like:

$$FWHM = (A_3 + A_4E)^{1/2}$$

where A_3 and A_4 are FWHM calibration coefficients which have to be determined (IAEA-TECDOC-1190, 2000). Details of this double X-ray detectors system for PIXE Analysis have been described elsewhere (Sakai *et al.*, 2005).

RESULTS AND DISCUSSION

Forecasted AD Moving

The Chemical weather FORecasting System (CFORS) developed by Research Institute for Applied Mechanics, Kyushu University (Uno *et al.*, 2003) and intensively used during the ACE (Asia Pacific Regional Aerosol Characterization Experiment)-Asia shows AD inflows into East Asia including our sampling site (Fig. 6.4). Detailed description of CFORS such as general concept of model system and tracer modules can be found elsewhere (Uno *et al.*, 2003).

The Meteorological Data Explorer (METEX) (Center for Global Environmental Research, 2010) backward trajectories (1000, 2000, and 4000m heights of air parcel) for 72 hours trajectory length started at our sampling site at 09 UTC, April 12, 2003 is also displayed at right of Fig. 6.4. According to these model results (i.e., AD inflows into East Asia and the movements of air parcel during field event), a dense AD storm on April 11, 2003 was coming from the desert and loess regions in eastern China and southern Mongolia through urban Beijing metropolis by the prevailing winds originated from northwest. And it was extended to the Korean Peninsula after passing through the Yellow Sea.

Since four plants (a total power generating capacity of about 2.7 GW), owned by Huaneng Power International, Datang International Power Generation Co Ltd, China Shenhua Energy and Beijing Jingneng Thermal Power Co Ltd, exist in urban Beijing (China's Development Research Center of the State Council), the AD particles passed over urban Beijing metropolis easily contacted with the pollutants originated from coal-fired power plants.

However, there remain a lot of uncertainties regarding the linkage between chemical alteration of AD particles and the emission sources of receptor region such as a large scale a coal-fired power plant, in particular under the stable meteological condition. Therefore, in the present study, the National Oceanic Atmospheric Administration (NOAA) HYSPLIT (HYbrid

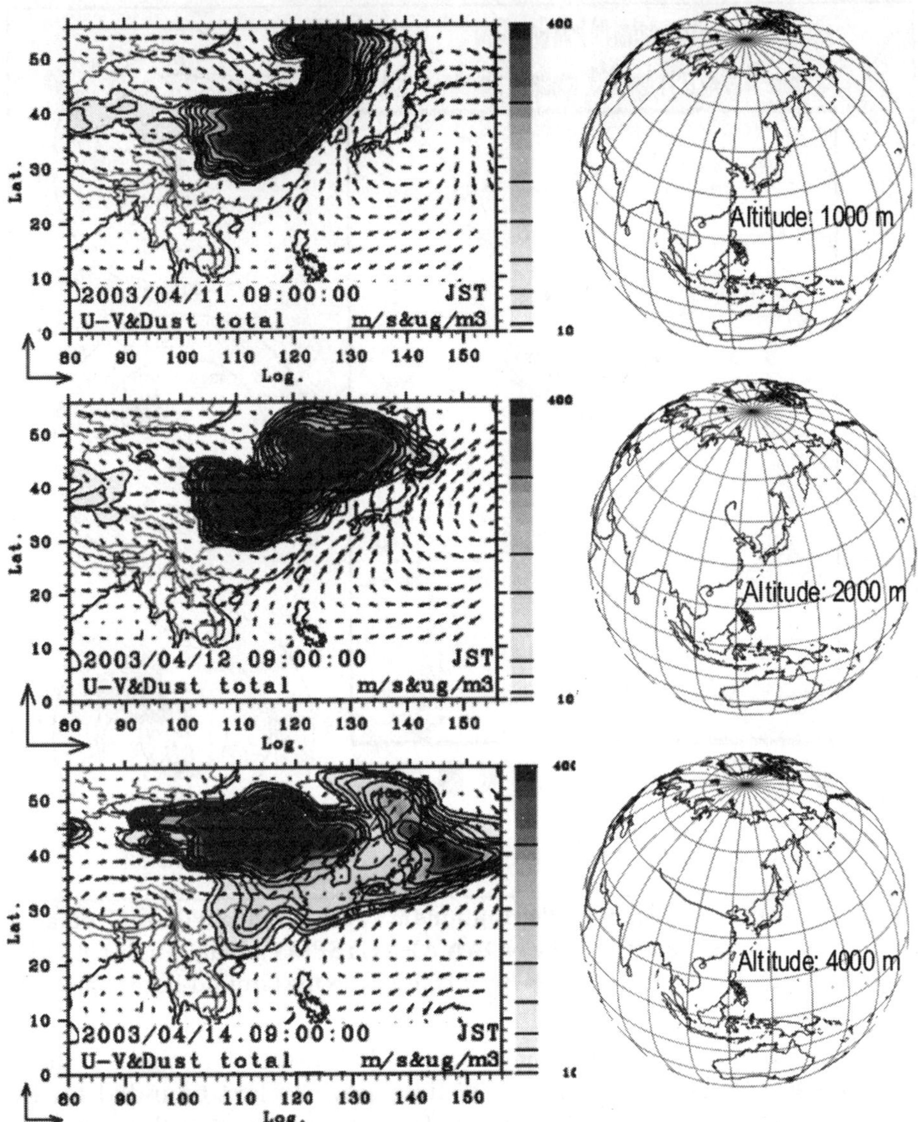

Fig. 6.4: Forecasted Dust moving and Concentration by the CFORS Model (Left) and the METEX Backward Trajectories Started at Our Sampling Site (Right)

Single-Particle Lagrangian Integrated Trajectory) dispersion model (Rolph, 2003) was run to estimate the impact of locally emitted air pollutants from the Taean thermal power generation station on chemical transformation of AD particles. A detailed model description of HYSPLIT was given by Rolph (2003). Fig. 6.5 displays the simulated forward aerosol dispersion (composited aerosol layer from the surface to 500 m) started from Taean thermal power

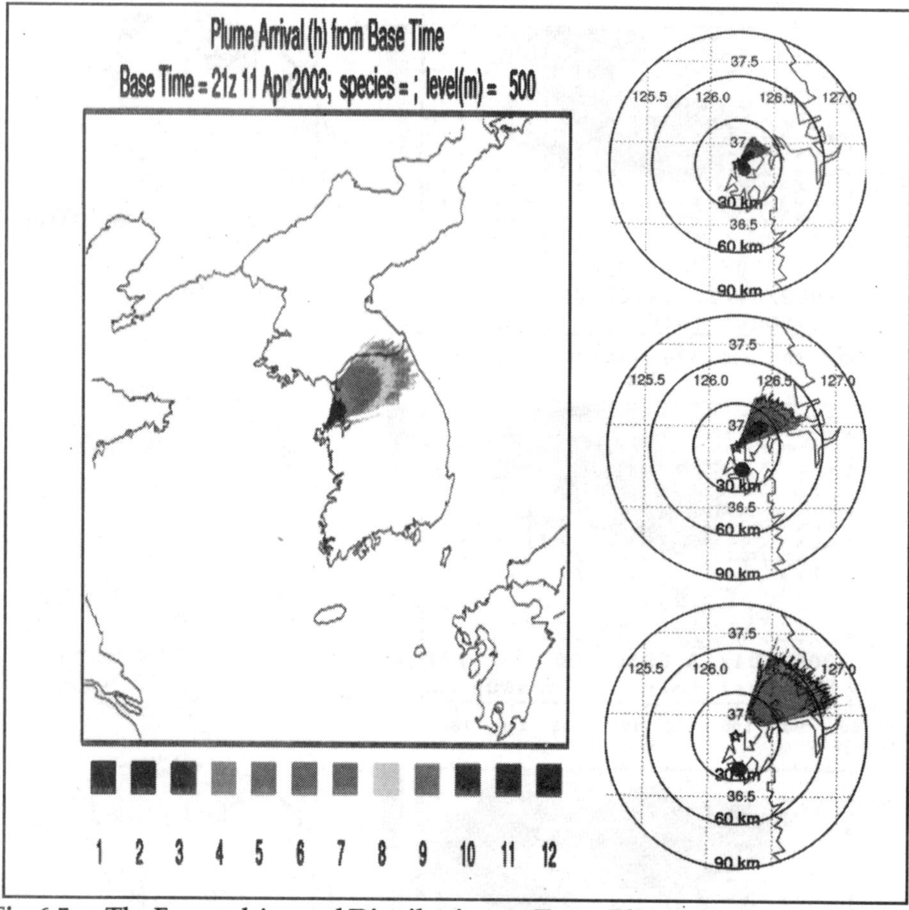

Fig. 6.5: The Forward Aerosol Distributions at Taean Thermal Power Generation Station Simulated by the NOAA ARL HYSPLIT Model (Right). A Filled Circle in HYSPLIT Model Results Indicates the Ground-based Sampling Site.

generation station. The results of this HYSPLIT dispersion model indicate that the aerosols emitted from a coal-fired power plant bounded for the northeast part of the Korean Peninsula. Thus it suggests that the pollutants emitted from the Taean thermal power generation station did not directly affect the aging processes of AD particles.

Fig. 6.6 shows an illustrative explanation of the transformation processes of the AD particles between source area and our sampling site during long-rage transport. After finishing the first aging process, AD particles are often condemned to get together with sea-salts (i.e., second aging process) then experienced the third aging process. Hwang *et al.* (2008) reported that AD particles were mixed with sea-salts entrained over the Yellow Sea, as well as air pollutants from the eastern China coastal areas.

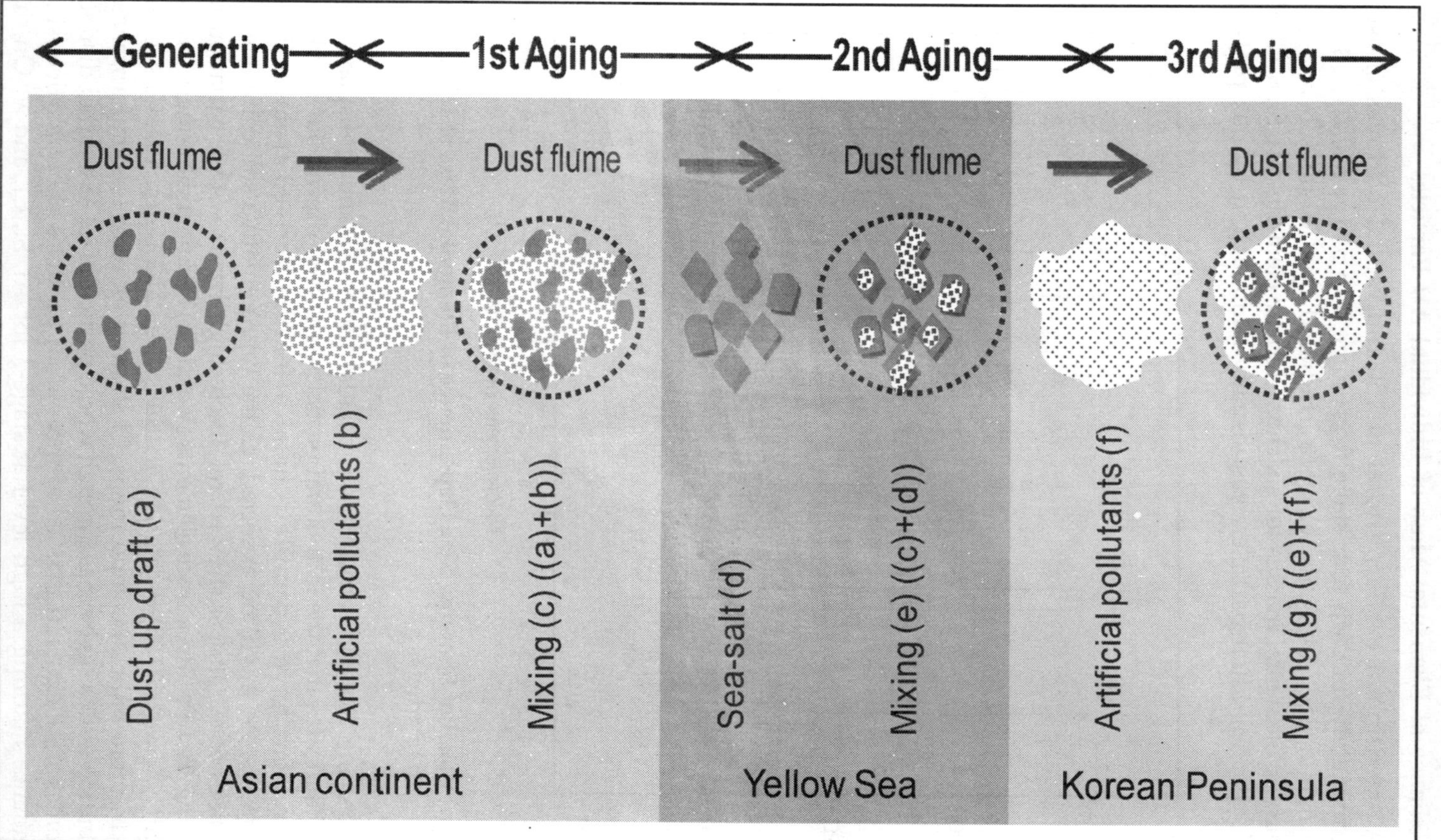

Fig. 6.6: An Illustrative Explanation of the Transformation Processes of the AD Particles during Long Range Transport

Size Reliance of Elemental Mass of Individual AD Particles

As mentioned earlier, a total of 150 individual particles chosen indiscriminately for each four-stage from stage 2 to 5 (4.7, 3.3, 2.1, 1.1 μm aerodynamic size, respectively) were irradiated by XRF microbeam. The summary of elemental masses for six characteristic elements (Al, Si, S, Cl, V, and Cr) in individual particles was visually summarized by box plots in Fig. 6.7.

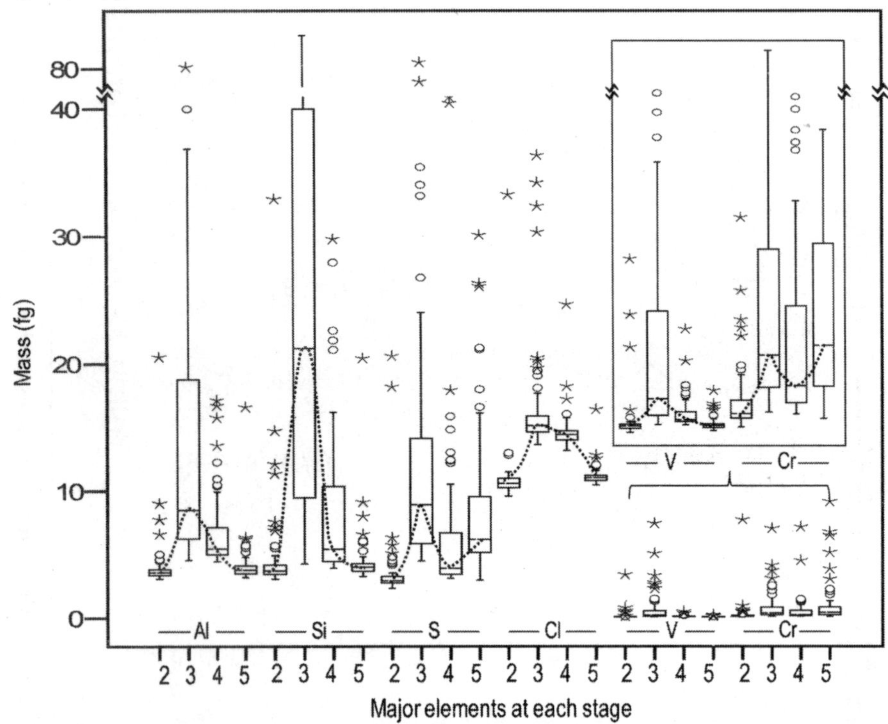

Fig. 6.7: Box Plot Showing Size Dependence of Elemental Mass of Individual AD Particles

The long box and whisker, in particular for Al, Si, and S, displayed in Fig. 6.7 indicates that the individual particles collected during our intensive measurement have a complex chemical nature derived from various mechanisms. As might be expected, as the representative soil components, the masses of Al and Si showed relatively high levels with a variation in wide range, while minor trace elements (V and Cr) had negligible mass within a small variation range relative to the other elements. Elsewhere, in comparison to mineral compositions, Cl showed more or less uniform mass distribution with a high mass through whole particle size. As a rather distinct phenomenon, elemental masses of individual particles show particle size dependence marking a high level at stage-3 for Al, Si, Cl, and V. On the other hand, the masses of S and Cr were observed to increase in the fine particle fraction (1.1 - 2.0 μm).

For the purpose of thorough estimating of the change in chemical quality of AD particles, the ratios of four kinds of elemental masses to Si mass for size-resolved individual particles were determined (Fig. 6.8). The numerical levels on upper adjacent refer to the medians. The elemental mass ratio of desert sand is the referential average value of desert sands collected at four different desert regions (Yinchuan, Wuwei, Dulan, and Yanchi) in China (Ma *et al.*, 2008). This box plot, comparing four size fractions and desert sand for the output of mass ratio of element to Si, shows that ratios have a significant fluctuation with respect to particle size. As compared with the median value of dust sand, with the exception of V in particle size range from 3.3 to 4.7μm, there was a tendency towards overwhelmingly higher ratios in size-resolved ambient particles. It could therefore be suggested that AD particles collected in the present study might be actively engaged in chemical transformation. The fine particles collected on stage-5 (1.1 - 2.0 μm) has the highest ratio; the particles deposited on stage-3 (3.3 - 4.7 μm) have the least value of ratio. As described earlier, high mass ratios of S and Cr are likely responsible for the unusually high levels in fine fraction of particle. The increase of S mass ratio in fine mode particle can be explained by the inflow of artificial S containing fine particles into our sampling site. It is well known that SO_2 can be emitted from the fossil fuel-fired generating facilities like coal-fired power plants. The reason for the high elevating of Cr mass ratio in fine fraction of particle might be that the harmful substances like mercury and chromium can emitted via coal power station flues (Griffin, 2010) and they can also inflow into receptor area during AD event.

It is noteworthy that the ratio of Cl to Si is quite high (from 0.724 to 2.836) compared to other elements. This Cl enrichment can be apparently explained by the fact that AD particles aged by gaseous and particulate Cl emitted from the China's domestic sources were additionally reacted with sea-salt. Although various polluters such as automobiles and municipal incinerators can also be considered as the sources of ambient Cl, one cannot rule out the possibility that Cl was driven from coal consumption (e.g., coal-fired power plant). About this Cl enrichment of individual particles, details are discussed at the final part of this manuscript.

Classification of Individual AD Particles

By Cluster Analysis

In order to classify individual AD particles, the elemental masses measured by XRF microbeam were subjected to cluster analysis. Most particles could be clustered with highly dissimilar dendrogram which summarizes the process of clustering. It could therefore be suggested that elemental compositions were chemically heterogeneous throughout the whole individual AD particles.

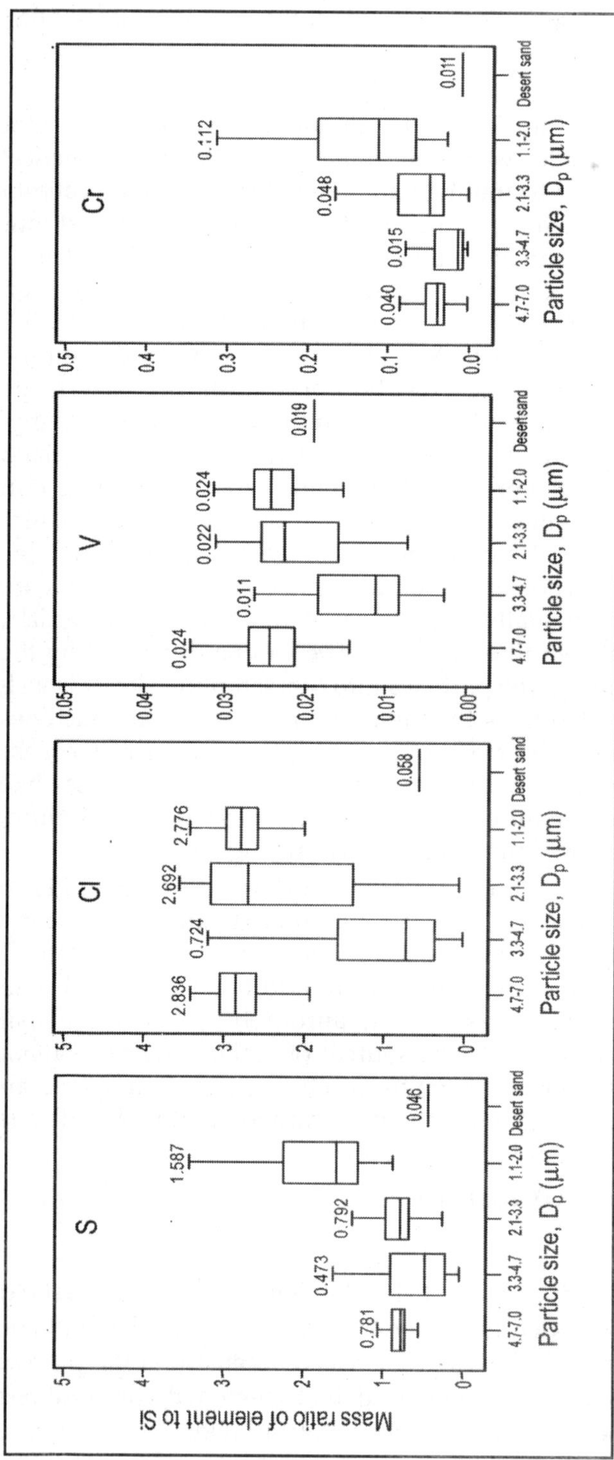

Fig. 6.8: Ratios of Four Kinds of Elemental Masses to Si mass for Size-resolved Individual AD Particles. Dp mm means the 50% Cut-off Size of Andersen Sampler

Fig. 6.9 shows the result of cluster analysis for the individual AD particles collected on the 2nd stage of Andersen sampler. Individual AD particles can be categorized into six clusters. Cluster I (Si>Cl>Al>K>SP) with a small portion of total particle population was found to be high mass for soil components and Cl. Cluster II (Cl>Si>Al>S>P) and Cluster III (Cl>Si>Ca>Al>S) with also a small account rate of total particle population were showing Cl and mineral compositions-rich. Cluster IV (Cl>S>Si>Al) with a poor particle number had high mass for Cl and S with coexisting of crustal elements. Cluster V (Cl>>Si>Al>S>P) could be categorized as the particles mainly containing Cl with slight soil components. Cluster VI (Cl>Al>Si>S) showing absolute share of particles seemed to express the modification of AD particles with marine derived Cl, and/or artificial Cl especially drived coal-fired power plant, and S.

By Micro-PIXE Spectra

As discussed above, Cl-rich particles had an ascendancy over other types of AD particles and it would mainly be induced by the particle-to-particle homogeneous reaction between AD paricles and sea-salt particles. On the other hand, the gaseous HCl generated by the reaction between sea-salt and acids (e.g., heterogeneous reactions of sea salt with HNO_3 and H_2SO_4) might have relevance to this enrichment of Cl (Roth and Okada, 1998). It can also be considered that large amounts of other chloride-containing fine particles (e.g., NH_4Cl or the vaporized gaseous HCl from fine mode NH_4Cl druing the state of increased temperature) were mixed with AD particles and had a significant impact on the present results. Elsewhere, under the state of coal consuming (e.g., power plant) in China, the impact of HCl originated from coal combustion should also be actually considered.

Therefore, in dealing with Cl, one has to distinguish among sea-salt, HCl emitted from coal combustion at power plant, gaseous HCl derived from the adsorption of acids to sea-salt, and other Cl containing man-made particles.

The elemental spectra driven by the double detector system of micro-PIXE are useful for fractionating AD particles into internally mixed AD particle with Cl. Fig. 6.10 is displaying micro-PIXE spectra for several distinctive AD particles experienced different aging processes during a long-range transport to our sampling site.

Particles (a) and (f) were remarkable Cl-rich AD particles that might be traced back to below two aging processes. (1) artificially generated $HCl_{(g)}$ was adsorbed on an AD particle before getting out of China and then experienced a further aging process with sea-salt. As described earlier, the man-made $HCl_{(g)}$ was emitted mostly from coal combustion at power plants.

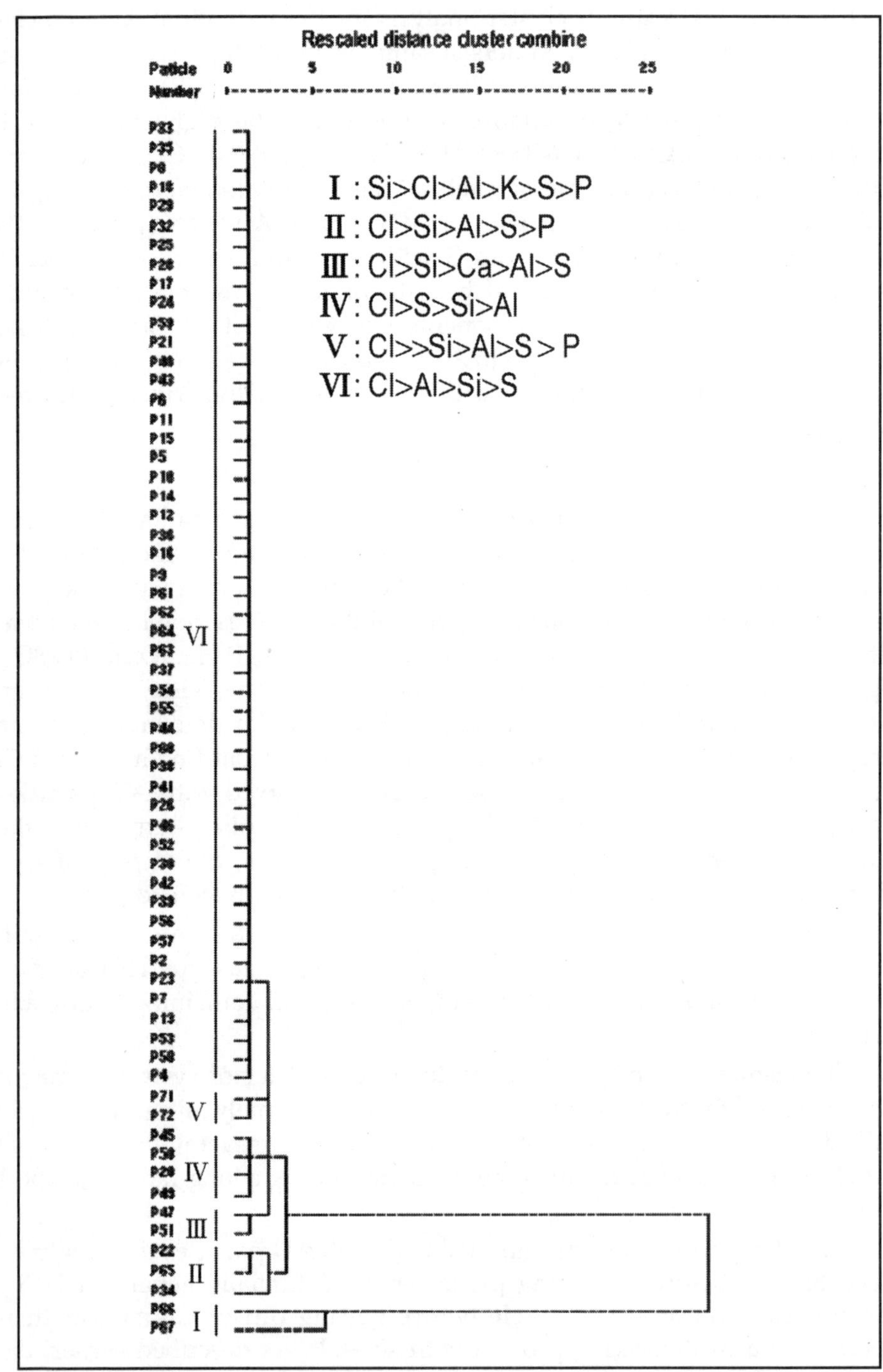

Fig. 6.9: Result of the Cluster Analysis for the Individual AD Particles Collected on the 2nd Stage of Andersen Sampler

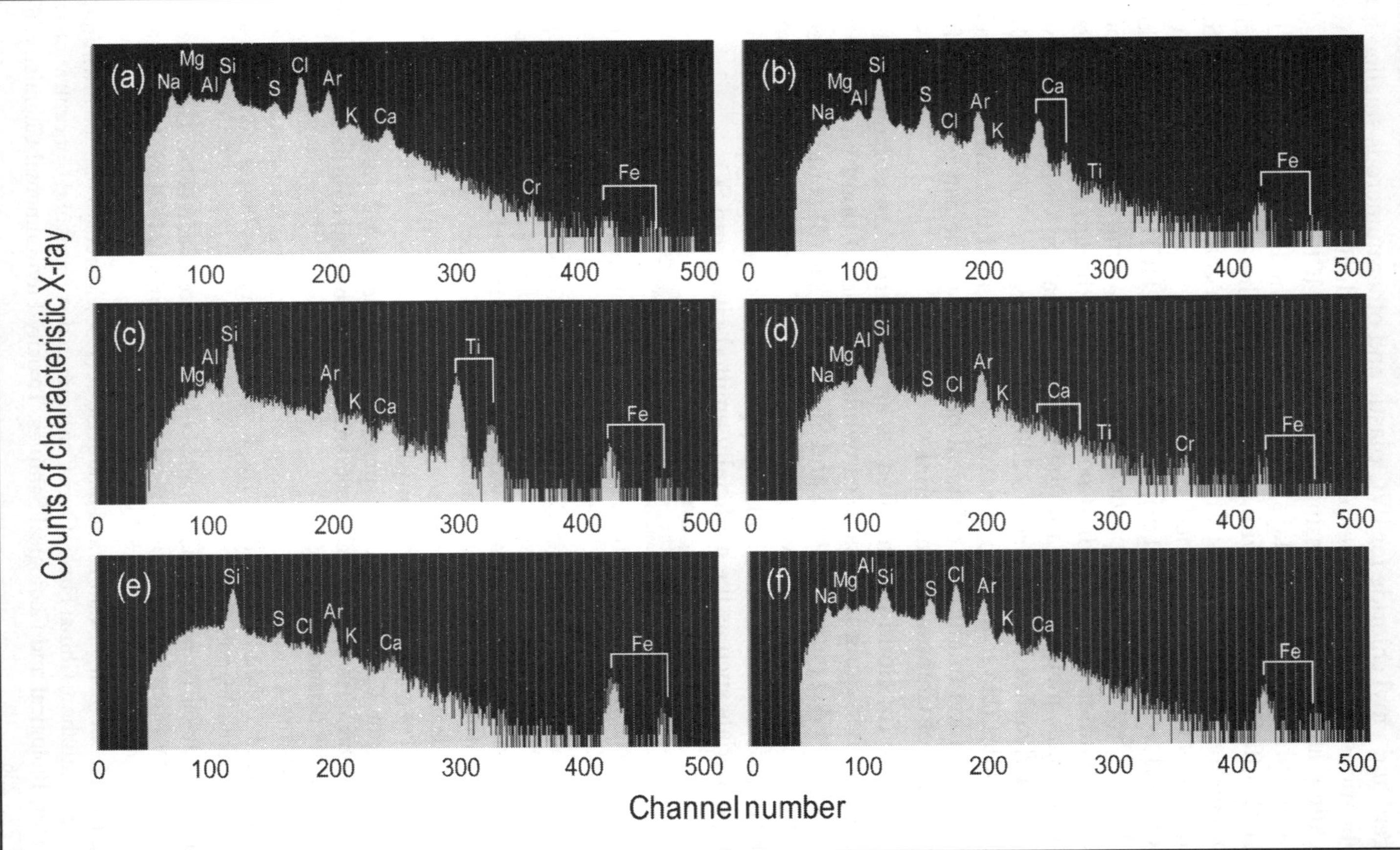

Fig. 6.10: Micro-PIXE Spectra of Individual AD Particles Experienced Different Aging Processes during Long-range Transport

It also diversely generated from the large-scale production of chemical reagent and vinyl chloride for PVC plastic and other numerous smaller-scale applications including household cleaning, production of food additives, descaling, and leather processing. Even though, HCl is fairly short-lived in the atmosphere (one to five days) (Griffin, 2010), the HCl generated in China and not sufficiently reacted with ammonia or alkaline cations such as calcium or potassium before outgoing China might have a chance to mixing with an aged AD particle. (2) enriched Cl by both $HCl_{(g)}$ generated by [2NaCl + H_2SO_4 (coal-fired power plant origin) →Na_2SO_4 + 2HCl↑] and sea-salt above the Yellow Sea. Especially, particle (a) was containing a small peak of Cr probably emitted from coal-fired power plant. Although Cr compounds are used in paints, metal polish, and the tanning of leather, Cr is often found in coal-fired flyashes (Llorens *et al*., 2001; Brigden *et al*., 2002). Also several earlier studies (He *et al*. 1998; Ma *et al*., 2010) indicated that the high level of Cr concentration might be a chemical peculiarity of the ash produced from combustion of Chinese coal material.

Particle (b) cloud be classified as an AD particle mixed with sea-salt without further aging process. Meanwhile, particle (c) cloud be categorized as a non-aged AD particle with Ti and Si-rich. Particle (d) could be classed as a Si and Al rich AD particle with anthropogenic Cr and disregardably small peaks of sea-salt. Particle (e) had the appearance of the aging processes with acidic materials such as the artificially emitted $HCl_{(g)}$ and SO_2.

REFERENCES

Baselt, R.C. (2008): Disposition of Toxic Drugs and Chemicals in Man (8th ed.). Foster City, Biomedical Publications, pp: 305-307.

Brigden, K., Santillo, D. and Stringer, R. (2002): Hazardous Emissions from Thai Coal-fired Power Plants: Toxic and Potentially Toxic Elements in Fly Ashes Collected from the Mae Moh nad Thai Petrochemical Industry Coal-fired Power Plants in Thailand, 2002, Technical note of Greenpeace Research Laboratory, UK, pp: 1-26.

Center for Global Environmental Research (2010): Calculate Air Trajectory, http://db.cger.nies.go.jp/metex/trajectory.html.

Duce, R.A., Unni, C.K., Ray, B.J., Prospere, J.M. and Merrill, J.T. (1980): Long-range Atmospheric Transport of Soil Dust from Asia to the Tropical North Pacific: Temporal variability. Science, 209: 1522-1524.

Griffin, J.R. (2010): A Review of the Impacts of Power Plants and Transmission Lines on Maryland's Natural Resources. The Report of Maryland Power Plant Research Programme, 15, pp: 99-107.

Hayakawa, S., Ikuta, N., Suzuki, M., Wakatsuki, M. and Hirokawa, T. (2001): Generation of an X-ray Microbeam for Spectromicroscopy at SPring-8 BL39XU. Journal of Synchrotron Radiation, 8: 328-330.

He, J., Tan, H., Sommar, J., Xiao, Z. and Lindqvist, O. (1998): Mercury Pollution in a Mining Area Guizhou, China: Fluxes Over Contaminated Surfaces and Concentrations in Air, Biological and Geological Samples. Toxicity Environmental Chemistry, 67: 225-236.

Hwang, H.J., Kim, H.K. and Ro, C.U. (2008): Single-particle Characterization of Aerosol Samples Collected Before and during an Asian Dust Storm in Chuncheon, Korea. Atmospheric Environment, 42: 8738-8746.

Iwasaka, Y., Yamamoto, M., Imasu, R. and Ono, A. (1988): Transport of Asian Dust (KOSA) Particles: Importance of Weak KOSA Events on the Geochemical Cycle of Soil Particles. Tellus, 40B: 494-503.

Li, F. and Okada, K. (1999): Diffusion and Modification of Marine Aerosol Particles Over the Coastal Areas in China: A Case Study Using a Single Particle Analysis. Journal of Atmospheric Science, 56: 241-248.

Llorens, J.F., Fermandez-Turiel, J.J. and Querol, X. (2001): The Fate of Trace Elements in a Large Coal-fired Power Plant. Environmental Geology, 40(4-5): 409-416.

Ma, C.J. (2010): Chemical Transformation of Individual Asian Dust Particles Estimated by the Novel Double Detector System of Micro-PIXE. Asian Journal of Atmospheric Environment, 4: 106-114.

Ma, C.J., Kasahara, M.,, Tohno, S. and Kim, K.H. (2008): Physicochemical Properties of Asian Dust Sources. Asian Journal of Atmospheric Environment, 2: 26-33.

Ma, C.J., Kim, J.H., Kim, K.H., Tohno, S. and Kasahara, M. (2010): Specification of Chemical Properties of Feed Coal and Bottom Ash Collected at a Coal-fired Power Plant. Asian Journal of Atmospheric Environment, 4: 80-88.

Nakai, I., Numako, C., Hayakawa, S. and Tsuchiyama, A. (1998): Chemical Speciation of Geological Samples by Micro-XANES Techniques. Journal of Trace and Microprobe Techniques, 16: 87-98.

Research Institute for Applied Mechanics, Kyushu University (2003): Chemical Weather Forecasting System, http://www-cfors.nies.go.jp/~cfors/index-j.html.

Rolph, G.D. (2003) Real-time Environmental Applications and Display system (READY) Website (http://www.arl.noaa.gov/ready/hysplit4.html). NOAA Air Resources Laboratory, Silver Spring, MD.

Roth, B. and Okada, K. (1998): On the Modification of Sea-salt Particles in the Coastal Atmosphre. Atmospheric Envornment, 32: 1555-1569.

Sakai, T., Oikawa, M. and Sato, T. (2005): External Scanning Proton Microprobe – a New Method for in-air Elemental Analysis. Journal of Nuclear and Radiochemical Sciences, 6: 69-71.

Uno, I., Carmichael, G.R., Streets, D.G., Tang, Y., Yienger, J.J., Satake, S., Wang, Z., Woo, J.H., Guttikunda, S., Uematsu, M., Matsumoto, K., Tanimoto, H., Yoshioka, K. and Iida, T. (2003): Regional Chemical Weather Forecasting System CFORS: Model Descriptions and Analysis of Surface Observations at Japanese Island Stations during the ACE-Asia Experiment. Journal of Geophysical Reseach, 108, 8668, doi:10.1029/2002JD002845.

Zhang, D. and Iwasaka, Y. (1999): Nitrate and Sulfate in Individual Asian Dust-storm Particles in Beijing, China in Spring of 1995 and 1996. Atmospheric Environment, 33: 3213-3223.

Zhang, J., Wu,Y., Liu, C.L., Shen, Z.B., Yu, Z.G. and Zhang, Y. (2001): Aerosol Characters from the Desert Region of Northwest China and the Yellow Sea in Spring and Summer: Observations at Minqin, Qingdao, and Qianliyan in 1995-1996. Atmospheric Environment, 35: 5007-5018.

Statistical Modeling of Noise from Urban Road Traffic Stream

Dibyendu Banerjee

ABSTRACT

The present study was conducted with the objective of evaluating the factors that significantly influence the equivalent road traffic noise level, L_{eq} and develop empirical models for its prediction using multiple linear regression analysis in the industrial town of Asansol, India. Noise measurements were recorded in 35 locations along the major roads across the town. The sampling also included the classified vehicle count, vehicular speed, road geometry and landuse information. The parameters were used to develop regression models that were statistically tested. The study shows that L_{eq} values are mostly influenced by the hourly traffic volume. Day time data provided with better statistical models in comparison with those using night time data.

Principal Component Analysis (PCA) was also used for identification of dominating variables that affects the L_{eq} values. The models developed using PCA factors were found to be statistically significant. Regression equations developed using log values of vehicle flow count gave highest correlation coefficient and were able to explain more than about 90% of variations in the dependent factor. The statistical evaluation tests shows

Department of Environment Science, Banwarilal Bhalotia College, (Constituent College of the University of Burdwan), Asansol, West Bengal, (INDIA).

that the models can predict the traffic noise level, L_{eq} within acceptable limits in comparison to observed noise values with certain degree of error.

Key Words: Road traffic noise, modeling, multiple regressions, factor analysis.

INTRODUCTION

Noise is unwanted sound and a serious cause of worry globally, especially in urban areas of developing and developed nations. In recent years heavy urbanization and industrialization has aggravated the environmental noise problem in India and all around the world. The sources of such noise are many and varied, but the most significant one is road traffic. Moving road traffic generates unrestrained noise pollution gives rise to associated auditory and non-auditory health effects. Such noise can cause both short term as well as long term psychological and physiological disorders, particularly among those living, work or remain in close proximity to roadways.

However because of complexity, variability, unpredictability and the interaction of noise with other environmental factors, the adverse health effects of noise prevent themselves to a straight forward analysis. Hence for proper assessment of road traffic noise, mathematical modeling and prediction is required. The prediction and assessment of noise from transport activities can be achieved either by measurement, by computation or by hybrid methods using measurement results in computations. Traffic noise modeling is also required for EIA of highway projects and also in other projects to assess the impact of increased transportation on the environment. Traffic noise models are required as aids in the design of highways and other roads and sometimes in the assessment of existing or envisaged changes in traffic noise conditions (Givargis and Mahmoodi, 2008).

Traffic noise models vary in several respects in feature but overall, the methodology is similar and the A-weighted equivalent noise level L_{eq} is the most preferred descriptor used to assess impact from traffic noise as found in literature. Research works conducted based on traffic noise modeling and prediction includes studies carried out by Banerjee at el, 2009; Bhattacharya et al, 2002; Calixto et al, 2003; Chakraborty et al, 1997; Chakraborty and Banerjee, 2007; Delany, et al, 1976; DOT, 1998; Givargis and Mahmoodi, 2008; Gupta et al , 1986; Kumara and Jain, 1998; Mehdi, 2002; Mohan et al, 2000; Nirjar et al, 2003; Pamanikabud and Vivitjinda, 2002; Qudais and Alhiary, 2007; Rao et al, 1989; Rao and Rao, 1991; Steele, 2001; Suksaard et al, 1999; To, 2002.

A mathematical model usually describes a system by a set of variables and a set of equations that establish relationships between the variables that can be practically anything; real or integer numbers, Boolean values or strings. The actual model is the set of functions that describe the relations between the different variables (Cohen et al, 2003). The models for road traffic noise are developed using the Multiple Linear Regression (MLR) technique that identifies a set of independent variables that explains a proportion of the variance in a dependent variable at a significant level. Another technique that can identify dominating factors from a vast array of independent variables is Factor Analysis. Factor analysis attempts to identify underlying variables, or factors, that explain the pattern of correlations within a set of observed variables.

Factor analysis is often used in data reduction to identify a small number of factors that explain most of the variance observed in a much larger number of manifest variables. A factor extraction method is used to form uncorrelated linear combinations of the observed variables. The first component has maximum variance, while the successive components explain progressively smaller portions of the variance and are all uncorrelated with each other. Principal Components Analysis (PCA) is used to obtain the initial factor solution. Scree plot, a plot of the variance associated with each factor, is used to determine how many factors to be selected. Varimax Method, an orthogonal rotation method that minimizes the number of variables that have high loadings on each factor is usually used and it simplifies the explanation of the factors.

Asansol, an urban-industrial town is situated in the eastern part of India in the state of West Bengal. The town has an area of 127 km^2 and a population density of 3737 persons per km^2. The problem of noise pollution was not a serious factor about five years back. But during the last five years the town has witnessed a sharp growth in vehicular population resulting in a significant increase in the noise pollution across the town. The simultaneous increase in the infrastructural activities has spilled on the roadways and free flow of traffic in majority of the roads has been hampered.

The noise pollution in the study area due to traffic movement has been studied in the past and overall the noise levels are higher than prescribed standards in most locations (Banerjee et al 2008; 2009) Unauthorized parking of vehicles along the roads and especially along roads where they have been widened causes frequent congestions and resultant high noise environment. The road transport vehicles in the area consists of trailers, trucks, mini-trucks, pick-up-vans, buses, mini-buses, SUV, jeeps, cars, taxis, tempos, auto-rickshaws, motorcycles along with the congestion producers, namely rickshaws (type of tricycle), bicycles, and pedestrians. The lack of footpaths, footpaths used as parking for 2-wheelers and over sprawling of commercial activities has added to the problem. This result in congestion and slow moving traffic, causing both air and noise pollution that vary according to the type of landuse.

The major objective of the investigation is to evaluate and determine the factors that considerably influence the equivalent road traffic noise level and develop empirical models for its prediction using Multiple Linear Regression Analysis. Statistical testing of the developed models was also desired.

MATERIAL AND METHODS

A. Data Collection

The design of the sampling was planned in such way so as to obtain sound-level information which was representative for each location and neighborhood. Measurements were made at thirty five locations, spread over the entire city. Hourly recordings of A-weighted sound-pressure level were made at an interval of 30 seconds during the day time (7 a.m.–10 p.m.) and night time (10 p.m.–7 a.m.). A digital sound level meter, Type 2 with frequency weighting network as per IEC651 specifications was used for the study. A 'B & K' multi-function acoustic calibrator (Model: 4226) was used for calibration before and after every sampling. All reading was taken on the 'A-Weighting' frequency network, at a height of about 1.5 meters from ground level and on the 'Fast' range Time Weighting. The 'A' weighting characteristic and 'Fast' range is simulated as 'Human Ear Listening' response. At each noise monitoring site, classified measurements of volume (per hour) and composition of road traffic were made simultaneously.

Average vehicular speed was also determined using manual methods. Vehicles in each location were categorized into Light vehicles (two-wheelers, auto rickshaw), Medium vehicles (car, van & jeep) and Heavy vehicles (bus and truck). All measurements were carried out during working days and under suitable climatic conditions. The landuse data, to be used as independent variable, was based on the Survey of India, Toposheet No. 73 I/14 (1:50000 scale), Aerial photograph and ground truth verifications. All noise sampling locations were considered for the study and site-specific landuse parameters were acquired within an area of 330 feet diameter around each site (Mehdi, 2002).

B. Data Computation

The data collected from field were recorded in MS. Excel worksheet and later transferred to SPSS (version 12) statistical software for further analysis. The sound level meter does not give a steady and consistent reading and it is quite difficult to assess the actual sound level over the entire monitoring period. To mitigate this shortcoming, the Continuous Equivalent Sound level, indicated by Leq, was estimated from sound pressure level recorded and used. It is defined as the level of that steady sound which over the same interval of time, contains the same total energy (or dose) as the fluctuating sound. Equivalent sound level, 'L_{eq}', can be obtained from variable sound pressure level, 'L', over a time period 'T' by using following equation:

$$L_{eq} = 10Log\,[(1/T)\int_0^T 10^{L/10}\,dt] \quad (1)$$

The locations of the sound level meter from the centre line of the road (r) were not equal for all the sites. The distance varied according to the site specific road geometry, road width, accessibility. Hence to maintain uniformity, all field recorded sound levels (L_{eq-r}) were transformed to values it would have been at a distance of 13 feet ($L_{eq-13ft}$), minimum sampling distance recorded, from the road centerline using following formula (Chakraborty et al, 1997):

$$L_{eq-13ft} = L_{eq-r} - 20Log\,(13/r) \quad (2)$$

C. Statistical Analysis and Modeling

Statistical analysis using correlation, multiple linear regression and principal component (PCA) were used to identify the factors that influence the traffic noise in the study area. Multiple Regression analysis using traffic and landuse data as independent variables was used to formulate a set of mathematical models for predicting the equivalent noise levels for day (L_{eq-d}) and night (L_{eq-n}) time. The variables to be used in the models were screened by three criteria statistical analysis of simple correlation matrix, scatter plots and t-test between equivalent noise level and independent parameters. Predictor parameters displaying strong association amongst themselves (collinearity) were not included in the modeling process. The modeling procedure is described below:

Step 1: Development of Scatter Plots and Simple Correlation Matrix of Equivalent Noise Levels and independent variables for selection of appropriate variables and elimination of collinearity and outliers.

Step 2: Multiple Linear Regression (MLR) analysis with selected parameters for two periods – Day and Night time. Three sets of Models developed using three data sets, namely – Traffic data, Landuse data and combined dataset.

Step 3: Principal Component Analysis (PCA) for identification of factors that influence the road traffic noise level. Regression analysis with parameters thus identified was conducted for day time data only.

Step 4: The selection of the best models from among the many developed was based on three criteria (Qudais and Alhiary, 2007):

- R^2 (Coefficient of Multiple Determination) and R^2_{adj} (Adjusted Coefficient of Multiple Determination). Less the difference between the R^2 and R^2_{adj} better the model
- F-test for the Regression Model and t-test for independent variables and their Significance values. Values with less than 0.05 indicating good fit.

- Standard Error of estimate with small values indicating low error and desirable model fits.

Step 5: The validity of the selected models were examined under three criterions, firstly the difference between the observed and predicted equivalent noise levels, secondly the correlation coefficient, and thirdly the paired t-test to examine the goodness of fit assuming a Null Hypothesis, where the mean value of difference between pair of measured and model predicted noise level is equal to zero

Principle Component Analysis

Principal component analysis (PCA) is a mathematical procedure that uses an orthogonal transformation to convert a set of observations of possibly correlated variables into a set of values of linearly uncorrelated variables called principal components (Wikipedia). The number of principal components is less than or equal to the number of original variables. This transformation is defined in such a way that the first principal component has the largest possible variance (that is, accounts for as much of the variability in the data as possible), and each succeeding component in turn has the highest variance possible under the constraint that it be orthogonal to (i.e., uncorrelated with) the preceding components. Principal components are guaranteed to be independent only if the data set is jointly normally distributed. PCA is sensitive to the relative scaling of the original variables. It is mostly used as a tool in exploratory data analysis and for making predictive models.

PCA can be done by eigenvalue decomposition of a data covariance (or correlation) matrix or singular value decomposition of a data matrix, usually after mean centering (and normalizing or using Z-scores) the data matrix for each attribute.[2] The results of a PCA are usually discussed in terms of component scores, sometimes called factor scores (the transformed variable values corresponding to a particular data point), and loadings (the weight by which each standardized original variable should be multiplied to get the component score). PCA is the simplest of the true eigenvector-based multivariate analyses. Often, its operation can be thought of as revealing the internal structure of the data in a way that best explains the variance in the data.

If a multivariate dataset is visualised as a set of coordinates in a high-dimensional data space (1 axis per variable), PCA can supply the user with a lower-dimensional picture, a "shadow" of this object when viewed from its (in some sense) most informative viewpoint. This is done by using only the first few principal components so that the dimensionality of the transformed data is reduced. PCA is closely related to factor analysis. Factor analysis typically incorporates more domain specific assumptions about the underlying structure and solves eigenvectors of a slightly different matrix.

Predictive modeling is the process by which a model is created or chosen to try to best predict the probability of an outcome. Such methods are part of an area of statistical analysis that deals with extracting information from data and using it to predict future trends. The core of predictive modelling relies on capturing associations between explanatory variables and the predicted variables from observed data and exploiting it to predict potential outcomes. For the present investigation the data collected at thirty five locations in the study area was used. The predictor variables were:

- Classified hourly vehicle count
- Percent heavy vehicles
- Average traffic speed
- Landuse pattern of location
- Road width

The validity of the selected models was examined under five criterions:

- Firstly the range of difference between the observed and predicted noise levels; less the range difference, better the fit.
- Secondly the correlation coefficient, at significance level of 0.05. Any value upto 0.5 is considered moderate whereas values of 0.7 and higher indicate strong association.
- Thirdly the paired 't-test', a parametric test for normally distributed data was conducted at 0.05 level of significance.
- 'Chi-square', a non-parametric (distribution free) test to examine the goodness of fit at significance levels of 5% (0.05) was also conducted. The tests was conducted at 0.05 level of significance

RESULTS AND DISCUSSION

The modeling outcome and results of analysis are discussed in this section. The computed data were subjected to descriptive statistical analysis and subsequent correlation analysis. The correlation coefficient, one of the most widespread and useful statistics, is a single numeral that describes the degree of association amongst two variables under study. The Table 7.1 give the descriptive statistics and summarize the data used for the present investigation, whose correlation matrix is given in Table 7.2. The Figure 7.1 and Figure 7.2 shows the correlation matrix.

A. Traffic Stream Character

As given in Table I, the traffic volume in most locations varied between moderate to heavy (346 – 4744 vehicles/hr) having mean value of 2176 ± 1190 vehicles/hour. The vehicle flow is significantly higher during the day time in comparison to evening and night and so also the noise environment.

Table 7.1: Descriptive Statistics of Predictor Variables (Traffic and Landuse) Used for Multiple Regression Analysis Using Road Traffic Noise as Dependent Variable for Model Development

Predictors	Units	Min	Max	Mean	Std. Error	Std. Diviation	Variance
Vehicles Count (X1)							
Day	Vehicles/hour	346	4744	2176	201.30	1190.95	1418381.69
Night	Vehicles/hour	77	2764	1190	125.58	742.95	551984.56
Heavy Vehicles (X2)							
Day	%	0.00	32.46	14.19	1.70	10.06	101.35
Night	%	0.00	36.78	16.29	1.90	11.24	126.45
Speed (X3)							
Day	Km/hr	22.06	72.82	41.46	2.16	12.80	163.89
Night	Km/hr	25.45	78.34	46.44	2.27	13.43	180.42
Road Width (X4)	Feet	12	60	23	2.06	12.20	148.98
Open (X5)	Acres	0.00	1.3170	0.4149976	0.0659747	0.3903119	0.152
Commercial (X6)	Acres	0.00	1.5349	0.5821271	0.0814488	0.4818574	0.232
Residential (X7)	Acres	0.375292	2.2940	1.4305821	0.0876353	0.5184575	0.269
Sensitive (X8)	Acres	0.00	1.0619	0.2678442	0.0583311	0.3450917	0.119
Roadways Area (X9)	Acres	0.0853994	0.8080	0.1841268	0.0234929	0.1389859	0.019
Built-up Area (X10)	Acres	0.9057209	3.3400	2.2805534	0.0903434	0.5344788	0.286

Table 7.2: Correlation Matrix (Pearson) of Road Traffic Noise Level and Predictor Variables, Using Data from Thirty Five Locations

	Leq_ Night	Vehicles_ Day	Vehicle_ Night	Speed_ Day	Speed_ Night	HV_ Day	HV_ Night	Road width	Open space	CM	RE	SE	BU
Leq_Day	.883	.877	.808	-.170	-.171	.462	.394	.527	-.395	.300	-.473	.241	.051
Leq_Night	1	.755	.734	-.108	-.078	.387	.387	.537	-.378	.250	-.250	.089	.100
Vehicles_Day	.755	1	.804	-.197	-.234	.493	.413	.499	-.365	.312	-.463	.202	.042
Vehicle_Night	.734	.804	1	-.126	-.119	.488	.401	.524	-.319	.367	-.331	-.113	-.031
Speed_Day	-.108	-.197	-.126	1	.902	.243	.393	.498	.717	-.392	-.186	-.130	-.784
Speed_Night	-.078	-.234	-.119	.902	1	.173	.310	.410	.655	-.373	-.059	-.183	-.670
HV_Day	.387	.493	.488	.243	.173	1	.897	.615	.015	.008	-.429	.088	-.382
HV_Night	.387	.413	.401	.393	.310	.897	1	.652	.123	-.090	-.355	.046	-.455
Roadwidth	.537	.499	.524	.498	.410	.615	.652	1	.135	-.026	-.458	-.046	-.575
Openspace	-.378	-.365	-.319	.717	.655	.015	.123	.135	1	-.549	-.039	-.131	-.810
Commercial	.250	.312	.367	-.392	-.373	.008	-.090	-.026	-.549	1	-.415	-.277	.476
Residential	-.250	-.463	-.331	-.186	-.059	-.429	-.355	-.458	-.039	-.415	1	-.377	.269
Sensitive	.089	.202	-.113	-.130	-.183	.088	.046	-.046	-.131	-.277	-.377	1	.159
Built-up	.100	.042	-.031	-.784	-.670	-.382	-.455	-.575	-.810	.476	.269	.159	1

CM – Commercial, RE – Residential, SE – Sensitive, BU-Builtup area

Units: L_{eq} – dB(A); Vehicles – vehicles/hr; Speed - kmph; HV (heavy vehicles) - %; Road-width – feet; Others - acres

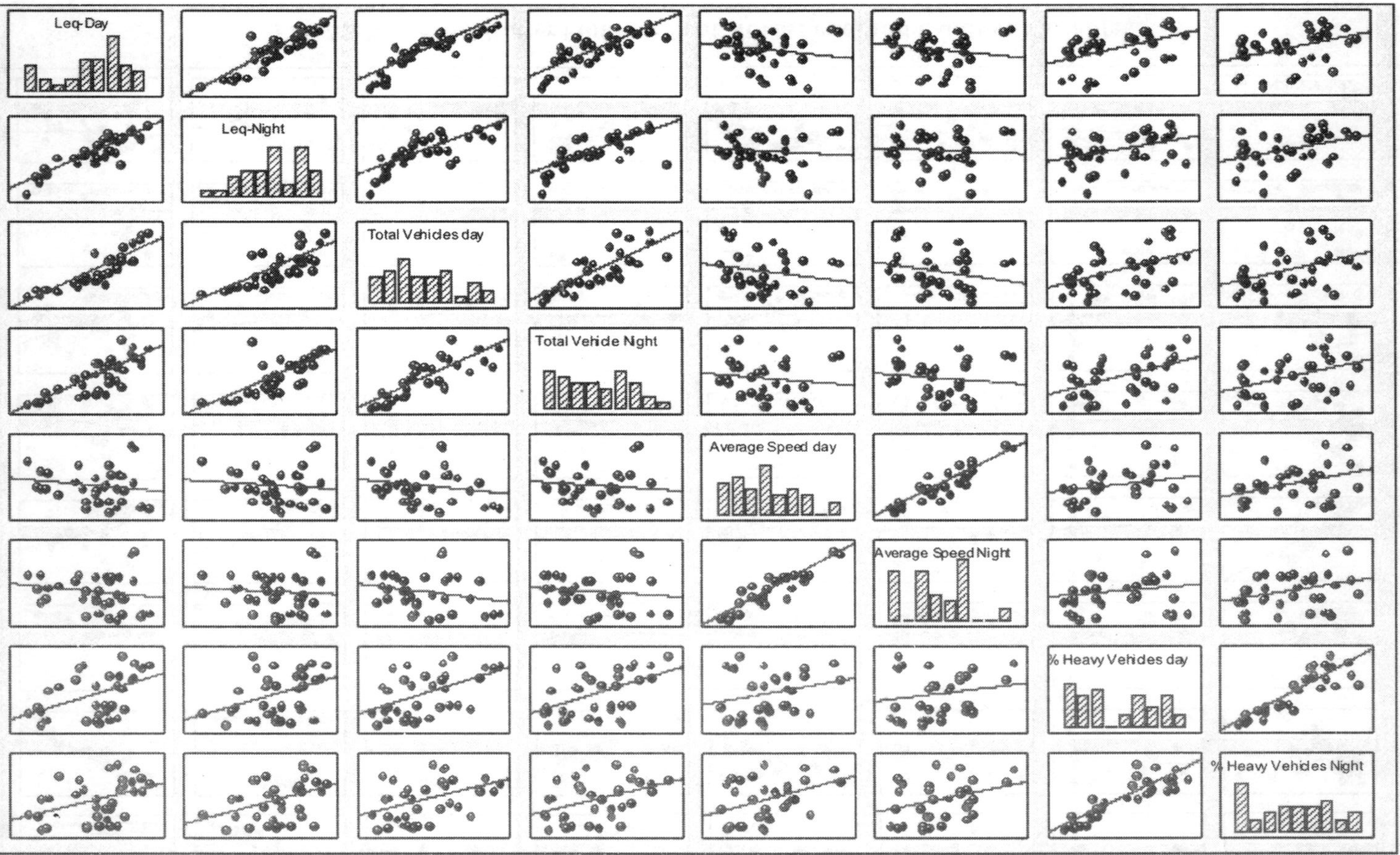

Fig. 7.1: Bivariate Scatter Plot Matrix of Noise Level and Traffic Variables

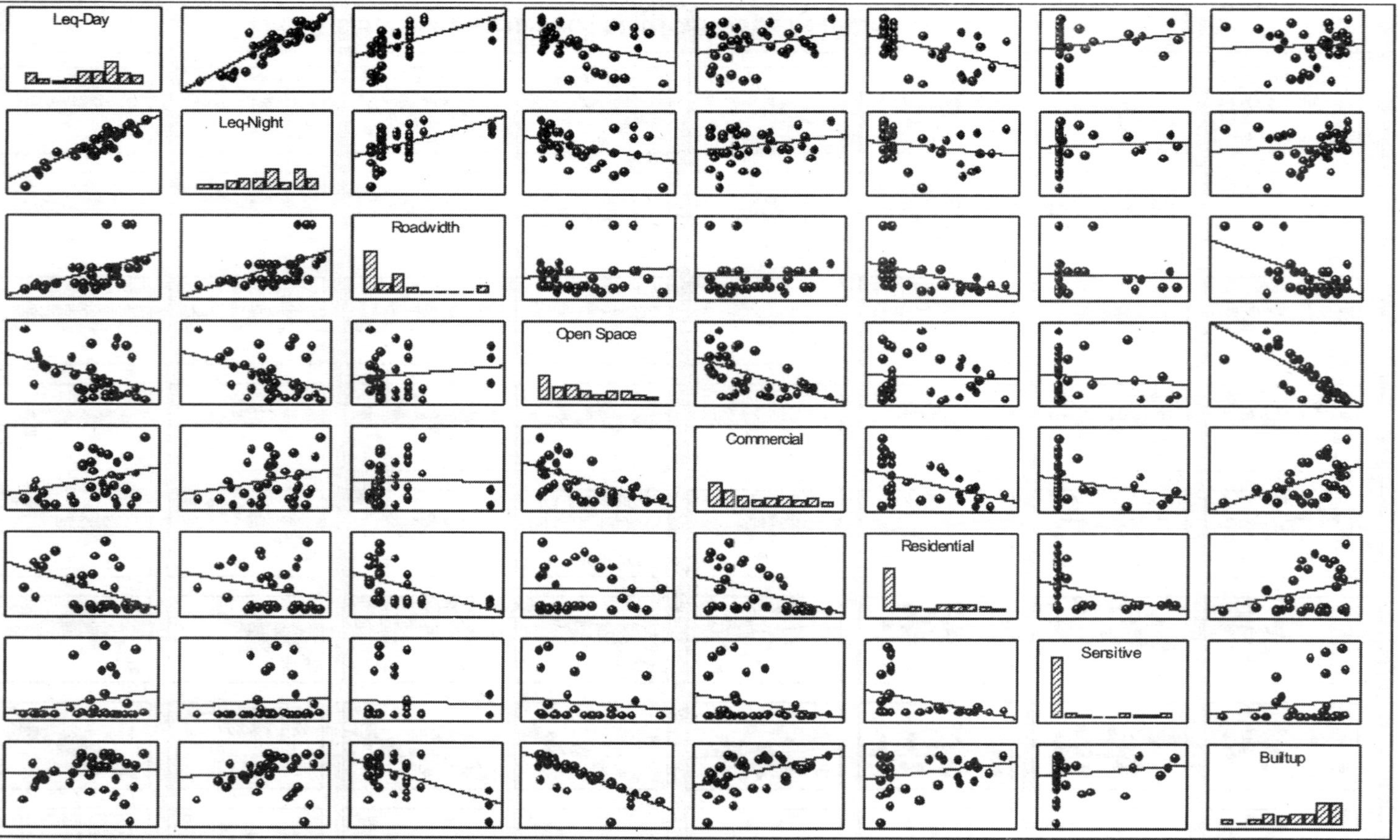

Fig. 7.2: Bivariate Scatter Plot Matrix of Noise Level and Landuse Variables

Slow moving vehicles tend to clog the roads and create frequent jams mostly in the commercial and market areas. Unauthorized and illegal parking of autos, 2-wheelers and sometimes cars, covers portion of the road and side walk and reduce the effective traffic moving space and result in heavy congestion. This gives rise with high noise pollution due to a variety of factors like blowing of horns, acceleration, deceleration, idling, type screeching, braking, exhaust noise, etc.

A classified vehicle data shows that in all locations 2-wheelers, including scooters, mopeds and bikes are predominant in almost all sampled sites. During night time the mean vehicle count was 1190 ± 742 vehicles/hour (77 – 2764 vehicles/hour). Heavy vehicles, which are the chief source of road traffic noise and influences it highly, ranged between nil and 32.46% with mean value of 14.19 ± 10.06 %. Some locations have 'No-Entry' for heavy vehicles during the day time and these locations had comparatively lower noise values. The night time movement of heavy vehicle ranged between nil and 36.78% with mean value of 16.29 ± 11.24%. Some locations had higher heavy vehicles movement during night time in comparison to day time and consequently higher noise level, as because the 'No-entry' is lifted after 21.00 hrs.

The noise level in those areas is comparatively higher in the post 2100 hours. The average vehicle speed in the sampling sites ranged between 22.06 and 72.87 kmph (mean 41.46 ± 12.80 kmph) during day time and 25.45 – 78.34 kmph (mean 46.44 ± 13.43 kmph) during night time. The width of the roads, an important noise influencing factor, ranged between 12 and 60 ft (mean 23 ± 12.20 ft). All roads are of asphalt built and can be classified in to arterial road (NH-2 and G.T.Road), secondary roads (Burnpur road), tertiary roads (Gorai road) and lanes and by-lanes. Based on present study it is observed that narrower roads have higher noise levels than broader roads, as because narrower roads cause more traffic congestions. Also since the main roads are frequented by congestions during the office hours, most medium and light vehicles divert and move along the secondary and other less wide roads, thus causing congestion and high noise pollution.

B. Predictors for Traffic Noise Modeling

The other predictor variables used for modeling included the land-use of the area covering a radius around the sampling site. The land use was classified into (a) Open Space (Space unoccupied, fallow, to be constructed upon, etc.); (b) Commercial (shops, departmental stores, cinema hall, offices, etc.); (c) Residential (apartments, office quarters, single and multistoried private houses, etc.), (d) Sensitive (educational and health establishments, court, etc.); (e) Built-up area (combination of commercial, residential, sensitive, industrial, etc.) and (f) Roadway area (area occupied by asphalt road within a 165 ft radius around the sampling station. Overall, dominating land use pattern was residential, followed by commercial. The built-up area had the highest mean value of 2.28 ± 0.5344 acres and ranged between 0.905 and 3.340 acres.

As given in Table 7.2, Noise Level defined by L_{eq}, is influenced by Total Vehicle Count, Percent Heavy Vehicles, Road Width and Residential land-use. The correlation with residential area variable shows a negative relationship, i.e. study locations in or near residential areas had has lower noise levels. This is because residential areas are in most cases away from the main roads. Also the roads passing across the residential areas are usually secondary type or lanes and thus have less vehicular movements and nearly no heavy vehicles. Weak negative correlation of L_{eq} with mean vehicle speed is observed. The more the smooth flow of traffic, higher the vehicle speed, less the congestion and lower the generated sound levels. Both commercial and sensitive landuse shows weak positive relation with L_{eq}.

Commercial areas, including market places, road side shops (temporary & permanent), hawkers, etc. encroach on a major portion of the footpath and onto the roads, thus reducing the effective road area. This causes heavy congestion and prevents free flow of traffic. The situation is worsened by the presence of heavy vehicles and peaks during the office hours. Greater the size of commercial activity, higher is the noise in most cases. But in certain areas the situation is not observed and free flow of traffic is ensured, hence noise is low. This variability in data explains the weak correlation result. Sensitive areas along road side mostly include school (primary, secondary and high) and health establishments (pathological laboratories, hospitals – public & private, nursing homes) with highly sensitive receivers.

The locations are frequently used by commuters and hence the noise environment is high in spite of the highly susceptible nature of the areas. Total absence of 'no horn' signs and very low awareness among the local community makes the locations more vulnerable. Sensitive locations away from road traffic have comparatively lower noise. Slow and unorganized movement of traffic, coupled with illegal parking along the roads, especially during school hours results in serious noise pollution in these areas.

C. Statistical Analysis and Modeling

For multiple regressions analysis the independent variable were identified into two groups, namely (a) Landuse; and (b) Traffic. The landuse parameters were Open Area (X1), Residential Area (X2), Commercial Area (X3), Sensitive Area (X4), Roadways Area (X5) and Total Built-up Area (X6). These landuse variables along with Hourly Traffic Flow (X7), Percent Heavy Vehicles (X8), Mean Vehicular Speed (X9) and Road-width (X10) were treated as independent parameters to compute the Equivalent Noise value (Y) using SPSS-12 (Statistical package for social science). The multiple regression equation developed for the prediction of L_{eq} values was in the following form:

$$Y = c + b1X1 + b2X2 + b3X3 + \text{———} + bnXn \quad (3)$$

Where, Y is the dependent variable, L_{eq}; 'c' is the constant, where the regression line intercepts the y axis and represents the amount the dependent Y will be when all the independent variables are 0. X1, X2, X3 ----Xn are the independent variables described and b1, b2 , b3 -- bn are the regression coefficients. The Equivalent Noise Level, L_{eq}, is the most recognized noise index in India and all standards are based on its day and night time values across various landuse zones and hence was used for the present study as the dependent parameter.

A number of regression models were developed for the accurate prediction of equivalent noise level under variable conditions like using traffic data only, using landuse data only and using a combined set of both types of data. The best models selected from the many developed are given in Table 7.3 A and Table 7.3 B. Each analysis was done separately for day and night time. For day time, using traffic data, the best model was found to be a function of Traffic Flow per hour (V), Percent Heavy Vehicles (H) and Road Width (Rw). Other variables like Mean Traffic Speed (S) negligibly increased the R^2 value and were thus found to have a less influence on L_{eq}. This regression equation can be written as:

$$L_{eq\text{-}d} = 62.903 + 0.006667V + 0.023770H + 0.107250Rw \quad (4)$$

Table 7.3 A: Statistical Characteristics of the Traffic Noise Prediction Models No. 4 to 9, Developed Using Multiple Regression Models and Using Traffic Variables and Landuse as Predictors and Road Traffic Noise Levels as Dependent Variables. (95% CI)

Statistical	Parameter	Models					
		Eqn. 4	Eqn. 5	Eqn. 6	Eqn. 7	Eqn. 8	Eqn. 9
Regression	S.S.	2466.361	815.716	2534.271	2603.748	1019.261	2887.977
	M.S.	822.120	271.921	422.378	867.916	339.754	481.330
	R	0.883	0.508	0.895	0.756	0.473	0.796
	R^2	0.780	0.258	0.801	0.571	0.224	0.633
	R^2 – Adj.	0.759	0.186	0.759	0.530	0.148	0.555
	S.E. of estimate	4.739	8.701	4.737	7.942	10.686	7.725
	F-Test	36.609	3.592	18.825	13.762	2.976	8.066
	Sig.	0.000	0.025	0.000	0.000	0.047	0.000
Constant	Estimate	62.903	79.084	57.464	53.846	82.436	58.374
	S.E.	2.099	4.589	5.130	3.397	6.625	6.947
	t-Test	29.971	17.234	11.202	15.852	12.442	8.403
	Sig.	0.000	0.000	0.000	0.000	0.000	0.000

Table 7.3 B: Statistical Characteristics of the Traffic Noise Prediction Models No. 10 to 15, Developed Using Multiple Regression Models and Using Traffic Variables and Landuse as Predictors and Road Traffic Noise Levels as Dependent Variables. (95% CI)

Statistical	Parameter	Models					
		Eqn.10	Eqn.11	Eqn.12	Eqn.13	Eqn.14	Eqn.15
Regression	S.S.	2550.556	2431.306	2743.027	2684.389	3200.249	2740.669
	M.S.	318.820	2431.306	2743.027	1342.195	3200.249	1370.334
	R	0.898	0.877	0.931	0.921	0.838	0.815
	R^2	0.806	0.769	0.867	0.849	0.702	0.664
	R^2 – Adj.	0.747	0.762	0.863	0.839	0.693	0.643
	S.E. of estimate	4.852	4.707	3.565	3.865	6.416	6.685
	F-Test	13.545	109.725	215.785	89.830	77.745	30.665
	Sig.	0.000	0.000	0.000	0.000	0.000	0.000
Constant	Estimate	67.174	64.459	- 25.786	-18.980	1.325	8.095
	S.E.	12.806	1.676	7.221	9.108	7.960	9.291
	t-Test	5.246	38.461	-3.571	-2.084	0.166	0.871
	Sig.	0.000	0.000	0.001	0.045	0.869[a]	0.390[a]

[a] Not significant

The regression parameters, namely R, R^2 and R^2_{adj} had values of 0.883, 0.780 and 0.759 respectably. About 78% of variations are explained by the day time traffic conditions, mainly total hourly vehicle and % heavy vehicles. Using landuse data, the best model was found to be a function of Commercial (LC), Residential (LR) and Sensitive (LS) space. The variables like Open and Built up area were found to have a lesser influence on L_{eq}. The regression equation can be written as:

$$L_{eq\text{-}d} = 79.084 + 0.0000920LC - 0.0001385LR + 0.0001005LS \quad (5)$$

The R, R^2 and R^2_{adj} for the equation had values of 0.508, 0.258 and 0.186 respectably. The landuse variables could only explain about 26% of variation in the noise level and rest was due to some other factors. The addition of another variable reduces the R^2 value to very insignificant level. Based on the result it can be said that landuse data may not have a high influence on the road traffic noise based on the present study condition. This is because throughout the town, some locational traffic noise will be significantly affected by the site landuse, while in others the affect is medium to low and hence does nt give a good regression fit model. The equation is improved by combining the variables of Eqn. 4 and Eqn. 5 and generating the model. This resulted in much better and statistically models having a highest R value of

0.895. The R^2 and R^2_{adj} for the best equation had values of 0.801 and 0.759 respectably and can be written as:

$$L_{eq}=57.464+0.000083LC-0.000059LR+0.000117LS+ 0.005747V-0.007137H+0.206274Rw \quad (6)$$

About 80% of the variability could be explained by this improved model and it can be said that road traffic noise is mostly a product of traffic character and certain landuse parameters. While the former is the source of the sound and hence more significantly related, while the later acts as the transmission path and may attenuate the propagation based on site specific features.

For night time, using traffic data input, the best model was found to be a function of Traffic Flow per hour (V), Percent Heavy Vehicles (H) and Road Width (Rw) and can be written as:

$$L_{eq\text{-}n} = 53.846 + 0.0097305V + 0.0000936H + 0.2051524Rw \quad (7)$$

The R, R^2 and R^2_{adj} for the above equation were 0.756, 0.571 and 0.530 respectably. The model statistics were less significant then the day time Eqn. 4. Using landuse data, the best model was found to be a function of Commercial (LC), Residential (LR) and Open space (LO) areas. Other variables were found to have a lower impact on the L_{eq}. The regression equation can be written as:

$$L_{eq\text{-}n} = 82.436 + 0.0000719LC - 0.0001756LR - 0.0003331LO \quad (8)$$

The R, R^2 and R^2_{adj} for the equation had values of 0.473, 0.224 and 0.148 respectably. The best equation has very low prediction power (22.4 %) of traffic noise and seems to be more dependent on the traffic data. The equations were improved when a combined data set of vehicular and landuse was used for modeling. The best equation had an R value of 0.796. The model fit was better than the two obtained (Eqn. 7 and Eqn. 8) using separate data sets. The R^2 and R^2_{adj} for the equation had values of 0.633 and 0.555 respectably. The regression equation can be written as:

$$L_{eq\text{-}n} = 58.374+0.0000447LC-0.0000078LR+0.0002189LO+ 0.007885V- 0.0216339H + 0.2973301Rw \quad (9)$$

From Table 7.3 A and Table 7.3 B it can be noted that models involving day time data were better than those developed with night time data. The variability in the models of day and night time is mainly due to the traffic parameters, since landuse data base was the same for both periods. Also the predictor models were significantly improved when a combination of traffic and landuse variables were used in the regression analysis.

Regression modeling with variables that significantly influence the L_{eq} value was also conducted such dominating variables were identified and interpreted using the 'Factor Analysis' tool. 'Principal Component' extraction method was used for factor analysis for the present study using the nine descriptive variables. The number of variables (components) required to elucidate the data dissimilarity was chosen based on 'Eigenvalues' (> 1.0), the Scree Plots and percent of total variation explained. The Eigenvalues, Percent of total variation explained, cumulative percent of total variance and rotated loadings for day time data is given in Table 7.4. The first Eigenvalue is 3.306 and explains 36.73% of the total variance. The second is 2.595 and explains 28.84% of total variance and third is 1.248 and explains 13.86% of total variance. The first three accounts for a total of 79% of variance and were identified as:

Component 1: Vehicular Speed, Open space, Built-up area.

Component 2: Total Vehicles, Percent Heavy Vehicles, Road Width, Residential Area.

Component 3: Sensitive Areas.

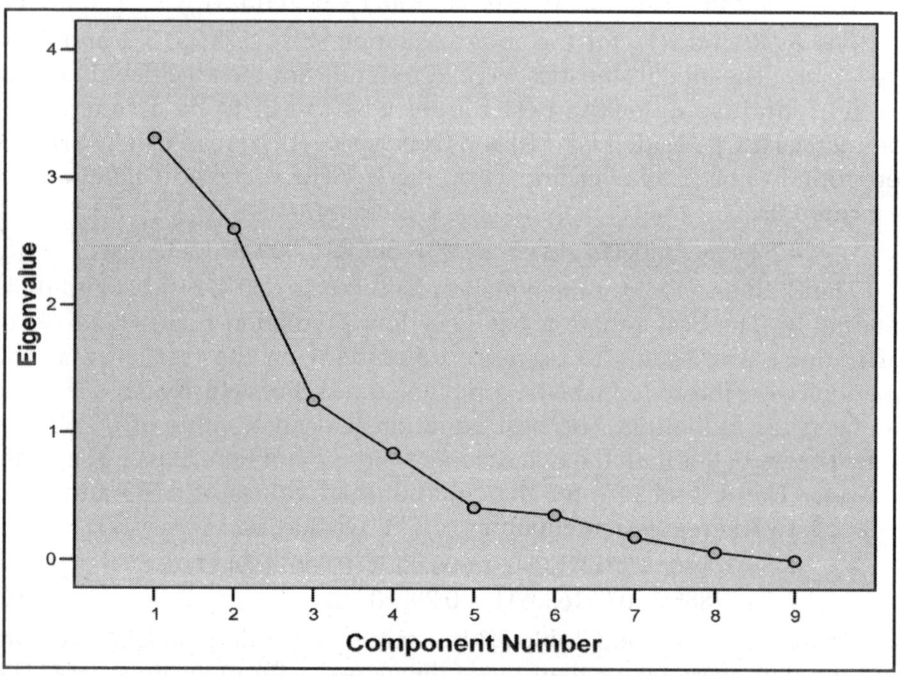

Fig. 7.3: Scree Plot Showing Position of Eigenvalues

The first component is characterized by about similar loading of Open space and Built-up area, followed by Vehicular Speed. Moderate negative loading of commercial space, lower loading of road width, total vehicle, heavy vehicles, sensitive space and negligible loading of residential area. This component may be interpreted as 'Congestion Barrier Factor'. The second component is characterized by about similar loading of total vehicles, percent heavy vehicles, road width and residential space. Moderate loading of commercial and built-up area and low to negative loading of remaining parameters. This component may be interpreted as 'Traffic Factor'. The third component is characterized by high loading of sensitive space and accounts for 13.87% of total variance. Moderate loading of commercial area and low to negative loading of remaining parameters. This component may be interpreted as 'Trip Generator Factor'.

Table 7.4: Principal Component Loadings for Three Factors (C1 - C3) by Varimax Rotation Using Kaiser Normalization Converged in Five Iterations Using the Factors Associated with Road Traffic Noise Emission and Propagation

Predictors	Component Loading		
	C1	C2	C3
Total Vehicles/hour	-.332	.782	.082
Mean Speed	.868	.196	-.122
% Heavy Vehicle	.186	.771	.016
Road width	.376	.789	-.154
Open space	.905	-.117	-.012
Commercial	-.682	.324	-.495
Residential	.001	-.787	-.168
Sensitive	-.116	.185	.961
Buildup	-.908	-.315	.097
Total Eigenvalues	3.306	2.595	1.248
% of Total Variance explained	36.729	28.837	13.862
Cumulative % of Variance	36.729	65.566	79.428

Using Factor Analysis, with the 3 component dataset, the regression equation obtained can be written as:

$$L_{eq} = 67.174 - 0.0301745S - 0.0000904LO + 0.0000090LB + 0.0055278V + 0.0293765H + 0.1749981Rw - 0.000233LR + 0.0000399LS \quad (10)$$

LB denotes Built-up area, a combination of residential, commercial, industrial and sensitive landuse in the sampling site. The R, R^2 and R^2_{adj} for the equation had values of 0.898, 0.806 and 0.747 respectably. Thus the Factor Analysis proves to be a useful statistical tool in improving the equation by identifying the best combination of independent variables. The R and R^2 values were much better than the previous models. Removal of other variables and using only hourly traffic count improved the model significantly. The statistical model developed was found to have R, R^2 and R^2_{adj} values of 0.877, 0.769 and 0.762 respectably. The developed model had the following form:

$$L_{eq} = 64.459 + 0.0071004V \quad (11)$$

The lower value of coefficient of variation is desirable, as because, if the vehicle count becomes zero then the constant will be the noise level. Although 'R' value in Eqn. 10 was higher than that of Eqn. 11, but the later was identified as the better model fit as because the difference between the R^2 and R^2_{adj} is lower in the Eqn. 11. Based on statistical characteristics of the model it can be said that it was significant and with a R^2 value of 0.769, it explains about 77% of the variation of the L_{eq}. As shown in Table 3b it can be said that multiple linear regression analysis using Factor Analysis can produce better models.

Statistical regression modeling of L_{eq} was also developed separately as function of logarithm of the Hourly Traffic Flow (V), Heavy Vehicles (H) and Light Vehicles (L) for the monitoring sites within the city. The vehicle count was categorized into the Heavy and Light types as because the type of vehicles has a dominating effect on the road traffic noise level. The light vehicles and heavy vehicles were classified as given below:

- Light vehicles including private cars, 2-wheelers, autos, tempos, taxi and all other light good vehicles.
- Heavy vehicles including private and public light buses, mini bus, trucks, container vehicles, etc.

The regression equation can be written as:

For day time traffic

$$L_{eq\text{-}d} = 32.395\text{Log}(V) - 25.786 \quad (12)$$

$$L_{eq\text{-}d} = 3.010\text{Log}(H) + 28.867\text{Log}(L) - 18.980 \quad (13)$$

For night time traffic

$$L_{eq\text{-}n} = 23.644\text{Log}(V) + 1.325 \quad (14)$$

$$L_{eq\text{-}n} = 4.005\text{ Log}(H) + 19.177\text{ Log}(L) + 8.095 \quad (15)$$

Modeling with log values of traffic count provided with excellent models that had good data fitting capacity. The models had high R, R^2 and R_{adj}, and low standard error. Comparatively, day time data was again significant in producing better models with respect to night time models. It was also observed that when modeling with only total vehicles, the equations were much better, than when heavy and light types of vehicles were used separately. This may be because the traffic flow in the study area is not homogenous and is of mixed type. Thus it is more about the impact of the total vehicles than the individual categories that tend to introduce error in the equations. Although the number of 2-wheelers is highest in any sampling site, but that does not mean that the noise is also very high in that location in comparison to a location where the 2-wheeler count is lower. The noise is more dependent and influenced by the congestion factor than the total or classified vehicle count. The daytime regression model had a high and significant R value of 0.931 a standard error (S.E.) of 3.565 while the night time model had an R value of 0.852 and S.E. of 6.445 as shown in Table 7.3B. As with the other model sets here also the day time variables proves to be better predictor of road traffic noise level, L_{eq}.

The multiple linear regression models were validated under the three criterions of measured-calculated difference in L_{eq}, secondly the correlation coefficient, and thirdly the paired t-test to examine the goodness of fit. The evaluation and test results are given in Table 7.5 for the 12 models, whose regression characters are given in Table 7.3 A and Table 7.3 B. The correlation coefficient value ranged between 0.440 and 0.931. A value of 0.7 and above for the statistical parameter indicates a good correlation between two sets of data (in this case the observed and predicted noise levels). The highest correlation was observed for the equation involving Log value of Hourly vehicle count and day time L_{eq}. This was the best predictive model amongst all the developed once and explained 93% of the variability in the noise level. The mean difference between pair of calculated and measured noise level was very low. The next best model was also a log based equation involving the day time total, heavy and light vehicle count, and accounting for about 92% of the variability in the L_{eq}. 50% of the tested models had correlation in the range of 0.8 to 0.9 and were statistically good in terms of predicting traffic noise level under the study conditions. Among them the model involving daytime vehicle count was best having correlation of 0.883 and paired mean difference of - 0.00029. The t-values for the equations were statistically significant in all the cases. Moderate to less significant correlations were observed in equations involving night time data or landuse variables. Among the equation involving both landuse data and night time traffic variables, the least significant had a correlation coefficient value of 0.440. The addition of landuse parameters in the regression equations, step wise, caused the lowering of the R value and such equations proved to be less significant in prediction of L_{eq}. Overall it can be said that hourly traffic flow was the most dominating in terms of influencing the road traffic noise index, L_{eq}.

The models involving the vehicular parameter was improved by using the log value instead of the absolute values and adding the breakup of the vehicles in to heavy and light, as shown by eqn. 13. The models get slightly less significant when night time data are used. This may be because of variability in night time data. In some locations the night time noise levels are higher than the day time noise, as because in these locations movement of heavy vehicles are prohibited during the day time period of 6.00 hours to 22.00 hours, hence noise is lower. The landuse data in the sampling locations also produces equations with low correlation and predictive value. Landuse data showed heterogeneity in terms of traffic noise.

This is because in most locations the landuse through which the road passes influences the noise spreading from the vehicles, but in some sites landuse had less predictive powers. For example in some residential areas the noise level is low as because the road passing is secondary type, whereas in most other locations the road is arterial and hence more noise prone.

Table 7.5: Comparative Statistical Evaluation of Road Traffic Noise Models for Evaluation of the most Suitable Ones that may give Better Results Using Traffic and Landuse as input Variables. The Correlation Data is for the Modeled and Actual Recorded Road Traffic Noise

Test Models	Correlation	Significance (95% CI)	Paired Differences			t-stat	Significance (2-tailed, 95% CI)
			Mean	Std. Deviation	Std. Error of Mean		
Eqn.4	0.883	0.000	-0.00029	4.5256	0.76497	-0.000373	0.999704
Eqn. 5	0.508	0.002	0.00086	8.30838	1.40437	0.000610	0.999517
Eqn. 6	0.875	0.000	2.29743	5.00212	0.84551	2.717201	0.010281[a]
Eqn. 7	0.756	0.000	0.00371	7.58253	1.28168	0.002898	0.997705
Eqn. 8	0.440	0.008	-4.06714	10.73782	1.81502	-2.240823	0.031678
Eqn. 9	0.597	0.000	-9.53914	9.41277	1.59105	-5.995507	0.000001[a]
Eqn. 10	0.848	0.000	4.11800	6.21410	1.05037	3.920509	0.000406[a]
Eqn. 11	0.877	0.000	0.00057	4.63730	0.78385	0.000729	0.999423
Eqn. 12	0.931	0.000	0.00000	3.51333	0.59386	0.000000	1.000000
Eqn. 13	0.917	0.000	-0.11353	0.64205	0.64205	-0.176823	0.860728
Eqn. 14	0.838	0.000	0.00057	6.32103	1.06845	0.000535	0.999576
Eqn. 15	0.815	0.000	-0.00088	6.47964	1.11125	-0.000794	0.999371

[a] Significant

The same works for some commercial and sensitive landuse areas. But overall the various landuse patterns had significant influence on the L_{eq} values and more so during the daytime. It can be said that the models would have been much better if they are developed for separate types of roads within the same urban area. This is beyond the scope of the present investigation.

Predictive Regression Model Validation

The best fitted mathematical models predicting L_{eq} noise level using the traffic and landuse variables were validated using observed data from the thirty five sampling locations in the study area. The Wilcoxon Matched Pair test was introduced in the validity exercise along with the other estimation criteria since some data was observed to be deviating from the normal distribution. The Wilcoxon matched pairs test is a nonparametric alternative to the paired t-test. The comparative results of the paired difference are given in Table 7.6 and t-test analysis is given in Table 7.7. The results of Wilcoxon matched pair test and Chi-square test is given in Table 7.8.

Table 7.6: Paired Difference of Mean Between Observed and Predicted Noise Data

Regression Model and Observed Data Pair		Paired Differences				
		Mean	Std. Deviation	Std. Error Mean	95% Confidence Interval of the Difference	
					Lower	Upper
Pair 1	Leq_Day – 01	-0.0003	4.52563	.76497	-1.55489	1.55432
Pair 2	Leq_Day – 02	0.0009	8.30838	1.40437	-2.85317	2.85489
Pair 3	Leq_Day – 03	2.2974	5.00212	.84551	.57914	4.01572
Pair 4	Leq_Night – 04	0.0037	7.58253	1.28168	-2.60098	2.60840
Pair 5	Leq_Night – 05	-4.0671	10.73782	1.81502	-7.75571	-.37857
Pair 6	Leq_Night – 06	-9.5391	9.41277	1.59105	-12.77254	-6.30574
Pair 7	Leq_Day – 07	4.1180	6.21410	1.05037	1.98338	6.25262
Pair 8	Leq_Day – 08	.0006	4.63730	.78385	-1.59240	1.59354
Pair 9	Leq_Day – 09	.0000	3.51333	.59386	-1.20687	1.20687
Pair 10	Leq_Day – 10	-.5703	4.57225	.77285	-2.14091	1.00034
Pair 11	Leq_Night – 11	.0006	6.32103	1.06845	-2.17078	2.17192
Pair 12	Leq_Day – 12	8.5909	5.34111	.90281	6.75612	10.42559

Table 7.7: Comparative Results of Paired t-Test, Pearson Correlation and Variance for the Regression Models and Observed Values

Models	01	02	03	04	05	06	07	08	09	10	11	12
Mean	79.91	79.91	77.61	70.85	74.92	80.39	75.79	79.91	79.91	80.48	70.85	71.32
Variance	72.54	24.00	104.44	76.56	60.54	71.46	137.02	71.51	80.68	66.47	94.13	81.26
Observations	35	35	35	35	35	35	35	35	35	35	35	35
Pearson	0.8831	0.5079	0.8747	0.7557	0.4402	0.5973	0.8478	0.8768	0.8353	0.8812	0.8379	0.7997
Correlation												
HMD	0	0	0	0	0	0	0	0	0	0	0	0
Df	34	34	34	34	34	34	34	34	34	34	34	34
t Stat	0.0006	0.0001	-2.7161	-0.0024	2.2411	5.9953	-3.9203	-0.0006	8.3696	0.7377	0.0004	0.3987
P (T<=t) one-tail	0.4998	0.5000	0.0052	0.4990	0.0158	0.0000	0.0002	0.4998	0.0000	0.2329	0.4998	0.3463
t Critical one-tail	1.6909	1.6909	1.6909	1.6909	1.6909	1.6909	1.6909	1.6909	1.6909	1.6909	1.6909	1.6909
P (T<=t) two-tail	0.9995	0.9999	0.0103	0.9981	0.0317	0.0000	0.0004	0.9996	0.0000	0.4658	0.9997	0.6926
t Critical two-tail	2.0322	2.0322	2.0322	2.0322	2.0322	2.0322	2.0322	2.0322	2.0322	2.0322	2.0322	2.0322

Values marked in red are significant at 0.05 level of confidence; HMD- Hypothesized Mean Difference

Table 7.8: Comparative Results of Chi-Square and Wilcoxon Matched Pair Test for the Pairs of Predicted and Observed Values

Pair		Chi-Square test		Wilcoxon Matched Pair test		
		X^2	p-level	T	Z	p-level
Pair 1	Leq_Day – PRED01	9.149	0.9999	307.00	0.1310	0.8957
Pair 2	Leq_Day – PRED02	30.145	0.6571	314.0	0.0164	0.9870
Pair 3	Leq_Day – PRED03	14.026	0.9990	174.0	2.3095	0.0209
Pair 4	Leq_Night – PRED04	27.091	0.7939	115.0	3.2758	0.0011
Pair 5	Leq_Night – PRED05	60.985	0.0030	314.0	0.0164	0.9869
Pair 6	Leq_Night – PRED06	76.409	0.0000	307.0	0.1310	0.8957
Pair 7	Leq_Day – PRED07	28.189	0.7476	301.0	0.2293	0.8186
Pair 8	Leq_Day – PRED08	9.517	0.9999	273.0	0.6879	0.4915
Pair 9	Leq_Day – PRED09	5.436	1.0000	186.0	2.1129	0.0346
Pair 10	Leq_Day – PRED10	9.162	0.9999	32.0	4.6353	0.0000
Pair 11	Leq_Night – PRED11	17.859	0.9896	285.0	0.4914	0.6232
Pair 12	Leq_Night_PRED12	22.201	0.9403	304.0	0.1801	0.8570

Values marked in red are significant at 0.05 level of confidence.

The General Road Traffic Noise Prediction Scenario

The predicted noise values for the study area of Asansol were compared with the field recorded data using various statistical tools. The overall outcome is summaries in Table 7.9.

CONCLUSIONS

Based on the present study which was aimed that identifying the factors that influences the road traffic noise levels using multiples regression models, under the urban Indian traffic stream, the following conclusions can be drawn:

1. The predicted noise levels are mainly influenced by the hourly traffic volume. The other factors that effect the L_{eq} includes percent heavy vehicles passing through the sites, the road width, log values of traffic count including heavy and light vehicles.
2. Data from day time monitoring provided with better statistical models in comparison with those using night time data.
3. Factor analysis using principal component extraction is useful tool for identification of dominating factors among the many that affects L_{eq}. The models developed using PCA identified factors were statistically significant

Table 7.9: Performance of Traffic Noise Prediction Models

Models	Prediction Range, d	Correlation, r	t-Stat	Chi-Square, X2	Wilcoxon test, Z	Score	Model Acceptability
FHWA	A	A	Sig.	Not Sig.	–	3/4	OK
CORTN	A	A	Sig.	Not Sig.	–	3/4	OK
PRED 01	A	A	Not Sig.	Not Sig.	Not Sig.	5/5	OK
PRED 02	NA	NA	Not Sig.	Not Sig.	Not Sig.	3/5	OK
PRED 03	MA	A	Sig.	Not Sig.	Sig.	2/5	NOT OK
PRED 04	NA	MA	Not Sig.	Not Sig.	Sig.	2/5	NOT OK
PRED 05	NA	NA	Sig.	Sig.	Not Sig.	1/5	NS
PRED 06	NA	NA	Sig.	Sig.	Not Sig.	1/5	NS
PRED 07	NA	A	Sig.	Not Sig.	Not Sig.	3/5	OK
PRED 08	A	A	Not Sig.	Not Sig.	Not Sig.	5/5	OK
PRED 09	A	A	Sig.	Not Sig.	Sig.	3/5	OK
PRED 10	MA	A	Not Sig.	Not Sig.	Sig.	3/5	OK
PRED 11	NA	A	Not Sig.	Not Sig.	Not Sig.	4/5	OK
PRED 12	NA	A	Not Sig.	Not Sig.	Not Sig.	4/5	OK

A – Acceptable, NA-Not Acceptable, MA – Moderately Acceptable; NS-Not Suitable; Not Sig. – No Significant difference between observed and predicted data (Null Hypothesis true); Sig. - Significant difference between observed and predicted data (Null Hypothesis Rejected)

4. Improved regression equations developed using log values of total, heavy and light vehicle count gave highest correlation coefficient and was able to explain about 93% (highest among all the models) of variations in the L_{eq}.

The statistical data analysis between predicted and observed noise levels collected from field investigation in the Asansol town was carried out to determine the suitability of the developed models for use under the Indian road conditions. It can be said that most of the models gives desirable results. The statistical evaluation tests shows that the models can predict the traffic noise level, L_{eq} within acceptable limits in comparison to observed noise values with certain degree of error.

REFERENCES

1. Banerjee D, Chakraborty S.K., Bhattacharyya S., and Gangopadhyay A, (2009). "Modeling of Road Traffic Noise in the Industrial Town of Asansol, India", Transport. Res. Part D, 13, 539-541.
2. Banerjee D, Chakraborty S.K., Bhattacharyya S., and Gangopadhyay A, (2009). "Appraisal and Mapping the Spatial-temporal Distribution of Urban Road Traffic Noise", Int. J. Environ. Sc. Tech., 6, 325-335.
3. Banerjee D, Chakraborty S.K., Bhattacharyya S., and Gangopadhyay A, (2008). "Evaluation and Analysis of Road Traffic Noise in Asansol: An Industrial Town of Eastern India", Int. J. Environ. Res. Public Health, 5, 165-171.
4. Bhattacharya, C.C., Jain, S.S., Singh, S.P., and Parida, M., (2002). "R & D Efforts in Prediction of Highway Traffic Noise", J. Inst. Engrs. India, 83, 7-13.
5. Calixto, A., Diniz, F.B., and Zannin, P.H.T., (2003). "The Statistical Modeling of Road Traffic Noise in an Urban Setting", Cities. 20, 23-29.
6. Chakrabarty, D., Santra, S.C., and Mukherjee, A., (1997). "Status of Road Traffic Noise in Calcutta Metropolis, India", J. Acoust. Soc. Am. 101, 943-949.
7. Chakraborty, S. K., and Banerjee, D., (2007). "A Study of Transport Related Noise Pollution in Asansol Town, West Bengal Using Modeling Techniques". Nat. Env. Poll. Tech. 6, 601-607.
8. Cohen, J., Cohen P., West, S.G., and Aiken, L.S., (1983). Applied Multiple Regression/ Correlation Analysis for the Behavioral Sciences, (Lawrence Erlbaum Associates, USA), pp. 453-466.
9. Delany, M.E., Harland, D.G., Hood, R.A., and Scholes, W.E., (1976). "The Prediction of Noise Levels L10 due to Road Traffic," J. Sound Vib. 48, 305-325.
10. DOT, (1988), Calculation of Road Traffic Noise, Department of Transport, Welsh Office, HMSO, UK, 1988, pp. 2-18.
11. Givargis, S., and Mahmoodi, M., (2008). "Converting the UK Calculation of Road Traffic Noise (CORTN) to a Model Capable of Calculating $L_{Aeq,1h}$ for the Tehran's Roads", Appl Acoust., 69, 1108-1113.
12. Gupta, A.K., Nigam., S.P., and Hansi, J.S. (1986). "A Study on Traffic Noise for Various Land Use for Mixed Traffic Flow", Indian Highways, 14, 30-48.

13. Kumara, K., and Jain, V.K., (1998). "A Predictive Model of Noise for Delhi", J. Acoust. Soc. Am. 103, 1677-1679.

14. Mehdi, M. R., (2002), Appraisals of Noise Pollution, Traffic and Land Use Patterns in Metropolitan Karachi Through GIS and Remote Sensing Techniques. Ph.D., Thesis, University of Karachi, Pakistan, http://eprints.hec.gov.pk/56/, (date last viewed 3/7/09).

15. Mohan S., Dutta, N., and Sarin, S.M., (2000). "Multiple Regression Analysis of Road Traffic Noise Data of Different Density Zones of New Delhi". J Indian Assoc. Environ. Management, 27, 117-121.

16. Nirjar, R.S., Jain, S.S., Parida, M., Katiyar, V.S., and Mittal, N., (2003). "A Study of Transport Related Noise Pollution in Delhi". J. Inst Engrs India, 84, 6-15.

17. Pamanikabud, P., and Vivitjinda, P, (2002). "Noise Prediction for Highways in Thailand". Transport Res: Part D., 7, 441-449.

18. Qudais, S.A., and Alhiary, A., (2007). "Statistical Models for Traffic Noise at Signalized Intersections", Building and Environment, 42, 2939-2948.

19. Rao, M.G.S., Rao, P.R., Dev, K.S., and Rao, K.V., (1989). "A Model for Computing Environmental Noise Level due to Motor Vehicle Traffic in Visakhapatnam City", Appl. Acoust. 27, 129-136.

20. Rao, P.R., and Rao, M.G.S., (1991). "Prediction of L_{A10T} Traffic Noise Levels in the City of Visakhapatnam. India", Appl. Acoust., 34, 101-110.

21. Steele, S., (2001). "A Critical Review of Some Traffic Noise Prediction Models". Appl. Acoust. 62, 271-287.

22. Suksaard, T., Sukasem, P., Tabucanon, S.M., Aoi, I., Shirai K., and Tanaka, H., (1999). "Road Traffic Noise Prediction Model in Thailand", Appl. Acoust., 58, 123-130.

23. To, W.M., Ip, C.W., Lam, C.K., and Yau, T.H, (2002). "A Multiple Regression Model for Urban Traffic Noise in Hong Kong", J. Acoust. Soc. Am., 112, 551-556.

Effects of Bioremediation on Physicochemical Properties of Crude Oil Contaminated Groundwater

*[1]W.O. Medjor; [2]V.O. Akpoveta
[2]V.U. Okojie; [2]F. Egharevba; [2]E.O. Jatto

ABSTRACT

The effects of bioremediation on physicochemical properties of crude oil contaminated groundwater using mixed culture microorganisms was investigated to ascertain the quality of groundwater and results were compared with the control values and W.H.O. Standard. Notable bioremediation markers; chemical oxygen demand (COD) was significantly reduced by 89.1% and biochemical oxygen demand (BOD) by 19.1%. Other physiochemical properties such as pH, dissolved oxygen (DO), salinity, nitrate, total suspended solids, and total solids of the treated samples indicated improvement within the control values or W.H.O Standards.

The method was not very effective in the treatment of heavy metals as there was no appreciable reduction in any of the metal concentration after treatment. The overall assessment was that although there was significant reduction in TPH as crude oil after treatment. In conclusion, 40% of the physiochemical properties (alkalinity, turbidity, electrical conductivity, phosphate, ammonia, total dissolved solids and heavy metals) examined needed post-treatment to make the groundwater safe for domestic and Agricultural uses.

1. Department of Chemistry Taraba State University, Jalingo, Taraba State, P.m.b. 1167, Nigeria.
2. Department of Chemistry Ambrose Alli University, Ekpoma, Edo State, Nigeria.

Keywords: Bioremediation; physicochemical properties; safe; W.H.O standard.

INTRODUCTION

Due to their complex composition, crude oils vary widely in their physical and chemical properties. The melting point, boiling point, vapour pressure, partition coefficient and water solubility characteristics of crude oils can differ between oil producing regions as well as within a specific production field. Despite these wide-ranging physical and chemical characteristics, some generalizations can be made regarding the environmental behaviour of crude oil. When a release to the environment occurs, components of crude oil will partition into various environmental compartments. The lower molecular weight components may dissolve in water or volatilize to the atmosphere, intermediate fractions may float and spread out on water where they may form emulsions and/or adsorb to soil and sediment, and the viscous, heavy components may agglomerate and float or sink in water or adhere to soil and sediment.

The rate at which partitioning occurs depends not only on the nature of the crude but also on the severity of the weathering processes it encounters. When components of crude oil disperse, they may undergo further chemical and physical transformations. Constituents that partition to the air interact with hydroxyl radicals in the atmosphere and thus are subject to indirect photodegradation. Atmospheric half-lives range from 0.4 days (e.g., n-dodecane) to 6.5 days (e.g., benzene). Crude oils are subject to biodegradation, but biodegradation rates vary considerably, and no crude oils would be considered to be readily biodegradable in standard tests. Low molecular weight components may readily biodegrade, but as molecular weight increases, hydrocarbons become increasingly insoluble in water, so that their bioavailability is limited (Concawe, 2001).

In general, hydrocarbons are regarded as being inherently biodegradable, although the degradation rates of the more complex high molecular weight fractions may be very slow. Spills in freshwater environments have been shown to adversely affect the diversity and abundance of the aquatic macro-invertebrate community, with the observed effects associated with oil sorption and substrate coating (Poulton *et al.*, 1997; Poulton *et al.*, 1998). Recovery of such communities in some habitats may be rapid (e.g., riffle areas of streams/rivers), while impacts to backwater areas may persist for months. Ultimately, the type of crude oil and the local conditions and habitats will dictate the potential and extent to which crude oil persists and cause effects in the environment. Crude oil is, in general, harmful to aquatic organisms.

In both marine and freshwater environments, a spill event may cause extensive mortality to non-motile susceptible species such as phytoplankton, crustaceans and larvae or eggs of fish and invertebrates. In contrast, spills of crude oil may not acutely affect highly mobile species such as adult fish, and mollusks and polychaete worms that have an apparent tolerance to oil contamination. Acute aquatic toxicity of crude oil ranged from 10 to >100 mg/L in studies of whole oil dispersions in water or as water-accommodated fractions (WAFs) (Concawe, 2001). Acute toxicity is attributed to those water-soluble hydrocarbon components that are either saturates (aliphatic and alicyclic) or mono-and di-aromatics. Polyaromatic hydrocarbons (PAHs) in crude oil are not expected to contribute significantly to acute aquatic toxicity due to limited bioavailability. However, their partition coefficients (log Kow 3 to > 6) indicate they have the potential to bio-accumulate, thus chronic toxicity of PAHs may be a concern. Other risks to aquatic species, semi-aquatic birds, and sea mammals include physical fouling of plumage, fur, gills etc, by floating oil product. This results in loss of buoyancy, insulation and smothering of inter-tidal animals. Ingestion of oil resulting from attempts by animals to clean contaminated body parts may result in severe enteritis and toxicity.

Spills in freshwater environments have been shown to adversely affect the aquatic macro-invertebrate community, with the observed effects associated with oil sorption and substrate coating. Recovery of such communities in some habitats may be rapid (e.g., riffle areas of streams/ rivers), while impacts to backwater areas may persist for months. Ultimately, the type of crude oil and the local conditions and habitats will dictate the potential and extent to which crude oil persists and cause effects in the environment. Human exposure to petroleum crude oils is primarily through skin contact; however some airborne exposure to crude oil components, such as hydrogen sulphide, mercaptans and gaseous and volatile hydrocarbons can occur via explosive events at wellheads, during transport and in the refinery. Known carcinogens such as benzene, certain polycyclic aromatic hydrocarbons, nickel and arsenic compounds are found in crude oil. Environmental exposure to marine organisms by dermal and oral routes occurs from accidental spills or spillage during loading or transport. Exposure to terrestrial species also occurs due to spillage and tank leakage.

MATERIALS AND METHODS

Materials

The petroleum contaminants used in the study was Brent crude oil. It was obtained from Shell Petroleum Development Company (SPDC) Flow Station, Kokori, Delta State, Nigeria. All plastics and glass wares utilized were pre-washed with detergent water solution, rinsed with tap water and soaked for 48 hours in 50% HNO_3, then rinsed thoroughly with distilled water and air-dried in the laboratory.

Sampling Method

Groundwater sample was obtained in pre-sterilized 10 litre container from the tap of a borehole located in Delta State University, Abraka, Nigeria. In the early hours of the morning, the borehole tap was allowed to run for about 2-3 minutes to eliminate impurities and then snap-shot sample were taken at once (grab sampling).Groundwater sample for the determination of dissolved oxygen (DO), chemical oxygen demand (COD) and biochemical oxygen demand (BOD) were collected in specialized glass wares.

Organic Supplement

Poultry, cow and piggery wastes were obtained from poultry and animal farms in Agbor.

The wastes were air-dried, grounded and thoroughly mixed in 1:1:1 ratio.

Preparation of Sample and Bioremediation Experiment

Pollution was simulated in the laboratory by contaminating groundwater sample with crude oil. A plastic container (microcosm) was filled with 900 cm^3 of the groundwater sample.

100 cm^3 of crude oil was added to the groundwater sample in the plastic container and stirred thoroughly using a magnetic stirrer to obtain 10% contamination. To the mixture, 25 g of the organic supplement was added which served as source of nutrients for the microorganisms and bioremediation was allowed to progress for 42 days.

Determinations of Physicochemical Parameters of Uncontaminated, Contaminated and Treated Groundwater Samples

pH

pH was determined using a digital Jenway pH model 3505. 100 cm^3 of the groundwater sample was measured into a beaker and the pH meter probe was rinsed with distilled water then followed by the sample to be tested and cleaned. The probe was then inserted into the sample and the pH meter was set on, care was taken not to allow the electrode come in contact with the sides and bottom of the beaker during measurement. The reading of the sample was displayed on the screen and recorded.

Turbidity

Turbidity of groundwater sample was determined using HI 93414 model turbidimeter after initial calibration of the instrument using the manufacturer's manual guide (< 0.1, 10, 100 and 750 NTU) following the procedure laid down in the manufacturer's manual guide and the instrument was turned to zero. A clean, dried cuvet was filled with 10 cm^3 of the water sample and the cap replaced. The cuvet was thoroughly wiped with a lint-free cloth to remove any fingerprints, dirt or water spots. The cuvet was placed into the instrument aligning the mark on the cuvet with the sign on the instrument top and the lid closed. The read/timer button was pressed, the instrument directly displayed turbidity value in Nephelometric Turbidity Units (NTU) on the screen and was recorded.

Dissolved Oxygen (D.O)

Dissolved oxygen of groundwater sample was determined using a model DO-5509 dissolved oxygen meter after initial calibration following the procedure provided in the manufacturer's manual guide.

The meter was powered and left at least for 5 minutes until the displayed reading value became stable with no fluctuation. Calibration procedure was made under wide and ventilating environment for best result. The probe was immersed to a depth of at least 10 cm of the measured water sample in order for the probe to be influenced by temperature and allowed automatic temperature compensation to take place. A magnetic agitator was used to ensure a certain velocity in the fluid. In this way, errors due to the diffusion of the oxygen present in the air into the solution were reduced to a minimum. The probe was rinsed with distilled water after each series of measurements. The reading of the sample was displayed on the screen and recorded in mg/l. The value that showed in the display was intended to measure the dissolved oxygen in the water that exist no salt. Therefore real dissolved oxygen value was re-calculated following the formula given in the manufacturer's manual guide:

$$DO = DO' \times [1 - (A\ mg/l\ /100{,}000)]$$

where:

DO′ = the dissolved oxygen value that shown on the instrument.

DO = the real dissolved oxygen value after be re-calculated.

A mg/l = the chloride value in mg/l that existed in the groundwater sample.

Biochemical Oxygen Demand (BOD)

The groundwater sample was thoroughly aerated. Dissolved oxygen determination was carried out on a portion of the groundwater sample as blank. A screw-topped incubator bottle was filled to the brim with a portion of the groundwater sample. The bottle was sealed and incubated for 5 days in the dark at 20°C in cooled incubator. Then the dissolved oxygen was determined in the incubated sample as was done on the blank. The BOD is the difference between the two determined DO levels.

Calculation: $DO_o - DO_5$ = mg/l BOD.

Chemical Oxygen Demand (COD)

Chemical oxygen demand was determined using the dichromate reflux method as described by Ademoroti, (1996b). 20 cm^3 of the groundwater sample was added to a refluxing flask containing 0.4 g of $HgSO_4$. 10 cm^3 of acidified 0.25M $K_2Cr_2O_7$ solution was then added to the mixture along with several glass beads. The flask was slowly and gently swirled after which 30 cm^3 of Ag_2SO_4 dissolved in H_2SO_4 solution was added. The flask was connected to a condenser and the mixture refluxed for 2 hours. A second set using distilled water in place of the groundwater sample was prepared as blank mixture and also refluxed for 2 hours.

At the end of the refluxing time each condenser was washed with distilled water into an Erlenmeyer flask and diluted to about 150 cm^3 using distilled water, allowed to cool at room temperature and then the excess dichromate was titrated against 0.1M iron(II) ammonium sulphate solution using 3 drops of ferroin indicator.

Equations:

$$\text{Organics} + Cr_2O_7^{2-} + \text{heat} + Ag^+ \rightarrow CO_2 + H_2O + 2Cr^{3+}$$

$$6Fe^{2+} + Cr_2O_7^{2-} + 14H^+ \rightarrow 6Fe^{3+} + 2Cr^{3+} + 7H_2O$$

Calculation:

$$\text{mg/l COD} = \frac{Vb - Vs \times M \times 16{,}000}{cm^3\,\text{sample}}$$

where: Vb = ml iron(II) ammonium sulphate used for blank;

Vs = cm^3 iron(II) ammonium sulphate used for sample

M = molarity of iron(II) ammonium sulphate

Total Dissolved Solids

The total dissolved solids of the groundwater sample were determined using total dissolved solids (TDS) meter. The meter was immersed into the groundwater sample up to the maximum immersion level without touching the bottom of the beaker. The solution was gently stirred with the meter until the reading displayed was stabilized.

Calculation: The value in mg/l on the display was multiplied by a factor of 10 as described in the manufacturer's manual guide.

Total Suspended Solids

The total suspended solids were determined using spectrophotometer. 3 cm^3 of distilled water was poured into a cuvet and read at zero at 810 nm. 3 cm^3 of the groundwater sample was poured into another cuvet and read with the meter. The reading in mg/l gave value for the total suspended solids.

Total Solids

Total Solids = Total dissolved solids + total suspended solids.

Salinity

The salinity values of the groundwater samples were determined using conductivity values extrapolated from a curve of known salinity concentrations of NaCl plotted against corresponding conductivity readings.

Electrical Conductivity

The Electrical Conductivity of the groundwater sample was measured using a digital Jenway conductivity meter model DDS 307. The instrument was switched on and allowed to stabilize for 10 minutes. The instrument was initially calibrated using the manufacturer's standard. The probe was immersed into the groundwater sample while completely submerging the holes of the sleeve. The probe was used to lightly tap the bottom of the beaker to remove any air bubbles trapped inside the sleeve. Temperature of the solution was measured with a thermometer and the instrument temperature knob was adjusted to the temperature coefficient value of the solution. The appropriate conductivity range was selected and allowed a few minutes for the reading to stabilize. The Liquid Crystal Display (LCD) displayed the temperature compensated conductivity reading. After every series of measurements, the probe was rinsed with tap water.

Inorganic Phosphate

Inorganic phosphate in the groundwater sample consisting of orthophosphate and polyphosphate was determined following procedures described by Ademoroti, (1996b). 100 cm^3 of the groundwater sample was measured into a conical flask and acidified with concentrated H_2SO_4 to methyl orange (i.e. pH 3.0 – 4.4) and boiled for 90 minutes and then cooled. The excess acid was neutralized with 6M NaOH until phenolphthalein colour in the solution became faint pink tinge. The solution was filtered through Whatman filter paper No. 42 and then transferred into 100 cm^3 volumetric flask and made up to the mark with distilled water. 25 cm^3 of the of the solution was taken in 50 ml volumetric flask to which 10 cm^3 of vandate-molybdate reagent was added and diluted to the mark with distilled water.

A blank was prepared using 25 cm^3 of distilled water instead of the groundwater sample. After 10 minutes of adding the vandate-molybdate reagent, the absorbance of the sample was measured against the blank at 470 nm using TG-60 model spectrophotometer. Standard phosphate solution was prepared by weighing accurately 0.2195g anhydrous potassium dihydrogen phosphate, KH_2PO_4 into 1 litre volumetric flask, dissolved with distilled water and made to mark. In this solution, 1 cm^3 = 0.05 mg PO_4^{3-} - P, various concentrations of 0, 2, 4, 6 and 8 mg/l were prepared. The spectrophotometer was calibrated using these standards. The reading displayed in mg/l gave the concentration of phosphate in the groundwater sample.

Ammonia

Ammonia in the groundwater sample was determined following procedures described by Ademoroti, (1996b). The pH of the solution was adjusted to about pH 7. 25 cm^3 of the sample was taken in 50 cm^3 volumetric flask to which 10 cm^3 of phenol-nitroprusside-buffer reagent was added, swirled gently to mix. Hypochlorite reagent was promptly added and made up to the 50 mark (a delay in adding the reagent may cause decrease in absorbance). The flask was stoppered and mixed well by inversion. Blue colour development was completed after 45 minutes at room temperature. Standard ammonia solutions of 0.2 mg/l, 0.4 mg/l, 0.6 mg/l, 0.8 mg/l and 1.0 mg/l were prepared and used to calibrate the spectrophotometer. The concentration of ammonia in mg/l was measured against a reagent blank carried out throughout the procedure along with the unknown samples using the instrument at 635 nm.

Nitrate

Nitrate in the groundwater sample was determined following procedures described by Ademoroti, (1996b). Flocculation (removal of interfering organic and metallic substance) was carried out by adding mercury (II) chloride and thoroughly mixed. Some of the groundwater sample was taken and its pH adjusted to between 11 and 11.5 with 50% NaOH and stirred for few minutes using magnetic stirrer. The sample was then allowed to stand for 5 minutes so that the flocculated particles may settle. The solution was then filtered but the first portion of the filtrate was discarded. Accurately, 2 cm^3 of the filtrate was pipette into a 50 cm^3 evaporating dish to which 1% sodium salicylate solution was added and evaporated to dryness. The residue was dried for 30 minutes in a drying oven at 105°C. The groundwater sample residue was removed from the oven, cooled and 2 cm^3 of concentrated H_2SO_4 added and quickly mixed well by swirling, allowed to stand for 10 – 15 minutes but swirled occasionally to ensure dissolution of all solids. When cold, 15 cm^3 of nitrate-free distilled water was added to the sample residue and swirled to mix. 15 cm^3 of sodium-hydroxide-potassium-sodium titrate was added, a yellow colour developed immediately indicating the presence of nitrate. The solution was swirled again and allowed to cool for an hour at room temperature. A blank groundwater sample was then prepared in the same manner. Stock nitrate solution was prepared by dissolving 0.7218 g anhydrous potassium nitrate, KNO_3 in a litre volumetric flask using distilled water and then made up to the mark. 1 ml of this solution = 8.86 mg NO_3^-. From the stock solution, 0, cm^3, 2 cm^3, 4 cm^3, 8 cm^3, 12 cm^3, 14 cm^3 and 16 cm^3 were pipetted into 50 cm^3 beakers and 1 cm^3 of 1% sodium salicylate solution was added to each beaker. Standards were treated exactly as the groundwater samples through the procedure namely: evaporation, drying and colour development. The standard solutions were employed to calibrate the spectrophotometer. The concentration of nitrate in the groundwater sample in mg/l was read at 420 nm as displayed by the instrument.

Total Alkalinity

Alkalinity in groundwater sample was measured following method described by (Ademoroti, 1996b). 50 cm^3 of the groundwater sample was pipetted into a 250 cm^3 Erlenmeyer flask, a drop of 0.05M sodium thiosulphate solution was added to remove free residual chlorine that may be present. Two drops of phenolphthalein indicator was then added to the solution and swirled. The solution was titrated with 0.02M standard HCl solution to a colourless end point, two drops of methyl orange was added to the solution obtained at the phenolphthalein end point and titrated against 0.02M standard HCl until a change from yellow colour to orange at end-point.

Calculation:

$$\text{Total Alkalinity as mg/l } CaCO_3 = \frac{(Vp + V) \times M \times 100{,}000}{cm^3\,\text{sample}}$$

where:

Vp = volume of acid used for phenolphthalein alkalinity determination

V= volume of acid used for titration after methyl orange indicator was added

HEAVY METALS ANALYSIS

Digestion and Analysis

Groundwater sample was digested using the standard proposed by the American Water Works Association (AWWA, 1985). 50 cm^3 of the groundwater sample was treated with 5 cm^3 of concentrated HNO_3 and heated on hot plate with gradual addition of concentrated HNO_3 as necessary until the solution boiled. It was then evaporated to about 20 cm^3; 5 cm^3 of concentrated HNO_3 was finally added, covered and allowed to cool and then filtered. The filtrate was poured into a 50 cm^3 standard volumetric flask and made up to the mark with distilled water. Portion of the solution was used for heavy metals (Cd, Cr, Cd, Ni, V, Hg, Se and As) analysis using atomic absorption spectrophotometer (AAS) [Carolina *et al.*, 2007]. A standard calibration curve for each of the heavy of interest was first constructed. The concentrations of heavy metals in the samples were determined by extrapolation from the curves.

Preparation of Standard for Cadmium

Standard Stock of 1000 mg/l was prepared by dissolving 1.41 g of $CdSO_4.8H_2O$ in distilled water in 1 litre volumetric flask and made up to mark with the distilled water. 10 cm^3 of the standard stock was taken in 100 cm^3 volumetric flask and made up to mark in order to have 100 mg/l. Working standards of 0 mg/l, 1 mg/l, 2 mg/l, 4 mg/l, 6 mg/l, 8 mg/l and 10 mg/l were prepared from the 100 mg/l by serial dilution.

Preparation of Standard for Chromium

Standard Stock of 1000 mg/l was prepared by dissolving 2.828 g of $K_2Cr_2O_7$ in 0.05M H_2SO_4 in1 litre volumetric flask and made up to mark with the acid. 10 cm^3 of the standard stock was taken in 100 cm^3 volumetric flask and made up to mark in order to have 100 mg/l. Working standards of 0 mg/l, 1 mg/l, 2 mg/l, 4 mg/l, 6 mg/l, 8 mg/l and 10 mg/l was prepared from the 100 mg/l by serial dilution.

Preparation of Standard for Nickel

Standard Stock of 1000 mg/l was prepared by dissolving 6.724 g of $Ni(NH_4)_2(SO_4)_3.6H_2O$ in distilled water in 1 litre volumetric flask and made up to mark.

10 cm^3 of the standard stock was taken in 100 cm^3 volumetric flask and made up to mark in order to have 100 mg/l. Working standards of 0 mg/l, 1 mg/l, 2 mg/l, 4 mg/l, 6 mg/l, 8 mg/l and 10 mg/l were prepared from the 100 mg/l by serial dilution.

Preparation of Standard for Lead

Standard Stock of 1000 mg/l was prepared by dissolving 1.60 g of $Pb(NO_3)_{2-}$ in distilled water in 1 litre volumetric flask and made up to mark. 10 cm^3 of the standard stock was taken in 100 cm^3 volumetric flask and made up to mark in order to have 100 mg/l. Working standards of 0 mg/l, 1 mg/l, 2 mg/l, 4 mg/l, 6 mg/l, 8 mg/l and 10 mg/l were prepared from the 100 mg/l by serial dilution.

Preparation of Standard for Vanadium

Standard Stock of 1000 mg/l was prepared by dissolving 2.297g of NH_4VO_3 in distilled water in 1 litre volumetric flask and made up to mark with the distilled water. 10 cm^3 of the standard stock was taken in 100 cm^3 volumetric flask and made up to mark in order to have 100 mg/l. Working standards of 0 mg/l, 1 mg/l, 2 mg/l, 4 mg/l, 6 mg/l, 8 mg/l and 10 mg/l were prepared from the 100 mg/l by serial dilution.

Preparation of Standard for Mercury

Standard Stock of 1000 mg/l was prepared by dissolving 1.000 g of mercury metal in 20 cm^3 5M-HNO_3 in 1 litre volumetric flask and made up to mark with distilled water. 10 cm^3 of the standard stock was taken in 100 cm^3 volumetric flask and made up to mark in order to have 100mg/l. Working standards of 0 mg/l, 1 mg/l, 2 mg/l, 4 mg/l, 6 mg/l, 8 mg/l and 10 mg/l were prepared from the 100 mg/l by serial dilution.

Preparation of Standard for Selenium

Standard Stock of 1000 mg/l was prepared by dissolving 1.000 g of selenium metal in 15 cm^3 concentrated HCl + 5 cm^3 concentrated HNO_3 in 1 litre volumetric flask and made up to mark with distilled water. 10 cm^3 of the standard stock was taken in 100 cm^3 volumetric flask and made up to mark in order to have 100 mg/l. Working standards of 0 mg/l, 1 mg/l, 2 mg/l, 4 mg/l, 6 mg/l, 8 mg/l and 10 mg/l were prepared from the 100 mg/l by serial dilution.

Preparation of Standard for Arsenic

Standard Stock of 1000 mg/l was prepared by dissolving 1.320 g of As_2O_{2-} in 50 cm^3 of concentrated HCl in 1 litre volumetric flask and made up to mark with distilled water. 10 cm^3 of the standard stock was taken in 100 cm^3 volumetric flask and made up to mark in order to have 100 mg/l. Working standards of 0 mg/l, 1 mg/l, 2 mg/l, 4 mg/l, 6 mg/l, 8 mg/l and 10 mg/l were prepared from the 100 mg/l by serial dilution.

Total Petroleum Hydrocarbon (TPH)

Changes in total petroleum hydrocarbon (TPH) was determined using T-60 UV/Visible spectrophotometer (2007 Model) at a wavelength of 460 nm following standard method adopted by Macgill,(2000) before and after contamination and at the end of bioremediation. Biogenic factor (TPH contributions from the organic supplement) was neglected and therefore total hydrocarbon content (THC) was used as total petroleum hydrocarbon (TPH).

Physicochemical properties of groundwater sample before and after contamination, after bioremediation and W.H.O. Standard

The physicochemical properties of groundwater sample before and after contamination, after bioremediation and W.H.O. Standard are presented in Table 8.1.

pH is the measure of hydrogen ion activity of a solution and is mathematically expressed as pH = $-\log[H^+]$. pH is an important quality parameter which indicates the aesthetic quality of water such as taste and has no serious health significance . pH affects the degree of ionization of toxic substances such as ammonia (Stirling, 1985). The groundwater sample obtained at the end of bioremediation process had a pH range of 8.7. The pH of groundwater sample from bioremediation process was found to be within the permissible limit of 6.5 - 9.5 set by W.H.O., (1991) for quality drinking water/Agricultural uses. pH as physicochemical parameter for control, untreated, treated groundwater samples and W.H.O. Standard is shown in Figure 8.1.

Table 8.1: Mean Results ± Standard Deviations from Triplicate Analysis of Physicochemical Properties of Groundwater Sample Before and After Contamination, After Bioremediation and W.H.O. Standard

Parameters	Before Contamination	After Contamination	After Bioremediation	W.H.O. Standard
pH	8.60 ± 0.060	9.70 ± 0.010	8.20 ± 0.100	9.20
Electrical Conductivity (μS/cm)	100.00 ± 0.010	100 ± 0.000	2150 ± 5.10	1200
Turbidity (NTU)	0.20 ± 0.000	1200 ± 4.98	220.00 ± 19.405	5.00
Alkalinity (mg/l)	148.00 ± 0.01	140.00 ± 0.01	240.00 ± 2.320	100
Dissolved Oxygen (mg/l)	7.29 ± 0.133	3.80 ± 0.000	7.03 ± 0.133	15
BOD_5 (mg/l)	2.80 ± 0.133	8.5 ± 0.066	6.59 ± 0.066	7.5
COD (mg/l)	524.00 ± 0.010	244.00 ± 2.22	26.39 ± 0.200	10
COD/ BOD_5	–	28.71	4.01	–
% reduction in COD	–	–	89.1	–
Salinity (mg/l)	103.19 ± 0.000	60.29 ± 0.000	982.64 ± 34.689	1600
Nitrate (mg/l)	148.00 ± 3.440	17.00 ± 0.010	60.00 ± 0.01	50.00
Phosphate (mg/l)	0.28 ± 0.001	0.37 ± 0.003	0.23 ± 0.001	0.02
Ammonia (mg/l)	0.53 ± 0.001	0.28 ± 0.006	2.60 ± 0.02	0.5
Total Dissolved Solids (mg/l)	115.00 ± 8.086	180.00 ± 0.000	935.00 ± 8.086	500
Total Suspended Solids (mg/l)	1.089 ± 0.003	1.39 ± 0.023	6.87 ± 0.042	10.00
Total Solids (mg/l)	116.09 ± 7.76	181.39 ± 4.77	941.8 ± 5 .250	1500
Cadmium (mg/l)	0.21 ± 0.001	0.20 ± 0.0006	1.60 ± 0.01	0.001
Chromium (mg/l)	0.10 ± 0.0001	0.70 ± 0.006	0.70 ± 0.001	0.05
Nickel (mg/l)	0.62 ± 0.0003	0.85 ± 0.001	6.45 ± 0.010	0.02
Lead (mg/l)	BDL	BDL	BDL	0.05
Mercury (mg/l)	0.37 ± 0.001	0.23 ± 0.001	1.03 ± 0.001	0.02
Vanadium mg/l)	BDL	BDL	BDL	0.05
Selenium (mg/l)	BDL	BDL	BDL	0.05
Arsenic(mg/l)	0.03 ± 0.001	0.03 ± 0.001	0.30 ± 0.001	0.05
TPH(mg/l)	30.00 ± 0.010	5018.25 ± 2.180	411.99 ± 2.94	10.00

Key:

BDL = Beyond detectable level;
COD = Chemical oxygen demand
BOD_5 = Biochemical oxygen demand at day-5
TPH = Total petroleum hydrocarbon

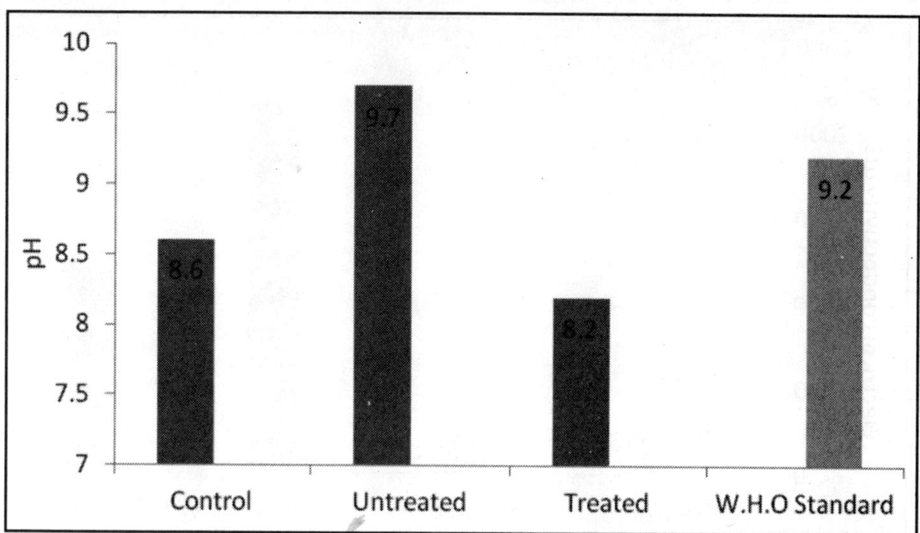

Fig. 8.1: pH as Physicochemical Parameter for Control, Untreated, Treated Groundwater Samples and W.H.O. Standard

Electrical conductivity is a good measure of the total amount of salts in solution (e.g., calcium, magnesium, sodium, potassium, carbonate, hydrogen carbonate, sulphate, chloride, nitrate, and others). Electrical Conductivity indicates the presence of dissolved solids and contaminants especially electrolytes but does not give information about specific chemical component (Esry *et al.*, 1986). The electrical conductivity value for the uncontaminated groundwater sample was 100μS/cm while that for the crude oil simulated groundwater sample was 0.00 μS/cm. The 0.00 μS/cm electrical cconductivity value for the crude oil contaminated groundwater sample may be due to a non-polar environment provided by the hydrocarbon thus helped in retarding the movement and immobilizing of ions present in the solution. The resultant effect was reduced ionic mobility, velocity and reduction of electrical conductivity. The crude oil being predominantly consisted of non-polar organic fractions had no tendency to conduct electrical current. The electrical conductivity value of the treated groundwater sample was 4150 μS/cm. This extremely high value of electrical conductivity was probably due to exogenous inputs from the animal wastes used in preparation of the treatment solution for the remediation work coupled with the removal of substantive amount of hydrocarbons which previously provided non-polar environment for ion-reduced mobility. Increased electrical conductivity value indicated that remediation occurred in treated groundwater samples even though the electrical conductivity value was above the required Standard for electrical conductivity (1200 μS/cm) set for quality drinking water (W.H.O., 1991). The electrical conductivity as physicochemical parameter for control, untreated, treated groundwater samples and W.H.O. Standard is displayed in Figure 8.2.

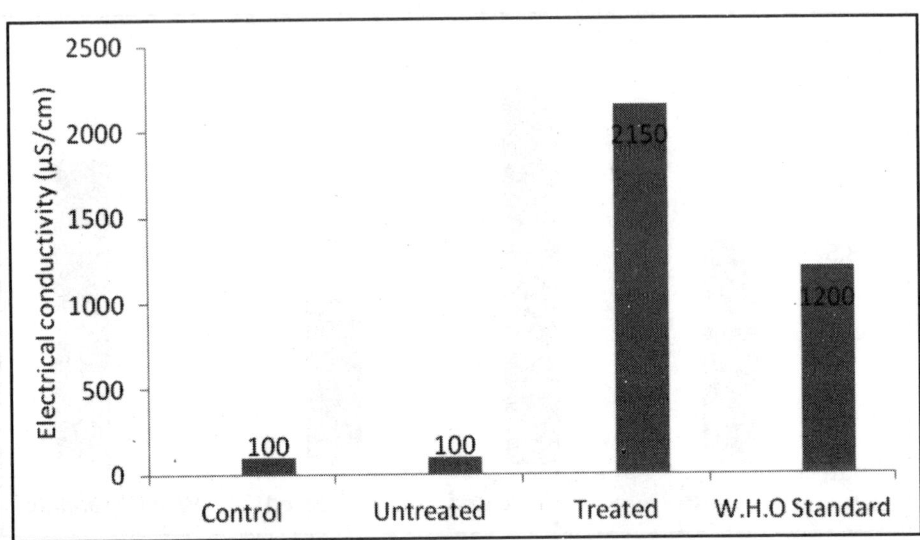

Fig. 8.2: Electrical Conductivity as Physicochemical Parameter for Control, Untreated, Treated Groundwater Samples and W.H.O. Standard

Turbidity of water is an optical property that causes light to be scattered and absorbed, rather than transmitted. The scattering of the light that passes through a liquid is primarily caused by suspended solids. Turbidity is directly proportional to the amount of scattered light. It is also true that even the molecules in a very pure fluid scatter light to a certain degree, as no solution has zero turbidity. The turbidity of crude oil simulated groundwater sample was 1200 NTU. This value was found to be astronomically high and an indicator that the prepared groundwater sample was extremely polluted compared to 100 - 275 NTU turbidity values of for highly polluted water reported by Rump, (1999).

Groundwater sample obtained from the bioremediation experiment had its turbidity value >1000NTU. This exceptionally high value of turbidity must be connected with the heavy organic load from the organic supplement used in the experiment and indicated high load of colloidal matter and by implication high concentrations of solids. The turbidity value from the bioremediation work was higher than the permissible turbidity limit of 5 NTU recommended by W.H.O., (1991).

This implied that groundwater sample needed post-treatment in terms of turbidity. The turbidity as physicochemical parameter for control, untreated, treated groundwater samples and W.H.O. Standard is shown in Figure 8.3.

Alkalinity is due to the presence of hydrocarbonate, carbonate and hydroxyl ions in water. It is the acid neutralizing capacity of water and a function of all titratable bases present in water. The initial unpolluted

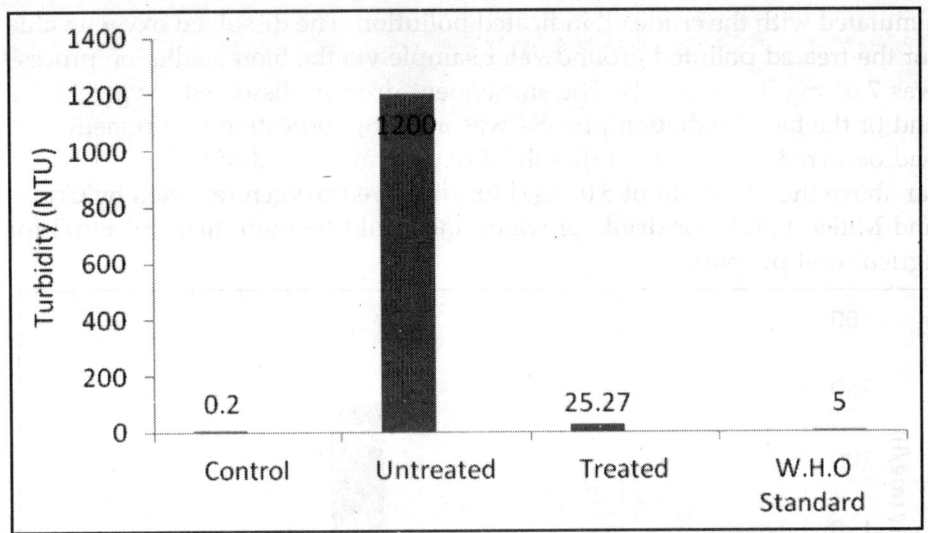

Fig. 8.3: Turbidity as Physicochemical Parameter for Control, Untreated, Treated Groundwater Samples and W.H.O. Standard

groundwater sample had an alkalinity concentration of 148 mg/l while that of crude oil simulated groundwater sample was 140 mg/l as shown in Table 8.1. The decrease in the alkalinity value recorded after contamination was likely due to chemical interaction between the acidic components of the contaminants and the carbonates or hydroxyl ions present in the groundwater sample. The alkalinity value for groundwater sample obtained from the bioremediation process was 240 mg/l (Table 8.1). For bioremediation process, alkalinity is the best indicator of biological activity that is for measuring the waste product of microbial activity. The increase in the alkalinity values for the groundwater sample obtained from the bioremediation process indicated biodegradation. The treated groundwater sample had its alkalinity level above the 100 mg/l desirable level recommended for quality drinking water in Nigeria (W.H.O., 1991). This is an indication that the treated contaminated groundwater needed post treatment in terms of alkalinity after remediation work. The Alkalinity as physicochemical parameter for control, untreated, treated groundwater samples and W.H.O. Standard is displayed in Figure 8.4.

Biological decomposition of organic matter uses dissolved oxygen. The concentration of dissolved oxygen is an important factor that determines the behaviour, growth and distribution of organisms due to their varying oxygen requirement (Collins, 1980). The dissolved oxygen value of the unpolluted groundwater sample (control) was 7.30 mg/l while those of crude oil simulated groundwater sample had its value as 3.80 mg/l. Table 8.1. The drop in the dissolved oxygen value after the groundwater sample was simulated with the crude oil indicated pollution. The dissolved oxygen value for the treated polluted groundwater sample via the bioremediation process was 7.03 mg/l (Table 8.1). The subsequent drop in dissolved oxygen at the end of the bioremediation process was a strong indication that remediation had occurred. The value of dissolved oxygen at the end of remediation was far above the threshold of 5.0 mg/l for dissolved oxygen reported by Cruise and Miller, (1994) for drinking water and could be more than 5.0 mg/l for agricultural purposes.

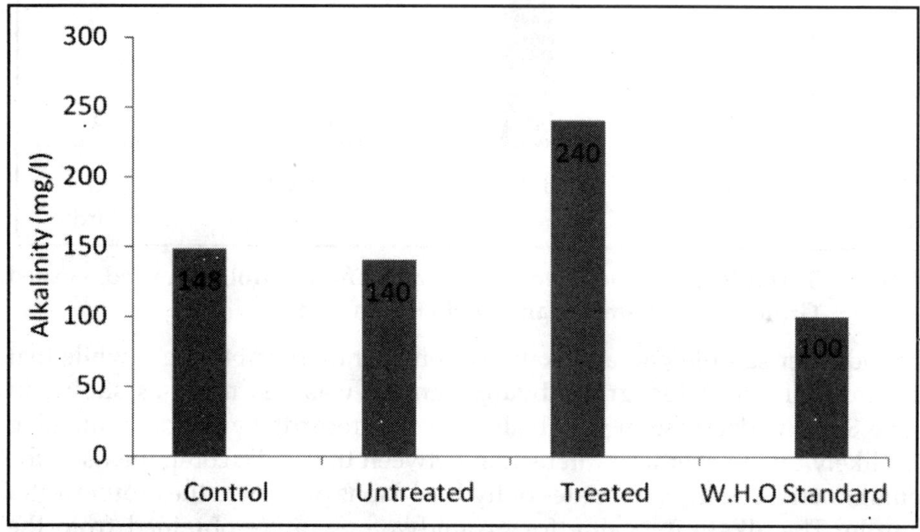

Fig. 8.4: Alkalinity as Physicochemical Parameter for Control, Untreated, Treated Groundwater Samples and W.H.O. Standard

However, dissolved oxygen value > 6 mg/l is the requirement for good quality water reported in literature by Rump, (1999). According to EPA classification (dissolved oxygen < 2 mg/l) could be fatal to most aquatic species while 5 mg/l - 6.0 mg/l are sufficient for the aquatic species, the latter condition was satisfied. Low dissolved oxygen may result in anaerobic conditions that cause bad odours. The treated contaminated groundwater therefore needed no post-treatment in terms of dissolved oxygen after remediation. The dissolved oxygen as physicochemical parameter for control, untreated, treated groundwater samples and W.H.O. Standard is given in Figure 8.5.

The Biochemical Oxygen Demand (BOD_5) measures the amount of oxygen required by microorganisms to oxidize the biodegradable organic constituents present in water and wastewater. It establishes direct relationship between the concentration of organic matter and the amount of oxygen used to oxidize the pollutants to water, carbon dioxide and oxygen inorganic nitrogenous compounds. The oxygen demand of water and wastewater is proportional to the amount of organic matter present (Nielson, 2002). A high oxygen demand indicates the potential of developing dissolved oxygen sag as the microbiota oxidizes the organic matter in the water and wastewater.

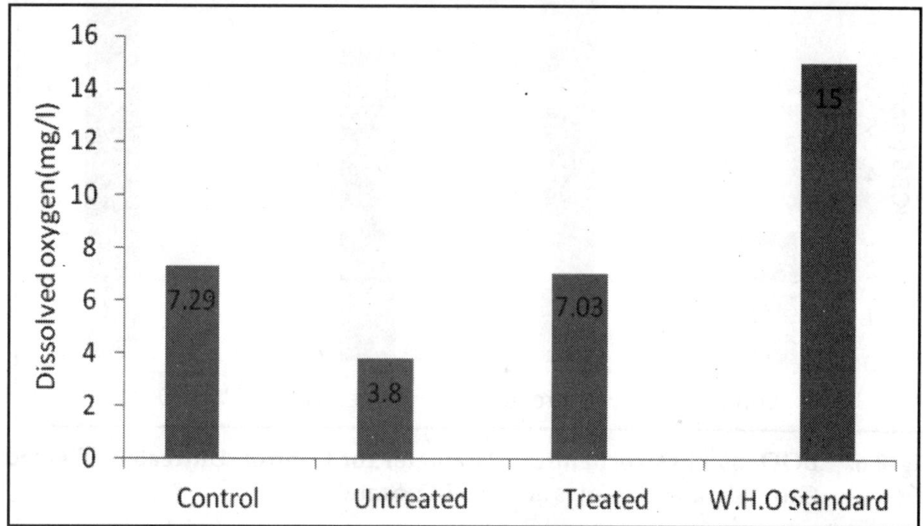

Fig. 8.5: Dissolved Oxygen as Physicochemical Parameter for Control, Untreated, Treated Groundwater Samples and W.H.O. Standard

The control groundwater sample had a BOD_5 value of 2.70 mg/l while that of the crude oil simulated groundwater sample was 8.15 mg/l (Table 8.1). The rise in BOD_5 after contamination showed that the groundwater sample was polluted. Oxygen containing compounds in crude oils have been reported to contribute to the total number of oil acids and are toxic to aquatic lives (John *et al.*, 2008). The BOD_5 value of the crude oil contaminated groundwater sample treated by bioremediation method was 6.59 mg/l and represented a BOD_5 reduction of 19.14%. The subsequent drop in BOD_5 value in the treated crude oil contaminated groundwater sample corroborated the fact that remediation had taken place at and is supported by the findings of earlier investigators (Yavuz and Koparal, 2006; Saien and Nejati, 2007). The treated contaminated groundwater sample had its BOD_5 value within the safe limit of (7.5 mg/l) recommended for quality drinking water by W.H.O., (1991). The biochemical oxygen demand (BOD_5) as physicochemical parameter for control, untreated, treated groundwater samples and W.H.O. Standard is illustrated in Figure 8.6.

Chemical Oxygen Demand (COD) provides a measure of the oxygen equivalent of that portion of the organic matter in a groundwater sample that is susceptible to oxidation under test condition (Bertram and Balance, 1996). The load of pollutants present in wastewater is regularly expressed in terms of chemical oxygen demand (COD).The COD value of the unpolluted

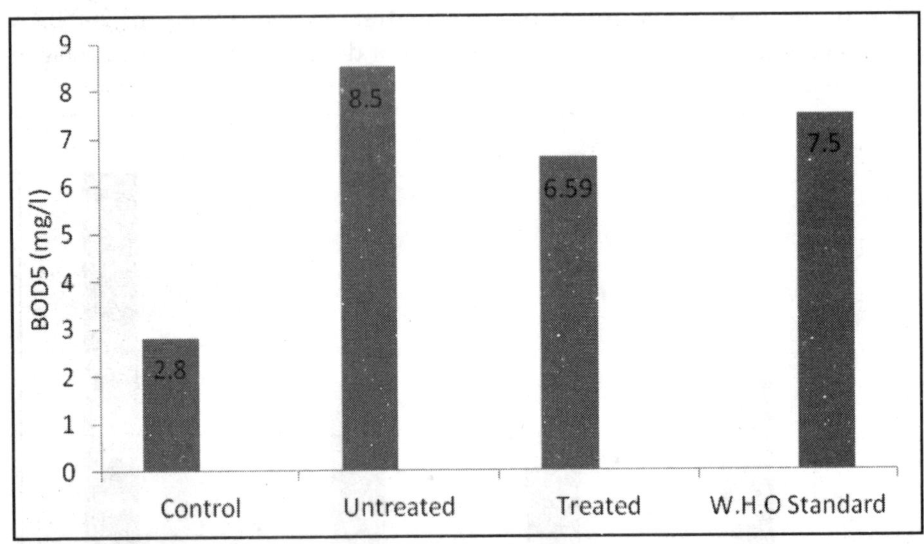

Fig. 8.6: BOD_5 as Physicochemical Parameter for Control, Untreated, Treated Groundwater Samples and W.H.O. Standard

groundwater sample was 524 mg/l and that of the crude oil simulated groundwater sample was 244 mg/l (Table 8.1). The COD being a measure of the total oxidizable organic matter is expected to increase on addition of the contaminants. The observed COD drop for crude oil simulated groundwater sample was possibly due to some aromatic hydrocarbons, straight-chain aliphatic and nitrogenous compounds present in crude oil which were not readily oxidizable. The COD value of the treated crude oil contaminated groundwater sample was 26.39 mg/ with 89.1% reduction in COD. The COD/BOD ratio of the treated contaminated groundwater sample was 4.01 and relatively low compared with value obtained for the polluted crude oil groundwater sample (28.71). Low COD/BOD ratio shows low concentration of oxidizable organic matter and high ratio indicates high levels of oxidizable organic matter in water/wastewater (Neilson *et al.*, 2002). The significant reduction in COD in the treated crude oil contaminated groundwater sample indicated effective remediation had taken place although its value was above the 10 mg/l safe permissible limit for quality drinking water set by W.H.O., (1991). The Chemical oxygen demand as physicochemical parameter for control, untreated, treated groundwater samples and W.H.O. Standard is depicted in Figure 8.7.

Salinity was determined as chloride. Chlorine gas is highly toxic but chloride ions are essential for life (Duffus, 1996). Chloride occurs in all natural waters in varying concentrations depending on the geochemical conditions. Chlorides are the most stable components in water and its concentration is largely unaffected by most natural physicochemical and biochemical processes.

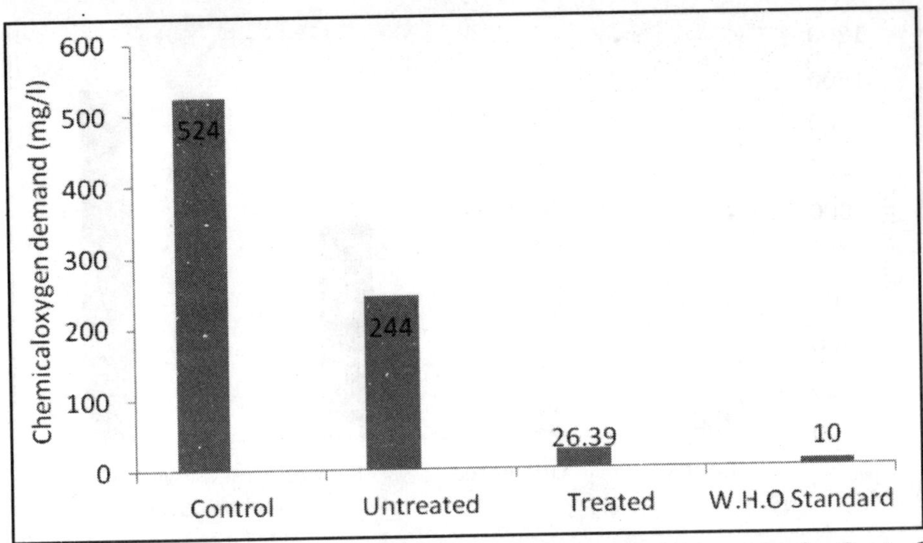

Fig. 8.7: Chemical Oxygen Demand as Physicochemical Parameter for Control, Untreated, Treated Groundwater Samples and W.H.O. Standard

Chloride in small concentrations are not harmful to humans in drinking water, and with some adaptation, the human body can tolerate water with as much as 200 mg/l chloride ion. However, above a concentration of 250 mg/l chloride, the water may taste salty (Hauser, 2001). The chloride ion concentration in the unpolluted groundwater sample was 103.19 and the salinity level for the crude oil simulated groundwater sample was 60.29 mg/l (Table 1). The salinity of the ccontaminated groundwater sample obtained from the bioremediation process had its value as 982.64 mg/l (Table 8.1) also the salinity as physicochemical parameter for control, untreated, treated groundwater samples and W.H.O. Standard is shown in Figure 8.8.

This concentration was far above the W.H.O., (1991) recommended standard (100 mg/l-250 mg/l) for chloride ions in drinking water. The contribution of salts from the animal waste may have led to the high salinity value for the treated groundwater sample. The Elevated salinity likely contributed to the reduced microbial activity towards the end of the bioremediation experiments. Removal of chloride from potable water is a very difficult task and generally requires desalination.

The uncontaminated groundwater sample had nitrate concentration of 148 mg/l while that of crude oil simulated groundwater sample was 17 mg/l (Table 8.1). The treated crude oil contaminated groundwater sample had a nitrate value of 13 mg/l. The treated crude oil contaminated groundwater sample had its nitrate concentration within the maximum permissible level of 250 mg/l recommended for quality drinking water by W.H.O., (1991).

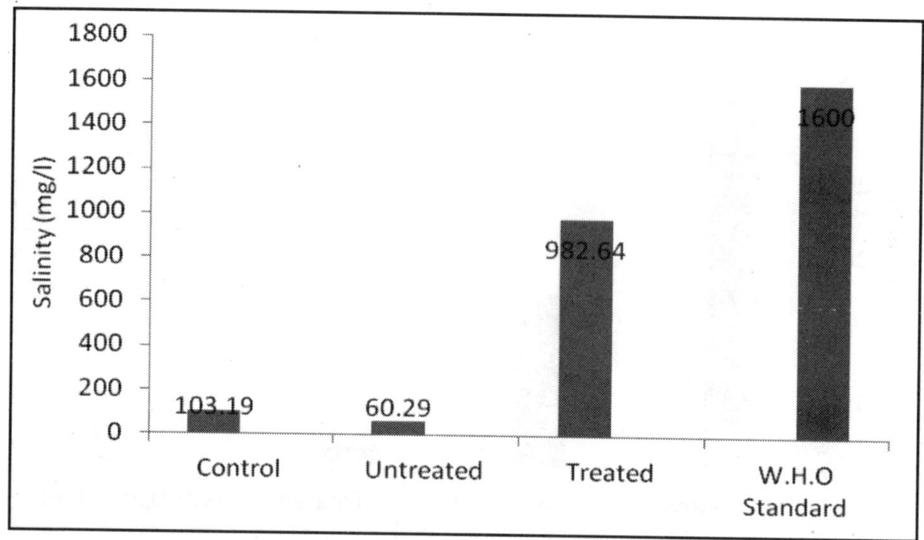

Fig. 8.8: Salinity as Physicochemical Parameter for Control, Untreated, Treated Groundwater Samples and W.H.O. Standard

Nitrate concentration above the W.H.O. recommended value of 10 mg/l (minimum) is dangerous to pregnant women and poses a serious health threat to infants less than 3-6 months of age. Nitrate, by itself is not harmful but when converted to highly toxic dioxonitrate (III), NO_2^- by certain bacteria commonly found in the intestinal tract of infants has devastating effects on infant health. Nitrate III causes a disease condition known as methemoglobinemia (blue baby syndrome) (Fecham *et al.*, 1986; Groen *et al*, 1988). Nitrates have the potential to cause dieresis, increased starchy deposits and haemorrhaging the spleen following a lifetime exposure.

Nitrates have a high potential to migrate to water since they are very soluble in water and do not bind to soil (Punmia and Jain, 1998). The Nitrate as physicochemical parameter for control, untreated, treated and W.H.O. Standard is illustrated in Figure 8.9.

The phosphate concentration in the control groundwater sample was 0.28 mg/l and that of crude oil simulated groundwater sample had a concentration of 0.37 mg/l (Table 8.1). The increase in the phosphate level in the crude oil simulated groundwater sample compared with that of the unpolluted groundwater sample may be due contributions of phosphate as chemical components from the contaminant. The treated contaminated groundwater sample had its phosphate concentration as 0.23 mg/l. Phosphate concentration was high and above the 0.02 mg/l maximum acceptable limit. Traces of phosphate increase the tendency of troublesome algae bloom in water (Esry *et al.*, 1991). This causes eutrophication or over – fertilization as it chokes waterways and uses up large amounts of dissolved oxygen.

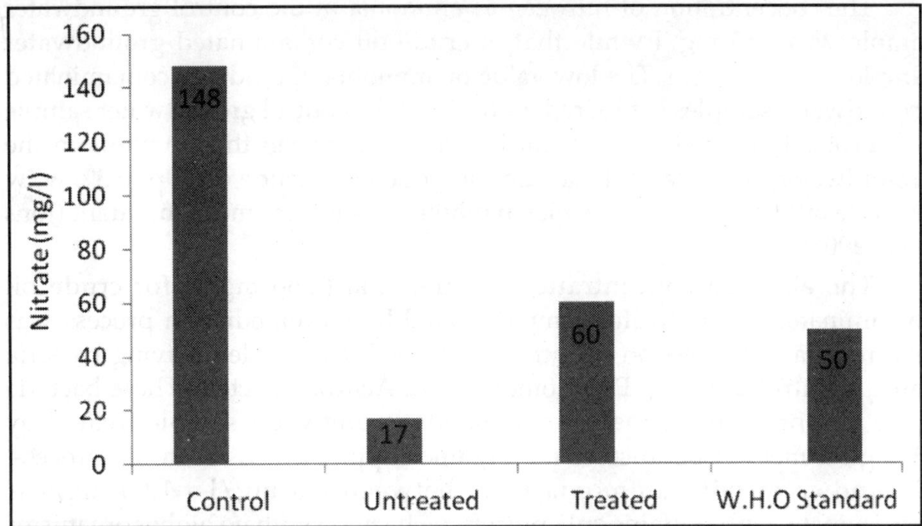

Fig. 8.9: Nitrate as Physicochemical Parameter for Control, Untreated, Treated Groundwater Samples and W.H.O. Standard

At this rate, the water bodies are being aged at much faster rate than the geologic forces can create new ones. When these water plants die, there will be excessive decay and putrefaction which may also kill fishes. However, appreciable increase in phosphate may be used as a source of nutrient and mineral enrichment for water needed for agricultural purposes. Phosphate as physicochemical parameter for control, untreated, treated groundwater samples and W.H.O. Standard is shown in Figure 8.10.

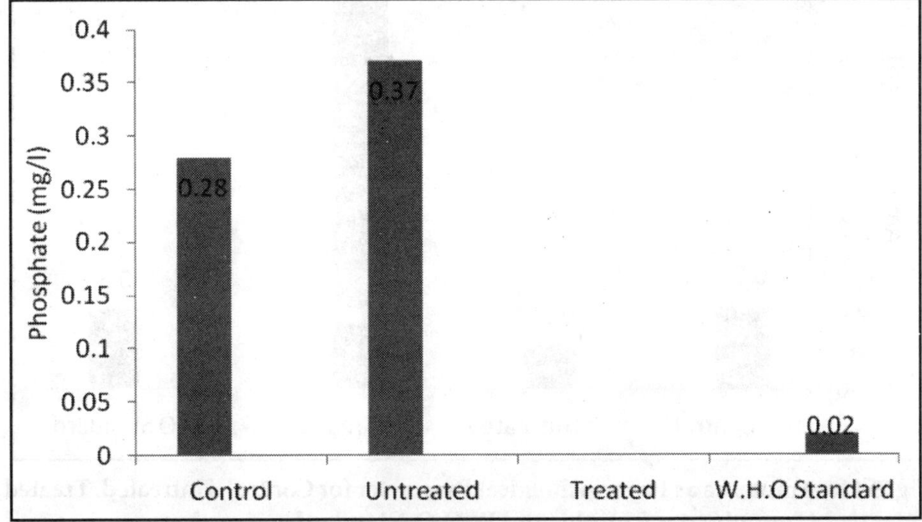

Fig. 8.10: Phosphate as Physicochemical Parameter for Control, Untreated, Treated Groundwater Samples and W.H.O Standard

The concentration of nitrogen as ammonia in the control groundwater sample was 0.53 mg/l while that of crude oil contaminated groundwater sample was 0.28 mg/l. The low value of ammonia of crude oil contaminated groundwater samples compared with that of the control groundwater sample was probably owned to chemical interaction between the ammonia in the groundwater sample and the acidic components in crude oil. Up to 3% w/w of crude oil may be acids of which naphthenic acids are most abundant (Jons *et al.*, 2001).

The elevated concentration of ammonia (2.60 mg/l) for crude oil contaminated groundwater sample treated by bioremediation process was as a resultant conversion of nitrates into NH_3 by the denitrifying bacteria called denitrificans (e.g. Pseudomonas and Achromobacter). These bacteria were predominant in the contaminated groundwater sample treated by biological method because of the organic supplement used in the process. Groundwater with ammonia level between 0.3 mg/l - 1.00 mg/l is contaminated and contains only putrefying bacteria with no higher organisms (Rump, 1999). The ammonia concentration of the treated crude oil contaminated groundwater sample was found to be higher than (0.5 mg/l) recommended level for ammonia for quality drinking water by W.H.O., (1991). Ammonia as physicochemical parameter for control, untreated, treated groundwater samples and W.H.O. Standard is depicted in Figure 8.11.

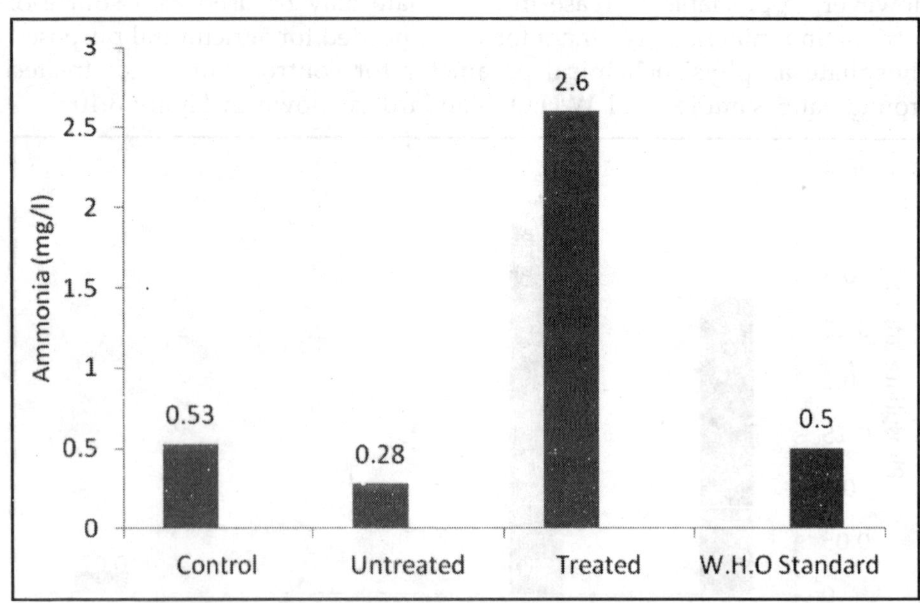

Fig. 8.11: Ammonia as Physicochemical Parameter for Control, Untreated, Treated Groundwater Samples and W.H.O. Standard

Total dissolved solids; defines the concentration of dissolved organic and inorganic chemical. Dissolved solids commonly found are calcium, magnesium, sodium, potassium, hydrogen carbonate, sulphate, chloride and silica (and were used to reflect salinity). The concentration of the total dissolved solids in the control groundwater sample was 115 mg/l while that of the crude oil contaminated groundwater sample was 160 mg/l – 180 mg/l. This value was within the desirable level of 200 mg/l set by W.H.O., (1991) for quality drinking water. The treated crude oil contaminated groundwater sample obtained from the biological process showed high value for total dissolved solids (935 mg/l). The high TDS value may be due to the heavy organic load of the animal waste. The removal of hydrocarbons from the system eradicated the non-polar environment thereby increased the solubilization of the solutes present thus increased TDS values. The implication was that the treated crude oil contaminated groundwater sample showed that reasonable remediation had occurred. The TDS value was far above the Standard (500 mg/l) set by W.H.O., (1991) for quality drinking thus needed for post treatment. Total dissolved solids as physicochemical parameter for control, untreated, treated groundwater samples and W.H.O. Standard is illustrated in Figure 8.12.

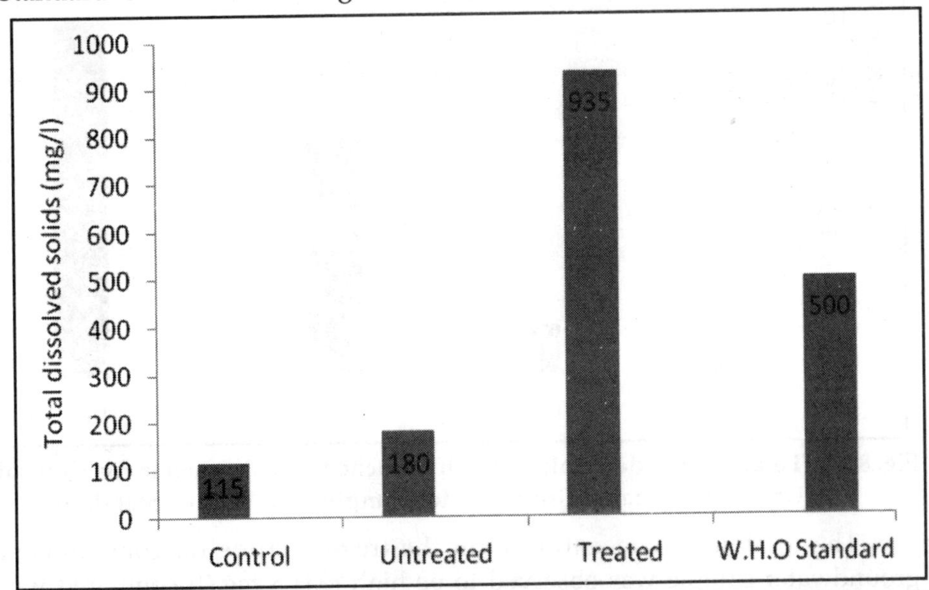

Fig. 8.12: Total Dissolved Solids as Physicochemical Parameter for Control, Untreated, Treated Groundwater Samples and W.H.O. Standard

The total suspended solids (TSS) level for the unpolluted groundwater sample was 1.089 mg/l while that of crude oil contaminated groundwater sample was 1.39 mg/l. as given in Table 8.1. The introduction of crude oil into the groundwater sample made the medium to have a non-polar hydrophobic environment and decreased solubility for solutes present may be mostly responsible for the high value of TSS in comparison with the value for unpolluted groundwater sample. The treated crude oil contaminated groundwater sample had TSS value of 6.87 mg/l. The treated crude oil contaminated groundwater sample had relatively high TSS compared with that of the untreated crude oil contaminated groundwater sample.

The higher TSS value in the treated crude oil contaminated groundwater sample was likely associated with the presence of microorganisms from the animal waste used as organic amendment. The treated contaminated groundwater sample had its TSS value less than the recommended value of >10 mg/l) by W.H.O., (1991). High presence TSS acts as points of attachment and may aid growth of bacteria (Rajim *et al.*, 2010). The value of the total suspended solids was relatively low and may not support the growth of bacteria.

The total suspended solids as physicochemical parameter for control, untreated, treated and W.H.O. Standard is displayed in Figure 8.13.

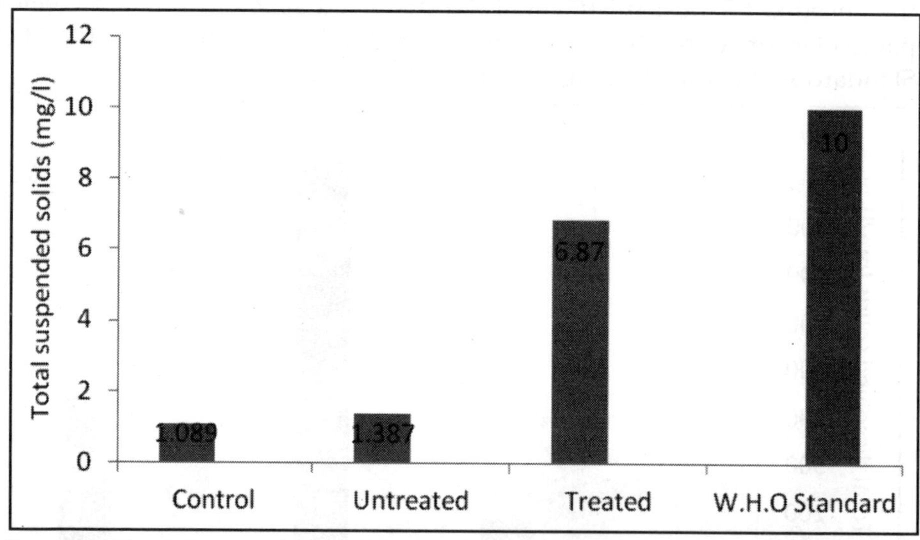

Fig. 8.13: Total Suspended Solids as Physicochemical Parameter for Control, Untreated, Treated Groundwater Samples and W.H.O. Standard

The total solid concentration in the treated crude oil contaminated groundwater sample was observed to be high (941.8 mg/l) compared with its value before contamination and treatment but within the recommended value of 1500 mg/l by W.H.O., (1991). The total solids as physicochemical parameter for control, untreated, treated groundwater samples and W.H.O. Standard is displayed in Figure 8.14.

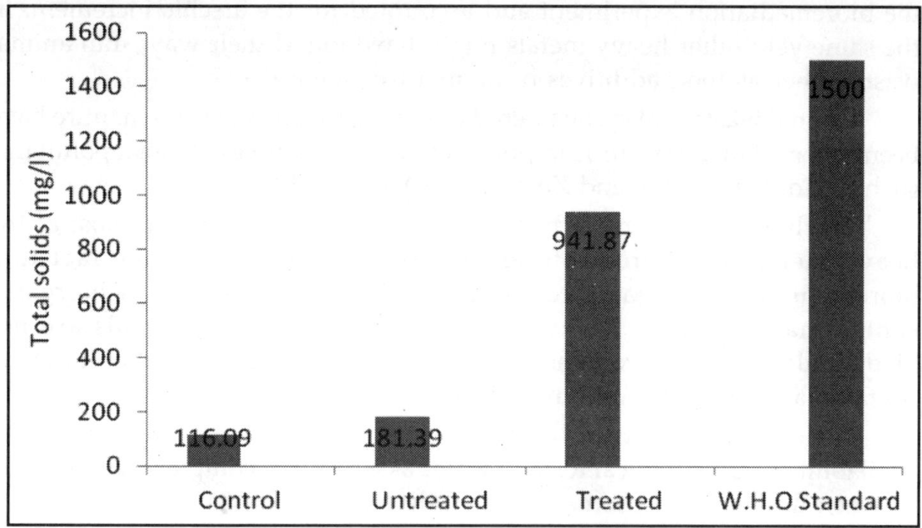

Fig. 8.14: Total Solids as Physicochemical Parameter for Control, Untreated, Treated Groundwater Samples and W.H.O. Standard

The uncontaminated groundwater sample had the following heavy metal concentrations Ni = 0.62 mg/l, Hg = 0.37 mg/l, As = 0.03 mg/l, Cd= 0.21 mg/l, Cr = 0.10 mg/l while V, Pb and Se were beyond detectable limit. The crude oil contaminated groundwater sample had heavy metals concentrations of: Ni = 0.85 mg/l; Hg = 0.23 mg/l

As=0.03 mg/l; Cd= 0.20 mg/l; Cr = 0.70 mg/l while V, Pb and Se were beyond detectable limit (Table 1). Increment in the concentration of Ni and Cr were observed in crude oil contaminated groundwater sample. The arsenic concentration in the uncontaminated groundwater sample was 0.03 mg/l and same concentration was found in the crude oil contaminated groundwater samples thus suggested that the arsenic contamination was from the groundwater and probably no arsenic contaminant was found in the crude oil. Lead, vanadium and selenium metals were beyond detectable limits in crude oil contaminated groundwater sample. The treated crude oil contaminated groundwater sample had concentrations of 1.60 mg/l (Cd); 0.70 mg/l (Cr); 6.45 mg/l (Ni); 1.03 mg/l (Hg); 0.30 mg/l (As); V and Pb were beyond detectable limits as shown in Table 8.1.

The treated crude oil contaminated groundwater sample showed significant increase in concentrations of the heavy metals due to the heavy metals present in the animal wastes. For example, the high concentration of arsenic noted was likely due to sodium arsenate applied in cattle dip to control infection by ticks and also arsenic acid used as feed additive to chickens, turkeys, and hog rations. These arsenic compounds were finally excreted as part of the animal waste that was used as organic supplement for the bioremediation experiment and accounted for the arsenic increment. In the same vein other heavy metals might have found their ways into animal waste either as food additives or animal treatment drugs.

Animal waste is also considered as manure. Composts and manure have been reported in literature as important non-point sources of metal pollutants such as Cd, Cu, Ni, Pb, and Zn and As (Alloway, 1990).

The bioremediation method was not capable of removing most of the heavy metals to appreciable level and is supportive by the fact that bioremediation of organic contaminants is easier than that of inorganic contaminants such as heavy metals because the heavy metals are not biodegradable and microorganisms can only change the speciation of metal contaminants (Pascale and Raina, 2000).

Generally, reduction in metal concentration was due to its less-availability of the chemical form in water as a result of complexation reaction between the metal and some of the crude oil components.

The increase in concentration of heavy metal in solution may have resulted to crude oil removal which in turn enhanced pH, redox potential and stimulated the bioavailability of heavy metals. Contributions from exogenous sources (organic supplement) may also be a crucial factor. The heavy metal concentration as physicochemical parameter for control, untreated, treated groundwater samples and W.H.O. Standard is shown in Figure 8.15.

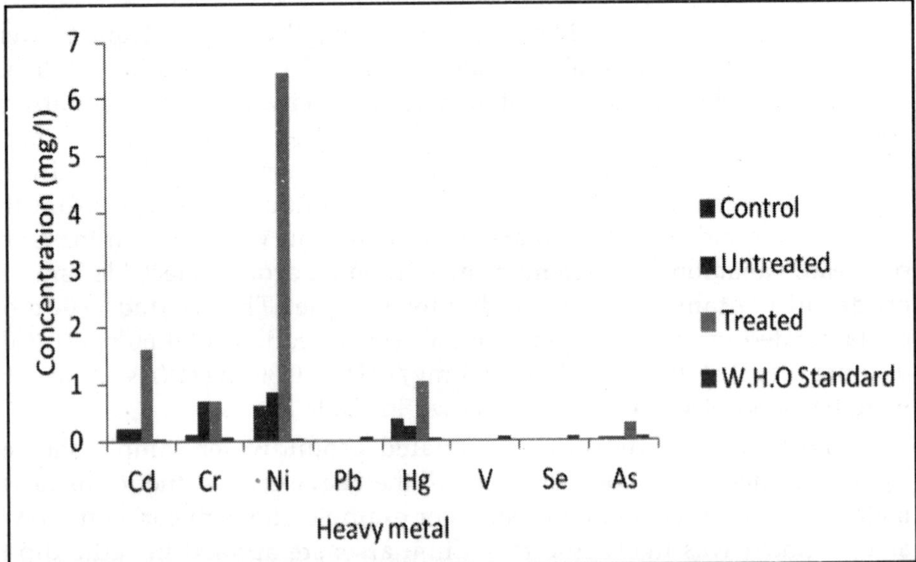

Fig. 8.15: Heavy Metal Concentration as Physicochemical Parameter for Control, Untreated, Treated Groundwater Samples and W.H.O. Standard

The treated crude oil contaminated groundwater sample had their heavy metal concentrations far higher than the permissible maximum limits set by W.H.O, (1991) for quality drinking water.

The reference total petroleum hydrocarbon (TPH) in the uncontaminated groundwater sample was 30 mg/l. The treated crude oil contaminated groundwater sample obtained from the bioremediation process had total petroleum hydrocarbon removal efficiency of 91.78% after 42 days (1008 hours) residence time. The Total petroleum hydrocarbon as physicochemical parameter for control, untreated, treated groundwater samples and W.H.O. Standard is shown in Figure 8.16.

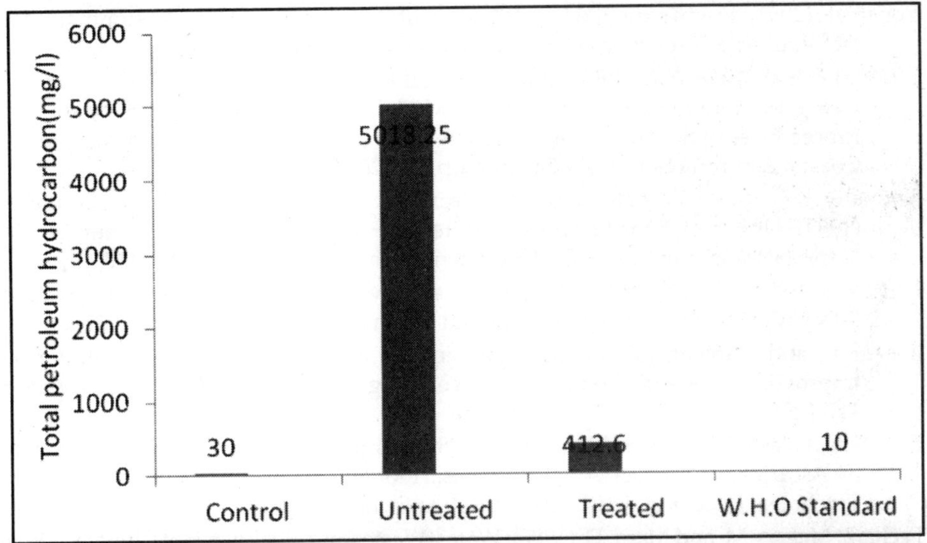

Fig. 8.16: Total Petroleum Hydrocarbon as Physicochemical Parameter for Control, Untreated, Treated Groundwater Samples and W.H.O. Standard

In conclusion, although very high remediation efficiency was attained after treatment, 40% of the physicochemical parameters especially the heavy metal contents were impaired and therefore the treated contaminated groundwater needed post treatment before it becomes safe for domestic and Agricultural uses.

REFERENCES

Ademoroti, C.M.A. (1996b): *Standard Methods of Treatment of Water and Wastewaters.* Ibadan Fodulex Press Ltd. pp. 41-83.

Alloway, B.J. (1990): *Heavy Metals in Soils.* 2nd Edition Blackic Publishers, Glasgow.

American Water Works Association, AWWA (1985): Standard Methods for the Examination of Water and Wastewater, 16th Edition.

APHA (American Public Health Association) (1998): Standard Methods for the Examination of Water and Wastewater, 20th edn, APHA, Washington DC.

Atlas, R.M. (1988). Microbiology: Fundamentals and Applications. 2nd ed. Mac Millan Publishing Co., New York.

Bertram, J.; Balance, R. (1996): A Practical Guide to the Design and Implementation of Freshwater, Quality Studies and Monitoring Programmes. Published on Behalf of United Nations.Environmental Programme (UNEP) and World Health Organisation (W.H.O.), E & FN Spoon Publishers pp. 172-177, 192-196.

Bumpus, J.A. (1993): White-rot Fungi and Their Potential Use in Soil Bioremediation Processes. In: J.M Bollag and G. Stotzky (Eds.) *Soil Biochemistry*, Marcel Dekker, New York, pp. 65-100.

Collins, R.T. (1980): The Ecology of Streams and Rivers in Biology Number 122. London, Edward Publishers Ltd. pp. 79.

Concawe, (2001). Environmental Classification of Petroleum Substances -summary data and Rationale. Report No. 01/54. Brussels: Concawe.

Cruise, J.F. and Miller, R.L. (1994): Interplaying the Water of Mayaguez Bay, Puerto Rico Using Remote Sensing, Hydrologic Modelling and Coral Reef Productivity. Proceedings of Second Thematic Conference on Remote Sensing for Marine and Coastal Environments, New Orleans. pp. 193-203.

Donnelly, K.C.; Chen, J.C.; Huebner, H.J.; Brown, K.W .; Autenrieth, R.L, and Bonne J.S. (1997): Utility of Four Strains of White-rot Fungi for the Detoxification of 2, 4, 6- trinitrotoluene in Liquid Culture. *Environ. Toxicol. Chem.*, 16, 1105-1110.

Duffus, J. (1996): Comments to Editor, Chemistry International, News Magazine of International Union of Pure and applied Chemistry (IUPAC), 18(6): 252-253.

Esry, S.A. and Habicht, J.P (1986): Epidemiologic Evidence for Health Benefits from Improved Water and Sanitation in Developing Countries. *Epidemiologic Reviews,* 8, 117-128.

Esry, S.A.; Potash, J.B. and Shiff, C. (1991): Effects of Improved Water Supply and Sanitation on Ascariosis, Diarrhea, Aracunculiasis, Hookworm Infection, Schitosomiasis and Trachoma. *Bulletin of the World Health Organisation* (5), 609-621.

Fecham, Mcgary M. and Mara, D. (1986): Water, Wastes and Health in Hot Climates. Wiley & sons, New York. p. 82.

Groen, J.; Schmann, J.B. & Gernaer, T.W. (1988): The Occurrence of High Nitrate Concentration in Groundwater in the Villages in North-western Burkinafaso. *J. Afri. Earth Sci.*, 7: 999-1009.

Hauser, B.A. (2001): Drinking Water Chemistry, a Laboratory Manual. Turbidity Herp II 2001, Lewis Publishers, A CRC Press Company Florida USA pp. 71.

Jamison, V.W.; Raymond, R.L.; and Hudson Jr., J.O. (1975): Biodegradation of high-octane.

John, V.H.; Kerry, M.P. and Mark, P.B. (2008). Mass Spectrometric Characterization of Naphthenic Acids in Environmental Samples: *A Review, Mass Spectrometry Reviews,* 28(1):121-134.

Jons, D.M., Watson, J.S.; Meredith, W.; Chen, M. and Bennet, B. (2001): Determination of Naphthenic Acids in Crude Oils Using Non-aqueous Ion Exchange Solid-phase Extraction", Analytical Chemistry, 73, 703-707.

Litchfield, D.R. and Clark, L.C. (1973): Bacterial Activity in Groundwaters Containing Petroleum Products. American Petroleum Institute Publication No. 4211. Washington D.C. API.

Lynch, J.M. (2002):, Resilience of the Rhizosphere to Anthropogenic Disturbance. *Biodegradation*, 13, 21-27.

Macgill (2000): Manual for Water/Wastewater/Soil/Sediments, Plant and Fish Analysis. Macgill Environmental Research Laboratory.

McMillen, S.J.; Magaw, R.I. and Carovillano R.L. (2001):"Risk-Based Decision-Making for Assessing Petroleum Impacts at Exploration and Production Sites," U.S. Department of Energy and Petroleum Environmental Research Forum, October.

Mills, A.I.; Beuil, C. and Cowell, R.R (1978): Enumeration of Petroleum Degrading Marine and Estuarine Microorganisms by most Probable Number Method.C and *J. Microbiol.* 4: 552-557

Mishra, S.; Jyot, J.; Kuhad, R.C.; and Lal, B. (2001): Evaluation of Inoculums Addition To Stimulate In Situ Bioremediation of Oily-Sludge-Contaminated-Soil. *Appl. Environ. Microbiol.*, 67, 1675.

Muller, P.H. J.G.; Rogers, J.C.; Kremer, F.V. and Glaser, J.A. (1992): 'Oil Spills Bioremediation: Experiences, Lessons and Results from the Exxon Valdez Oil Spill.

Nielson, S.S. (2002): Introduction to the Chemical Analysis of Foods. CBS. Publishers and Distributors 4596/1 –A, 11 Daryazanji, New Delhi – 110 032 (India). 1st Edition 2002.

Pascale, M. and Raina M.M. (2000): Rhamnolipid – Enhanced Mineralization of Phenanthrene in Organic – Metal Contaminated Soils. *Bioremediat. J.* 4(4), 295 308.

Prescott, L.M.; Harley, J.P. and Klein, D.A. (2002): Microbiology, Fifth Edition. McGraw-Hill Publication, pp. 106-107.

Rajim K.; Ronald P.; John C. and Vincent R. (2010): Microbiological and Physicochemical Analysis of Drinking Water in Georgetown, Guyana, *Nature and Science* 8(8):261-265.

Rump, H.H. (1999): Wiley-VCH:Weinheim. "*Laboratory Manual for the Examination of Water, Wastewater and Soil.*

Poulton, B.C.; Finger, S.E. and Humphrey, S.A. (1997). Effects of a Crude Oil Spill on the Benthic Invertebrate Community in the Gasconade River, Missouri. Arch. *Environ. Contam. and Toxicol.* 33: 268-276.

Poulton, B.C.; Callahan, E.V.; Hurtubise, R.D. and B.G. Mueller (1998). Effects of Oil Spill on Leaf Pack-Inhabiting Macro-invertebrates in the Chariton River, Missouri. *Environ. Pollut.* 99: 115-122.

Punmia, B.C. and Jain, A.K. (1998): Wastewater Engineering. Laxmi Publications, New Delhi.

Saien, J. and Nejati, H. (2007): Enhanced Photocatalytic Degradation of Pollutants in Petroleum Refinery Wastewater Under Mild Conditions. *Journal of Hazardous Materials*, Vol. 148, pp. 491-495.

Spain, J.C.; Pritchard, P.H.; and Bourquin, A.W. (1990): Effects of Adaptation on Biodegradation Rates in Sediment/Water Cores from Estuarine and Freshwater Environments. *Appl. Environ. Microbiol.* 40, 726.

Stirling, H.P. (1985):'Chemical and Biological Methods for Water Analysis for Aquaculturist".1st. Edition. Institute of Agriculture, University of Stirling, Stirling. Great Britian. pp. 118-119.

Sutherland, T.; Russel, R. and Selleck, M. (2002): Using Enzymes to Clean Pesticide Residues. *Pesticide Outlook*, 13, 149-151.

Walkley, A. and Black, I.A. (1934): Determination of Organic Carbon in Soil. Soil Sciences, 37: 28-29.

W.H.O. (1991): World Health Organizaion.

Zobell, C.E. (1946): Action of Microorganisms on Hydrocarbons. Bacterial. Rev. Vol. 10, pp. 149.

Impact of Abiotic Factors on the Benthic Macro-invertebrates Population of Kunda River (Madhya Pradesh), India

Shailendra Sharma[1]; Sudha Dubey[2]; Rajendra Chaurasia[2]

ABSTRACT

Physico-chemical parameters and macro-invertebrate fauna of Kunda River at Khargone district Madhya Pradesh, India were studied from August 2010 to January 2011. Surface water and benthic samples were collected monthly from four sampling stations along the river. Mean values of surface water temperature of 28.61°C, pH 8.32, Transparency 41.19, Dissolved Oxygen 6.86 mg/l, Biological Oxygen Demand (BOD) 4.28 mg/l, Total Hardness 141.04, Alkalinity 272.87, chloride 30.24 mg/l, nitrate 0.33 mg/l, phosphate 0.39 mg/l.

A total of Forty two (42) species of benthic macro-invertebrates were recorded of which three (3) major phyla (Arthropoda, Annelida and Mollusca) were identified namely; *L. truncatula* and *Chironomus sp.* were the most abundant with relative abundance of *Thiara tuberculata and Chaoborus* 5.61%, *Chironomus sp.*5.42%, *Lamellidens corricaunus* 5.26%, *Lymnea auricularia* 4.59%, *Dero dorsalis* 4.50%, *Lymnaea acuminate* 4.38%, *Tubifex albicola* 4.09% and *Chaoborus sp.* 4.04% respectively. The high values of BOD and the abundance of *Chironomus sp.*, a pollution-tolerant macro-invertebrate indicate that the river is likely under pollution stress.

1. Department of Biotechnology, Adarsh Institute of Management & Science Dhamnod (M.P.) India.

2. Department of Zoology, Govt. Holkar Science College, Indore - 452017, India.

Keywords: Physico-chemical parameters, Macro-invertebrates, Pollution, Kunda River.

INTRODUCTION

Benthic macro-invertebrates fauna are those organisms that live on or inside the deposit at the bottom of a water body (Idowu and Ugwumba, 2005). Water quality are those physical, chemical and biological factors that influence species composition, diversity, stability, production and physiological conditions of indigenous populations of a water body (Boyd, 1982). Studies on water quality management using macro-invertebrates in evaluating the impacts of specific pollutants in aquatic environments have been reported (Ogbeibu, 2001; Hart and Zabbey, 2005; Arimoro and Ikomi, 2007; George *et al.*, 2009; Esenowo and Ugwumba, 2010).

Benthic Macro-invertebrates have also been identified and the highest species number was recorded near tributaries due to the availability of food while the lowest are in the impacted areas where there are pollution discharges and gravel excavation (Beqiraj *et al.*, 2006). According to Danes and Hynes (1980), occurrence and distribution of macro-invertebrate are governed mostly by the physical and chemical quality of water and immediate substrate of occupation. Temperature, dissolved oxygen, pH and nutrients have considerable effects on the life of aquatic organisms. Macro-invertebrates play an important role in aquatic community which includes mineralization, mixing of sediments and flux of oxygen into sediment, cycling of organic matter and also in assessing the quality of inland water (George *et al.*, 2009). The distribution of macro-invertebrates fauna is determined by a number of factors such as the physical nature of the substratum, depth, and nutritive content, degree of stability and oxygen content of the water body. Macro-invertebrate organisms are threatened by changes in their habitat which are associated with pollution, erosion and siltation (Lydeard *et al.*, 2004). The use of macro-invertebrate diversity for bioassessment provides a simpler approach and this is due to the fact that they can be sampled quantitatively as well as the known relative sensitivity or tolerance of some of them to contamination (Adakole and Annune, 2003). Species vary in their degree of tolerance with the result that under polluted conditions, a reduction in species diversity is the most obvious effect (Rosenberg and Resh, 1993; Edokpayi *et. al.*, 2000; Emere, 2000; Olomukoro and Egborge, 2003).

Khargone District climate is changed thus water of Kunda River is absorbed and water pollution amount is increased day by day. All of them use Kunda river water for their water requirements and either directly or indirectly all their effluents reach Kunda river causing severe pollution, affecting agriculture and Effluent from waste dumps are discharged to receiving water bodies causing severe environmental damage.

The aims and objectives of this research is to assess the water quality of river Kunda using Physico-chemical Parameters Such as Temperature, pH,

Transparency, Dissolved Oxygen (DO), Biological Oxygen Demand (BOD), Total Hardness, Alkality, Chloride, Nitrate, Phosphate and Biological data of aquatic Benthic Macro-invertebrates.

MATERIALS AND METHOD

Study Area

River Kunda at Khargone district lies between longitude 75°36′4″E and latitude 21°49′16″ N. It's originated from Amba forest and Sirvel village. River Kunda has a length of approximately 169 Kms. and its catchment area of 3825 sq.km. Its river situated in the west directions of M.P. and its flows from South to North through four block of Khargone district Bhagwanpura, Goganwa, Khargone, and Kasrawad. The river is a dump site for domestic wastes and raw sewage due to high population and rapid urbanization. Four sampling stations were selected in the river (Map - 9.1).

1. DEJLA-DEVADA DAM

Dejla-Devada Dam is situated on Kunda River. It is 5 km. away from Bhagwanpura Tehsil in Khargone district of western Madhya Pradesh. Its total length is 6010 m. And Its 357.20 m. High from the deepest foundation level. Its Irrigation area is about 8000 hectare. Its water holding area is 335.40 sq. km. and its complete storage capacity is 56.35 million cubic meter, its total dam surface 383.20 m. And its maximum dam surface 38920 m.

Its latitude 21°36′45″ (DMS) N & longitude 75°37′30″ (DMS) E.

2. CONFLUENCE WITH UNDRI RIVER

Undri River is a tributary river of Kunda river. This place is situated 12km away From the Dejla-Devada dam. At this village Undri river confluence in Kunda River this village is called Bagdhari. At this place Garhi-Galtar project has made, which provided Irrigation facility to near about 1157 km. hectare Land.

Its latitude 20°41′30″ (DMS) N & longitude 75°52′15″ (DMS) E.

3. KHARGONE

Khargone district formerly known as West Nimar district. It is a district of Madhya Pradesh state in central India. The district lies in Nimar region, and is part of Indore Division. Khargone town is the headquarters of this district. It is situated on the bank of Kunda River. Khargone is located at South-West border of Madhya Pradesh, 283 meters above sea level. Area of the district is 8030 square km. The district is surrounded by Dhar, Indore and Dewas in the north, Maharashtra state in the south, Khandwa, Burhanpur in the east and Barwani in the west. The district forms almost the central section of Narmada valley which is bordered by Vindhachal ranges in the north and Satpura ranges in the south. Narmada is the main river flowing through the district. Its river flows in a path of 50 Km. inside the district.

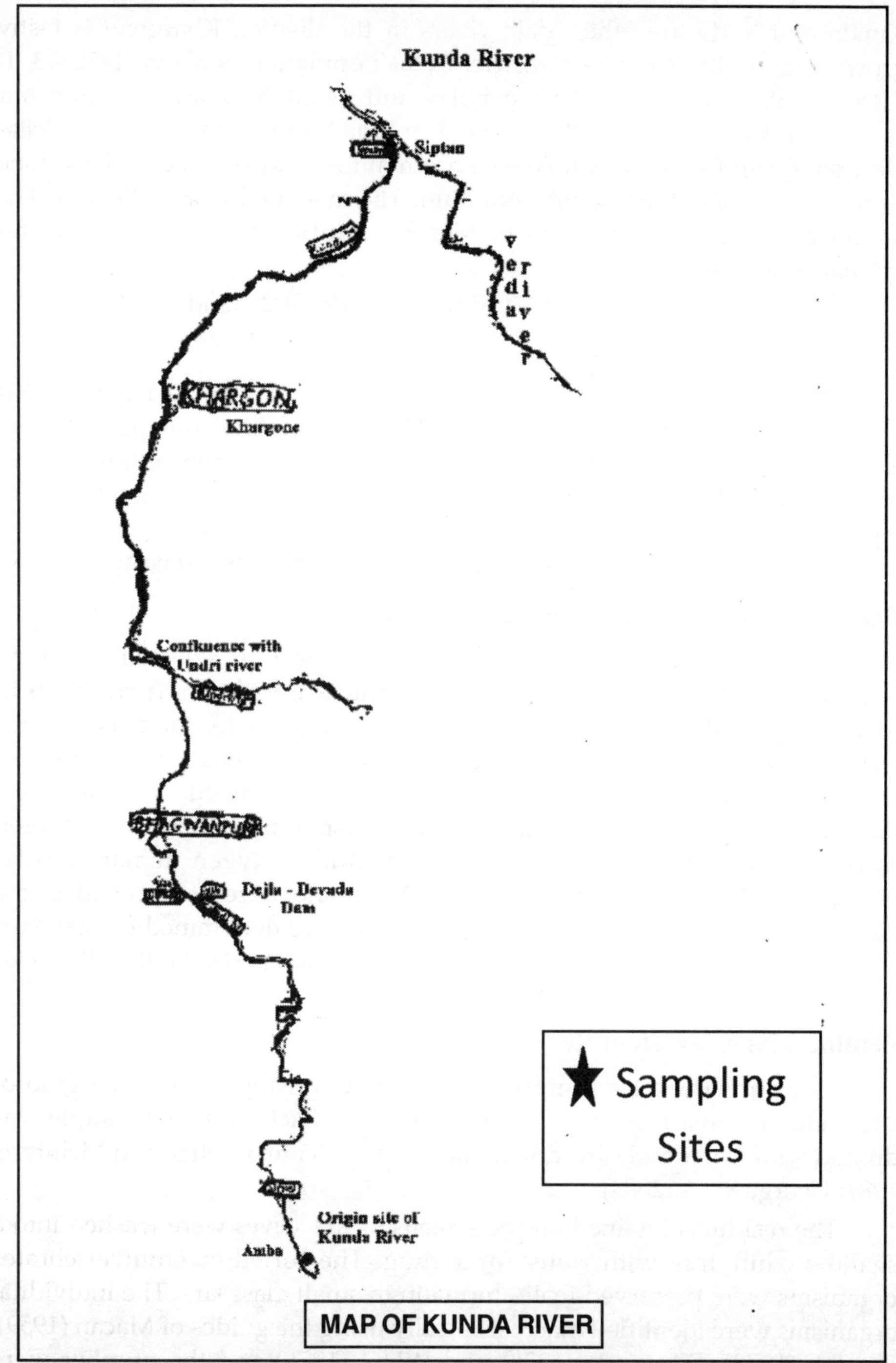

Map 9.1: Location Map Showing the Kunda River and Four Sampling Points, Khargone, M.P. India

Kunda and Veda are other main rivers in the district. Khargone is fastly growing as a city. Khargone district Total population is above 1872413. It district water use 141 Lac liter per day and its situated Intecvel its water capacity 1.062 Crore liter. It's situated in small and large 146 dam. Dejla-Devada, Garhi-Galtar & Ambaknala are main irrigation projects. Khargone generally has hot climate with little rain. The average rain fall 831mm. The summers are long ranging from March to July. Monsoon is brief and arrives in mid August.

Its latitude 20°22′ and 22°35′ N & longitude 74°25′ and 76°14′ E

4. SIPTAN

Siptan is a small town. It is a terminal point of Kunda river, At this point Kunda river confluence with the Veda River. After this place Kunda river is called Veda River. Siptan is situated 35 km away from administrative headquarters of Khargone district. Siptan is near the village named Bhulgori. Siptan catchments area is about 798.10 sq.m.

Its latitude 21°41′30″ (DMS) N & longitude 75°41′30″ (DMS) E.

Determination of Physicochemical Parameters

The water samples were collected from the four selected sampling stations viz., Dejla-Devada Dam = S I, Confluence with Undri river = S II, Khargone = S III and Siptan = S IV in the Kunda River for the period of Six month from August 2010 to January 2011. In the analysis of the physico-chemical properties of water, standard method prescribed in limnological literature were used. Temperature, pH, Transparency, Dissolved Oxygen were determined at the site while Biochemical oxygen demand, Total Hardness, Alkanity, Chloride, Nitrate, Phosphate were determined in the laboratory. The Physico-Chemical parameters were determined by standard methods of APHA (2002), Welch (1998), Golterman (1991). All the chemicals used were of AR grade.

Benthic Macroinvertebrate

Macroinvertebrates samples were collected using a Van-veen grab of 0.6m^2 surface area from each sampling station. Each sediment sample was diluted with water and sieved with mesh sizes 0.5 mm (Holme and Mclntyre, 1984; George *et al.*, 2009).

The residuals retained on the screens of the sieves were washed into a shallow white tray with water for sorting. The sorted macroinvertebrates organisms were preserved in 4% formalin in small glass jars. The individual organisms were identified macroscopically using the guides of Macan (1959), Pennak (1978), Edmunds (1978) and WHO (1978) and the number were counted.

RESULTS AND DISCUSSION

Physico-chemical Analysis

The result of the physico-chemical parameters of the four sampling station analyzed is presented in Tables 9.1, 9.2, 9.3 and 9.4 and Monthly Fluctuation of physicochemical parameters is presented in figures 9.1-9.10.

Table 9.1: [Station I] Physico-chemical Parameters of River Kunda at Dejla-Devada Dam for Six Month (August 2010 to January 2011)

Month	August	September	October	November	December	January
Temperature (°C)	28	30	35	31	29	25
pH	9.1	8.7	8.2	8.5	7.61	7.84
Transparency (N.T.U.)	16	25	38	50.5	51.2	53
D.O. (Mg/l)	8.2	6.23	6.50	6.35	6.39	6.21
B.O.D. (Mg/l)	5.63	5.5	4.8	3.1	3.2	3.31
Total Hardness (Mg/l)	80	78	73	71	89	107
Alkalinity	245	255	230	250	235	250
Chloride (Mg/l)	49	38	0.3	25.4	21	26
Nitrate (Mg/l)	0.125	0.13	0.131	0.121	0.11	0.89
Phosphate (Mg/l)	0.46	0.49	0.5	0.16	0.17	0.21

Table 9.2: [Station II] Physico-chemical Parameters of River Kunda at Confluence with Undri River for Six Month (August 2010 to January 2011)

Month	August	September	October	November	December	January
Temperature (°C)	27.1	30.1	35	31.3	29.2	25.2
pH	8.5	8.2	8.7	8.5	8.2	8.0
Transparency (N.T.U.)	20	30	42	55	48	58
D.O. (Mg/l)	6.2	9.2	9.8	6.5	7.2	7.5
B.O.D. (Mg/l)	6.3	5.7	5.08	3.0	2.8	3.1
Total Hardness (Mg/l)	128	136	170	165	155	180
Alkalinity	365	415	390	415	385	255
Chloride (Mg/l)	30	18	20	23	38	32
Nitrate (Mg/l)	0.120	0.135	0.139	0.120	0.110	0.890
Phosphate (Mg/l)	0.66	0.40	0.55	0.16	0.20	0.31

Table 9.3: [Station III] Physico-chemical Parameters of River Kunda at Khargone for Six Month (August 2010 to January 2011)

Month	August	September	October	November	December	January
Temperature(°C)	25	31	33	32	28	22
pH	9.3	8.8	8.4	8.0	7.5	7.9
Transparency (N.T.U.)	19	28	40	55	52	58
D.O. (Mg/l)	7.8	6.50	6.25	6.65	6.89	6.10
B.O.D. (Mg/l)	5.63	5.5	4.8	3.1	3.2	3.31
Total Hardness (Mg/l)	115	125	165	188	165	190
Alkalinity	250	258	239	260	230	252
Chloride (Mg/l)	41	35	28	24	20	27
Nitrate (Mg/l)	0.140	0.125	0.135	0.115	0.105	0.095
Phosphate (Mg/l)	0.39	0.55	0.50	0.36	0.25	0.17

Table 9.4: [Station IV] Physico-chemical Parameters of River Kunda at Siptan for Six Month (August 2010 to January 2011)

Month	August	September	October	November	December	January
Temperature (°C)	22	30	32	30	26	20
pH	9.0	8.2	8.8	8.4	7.9	7.5
Transparency (N.T.U.)	21	25	35	50	59	60
D.O. (Mg/l)	6.9	6.5	6.0	6.5	6.2	6.0
B.O.D. (Mg/l)	5.0	5.7	4.5	3.6	3.8	3.0
Total Hardness (Mg/l)	135	145	185	195	165	180
Alkalinity	220	245	220	230	210	245
Chloride (Mg/l)	50	45	39	32	28	36
Nitrate (Mg/l)	0.130	0.115	0.145	0.125	0.115	0.090
Phosphate (Mg/l)	0.55	0.75	0.69	0.45	0.39	0.25

Temperature

Temperature is one of the most important parameters that influence almost all the physical, chemical and biological properties of water and thus the water chemistry. In the present study temperature varied from 20°C – 35°C. The minimum temperature was recorded in the month of January at S IV and maximum was recorded in the month of October at S II and S III. The mean value of the temperature recorded was 28.61°C. In the present study water temperature was recorded between 20°C – 35°C (Fig. 9.1). Sharma *et al.*, (2001), Yogesh *et al.*, (2001) also reported the same type of fluctuation in various freshwater bodies.

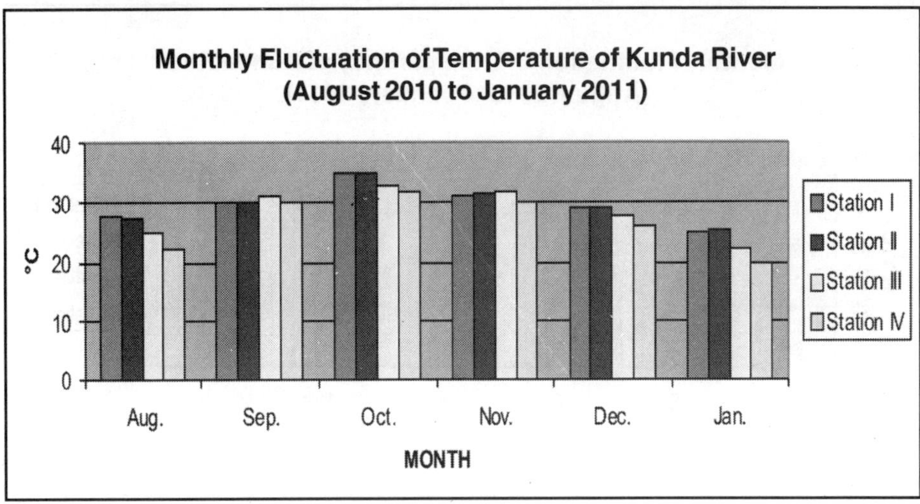

Fig. 9.1: Bar Diagram Showing Monthly Fluctuation of Temperature of Kunda River (August 2010 to January 2011)

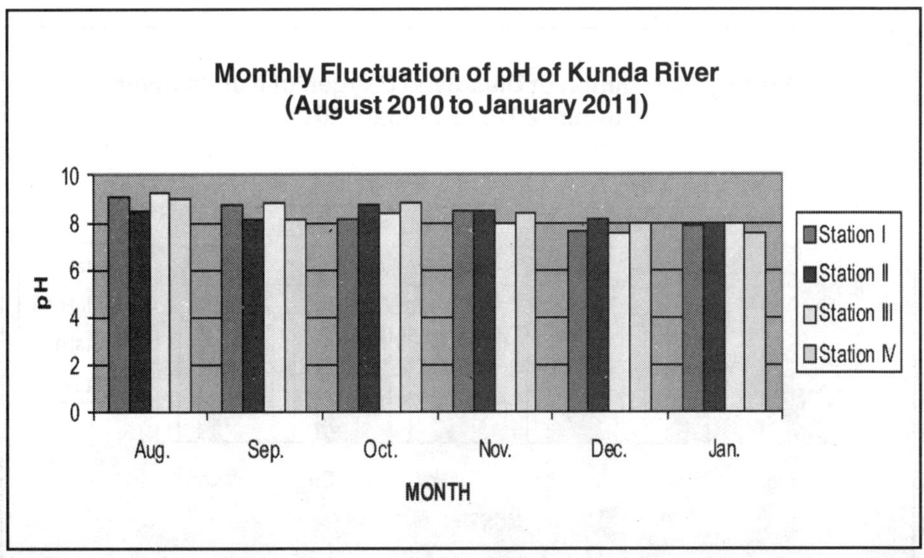

Fig. 9.2: Bar Diagram Showing Monthly Fluctuation of pH of Kunda River (August 2010 to January 2011)

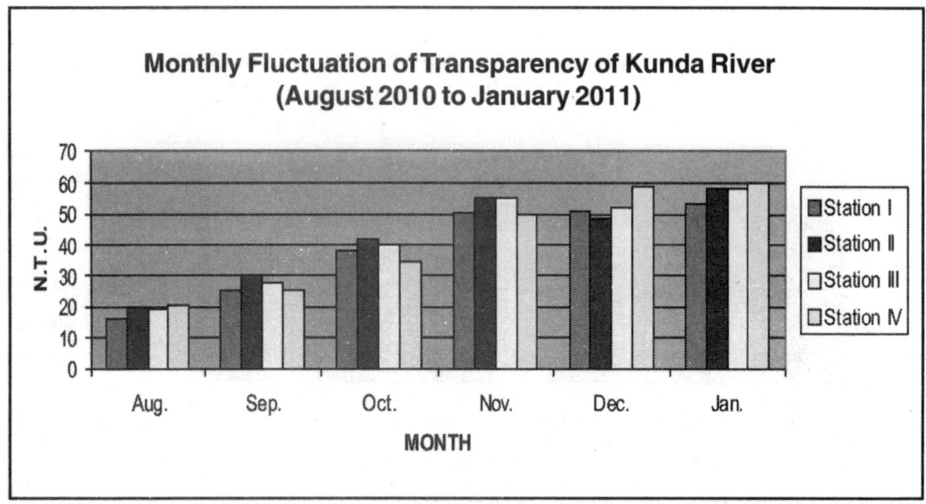

Fig. 9.3: Bar Diagram Showing Monthly Fluctuation of Transparency of Kunda River (August 2010 to January 2011)

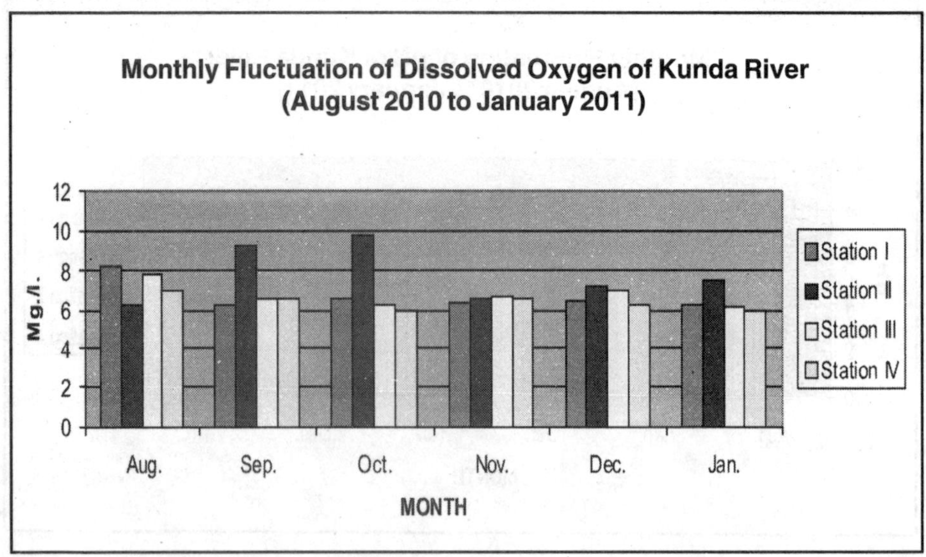

Fig. 9.4: Bar Diagram Showing Monthly Fluctuation of Dissolved Oxygen of Kunda River (August 2010 to January 2011)

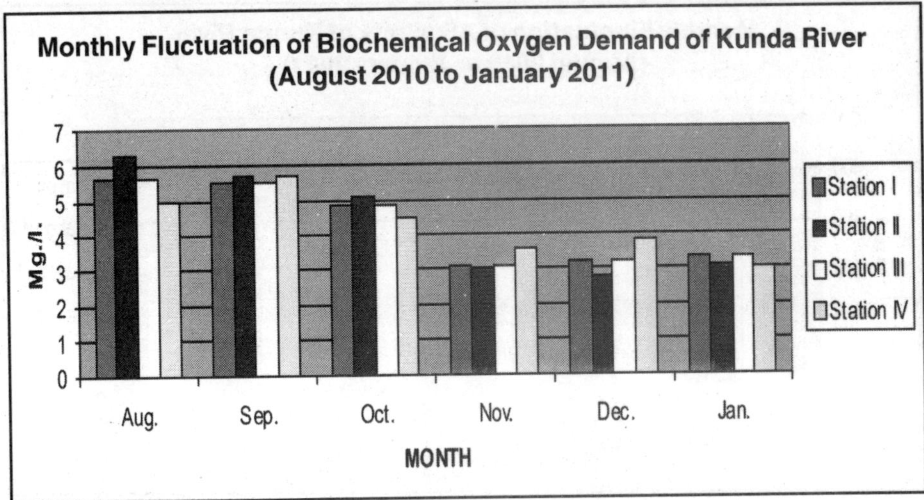

Fig. 9.5: Bar Diagram Showing Monthly Fluctuation of Biochemical Oxygen Demand of Kunda River (August 2010 to January 2011)

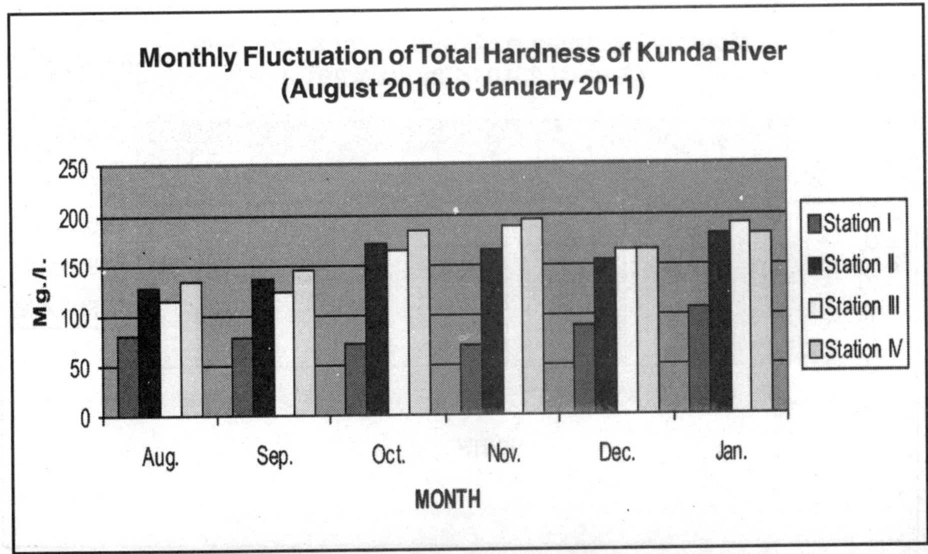

Fig. 9.6: Bar Diagram Showing Monthly Fluctuation of Total Hardness of Kunda River (August 2010 to January 2011)

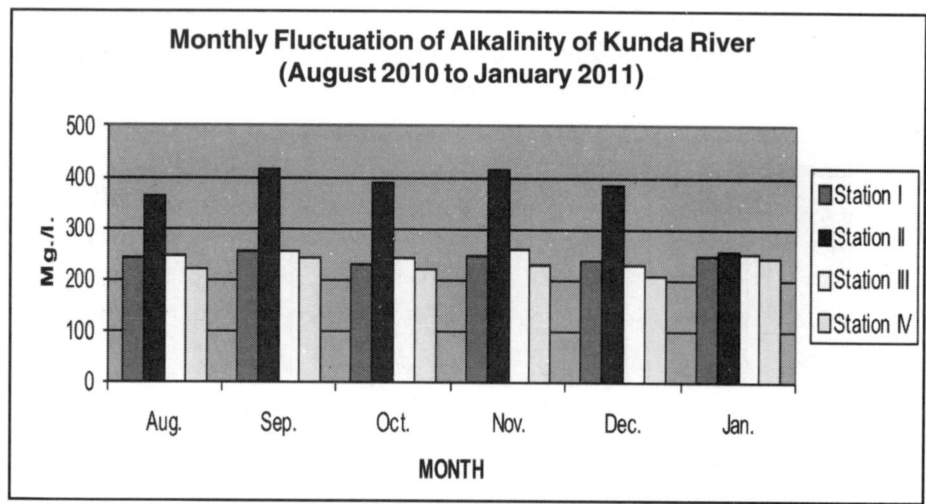

Fig. 9.7: Bar Diagram Showing Monthly Fluctuation of Alkalinity of Kunda River (August 2010 to January 2011)

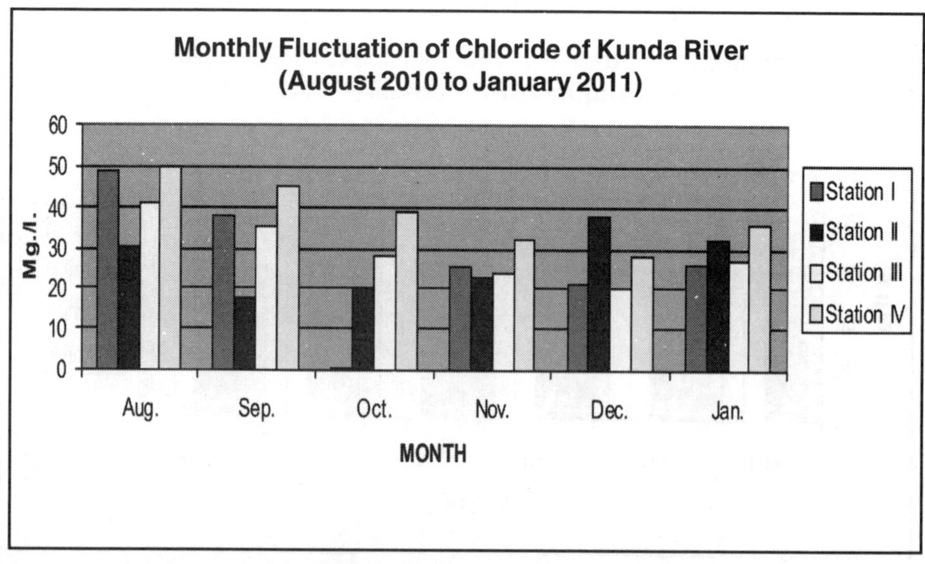

Fig. 9.8: Bar Diagram Showing Monthly Fluctuation of Chloride of Kunda River (August 2010 to January 2011)

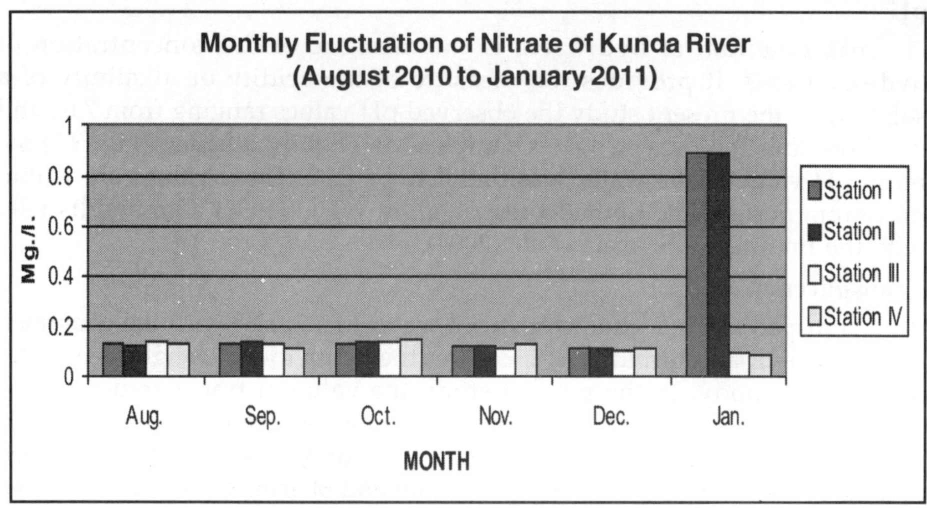

Fig. 9.9: Bar Diagram Showing Monthly Fluctuation of Nitrate of Kunda River (August 2010 to January 2011)

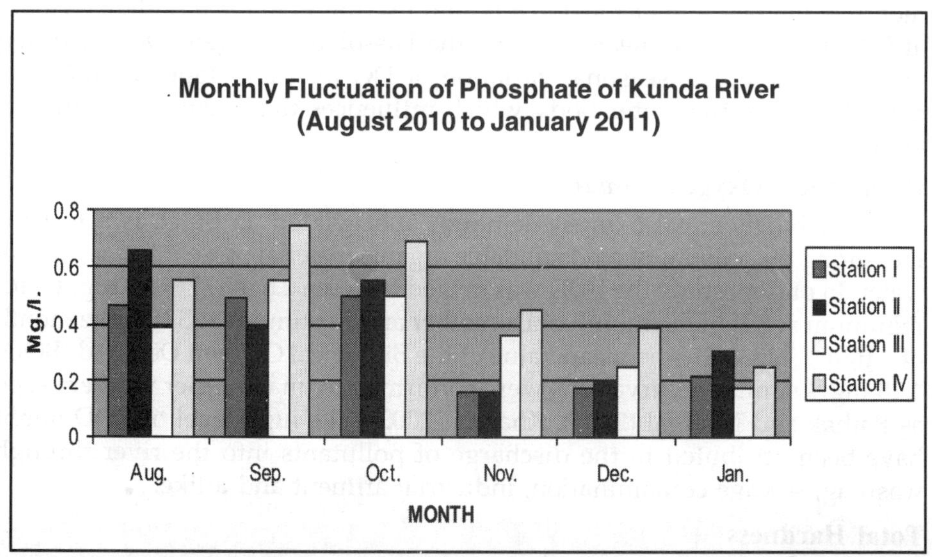

Fig. 9.10: Bar Diagram Showing Monthly Fluctuation of Phosphate of Kunda River (August 2010 to January 2011)

pH

pH–Potential of hydrogen, is the measure of the concentration of hydrogen ions. It provides the measure of the acidity or alkalinity of a solution. In the present study the observed pH values ranging from 7.61 and 9.3 show that the present water samples are slightly alkaline (Fig. 9.2).the mean pH value of the water was found to be 8.32. These values are within maximum permissible limited prescribed by WHO (1993). Our results tally with the findings of Sharma *et al.,* (2004).

Transparency

Transparency is a characteristic of water that varies with the combined effect of colour and turbidity. It measures the depth to which light penetrates in the water body. In the present study the value of transparency varied from 16 (NTU) – 60 (NTU) the mean value of the Transparency recorded was 41.19 (NTU). The highest Transparency unit was 60 (NTU) obtained and the lowest was 16 (NTU). (Fig. 9.3), Jain and Sharma (2000) also reported lowest transparency in rainy season and maximum in winter.

Dissolved Oxygen (DO)

Dissolved oxygen in natural and waste water depends on the physical, chemical and biological activities in the water body. Dissolved Oxygen (DO) content, plays a vital role in supporting aquatic life and is susceptible to slight environment changes. DO an important limnological parameter indicating level of water quality and organic pollution in the water body (Wetzel and Likens, 2006). In present study concentration of DO in Kunda river water samples varied from 6.0 mg/l to 9.8 mg/l with minimum in the month of January and October at S IV and maximum in the month of October at S II (Fig. 9.4). The mean value of the Dissolved Oxygen (DO) recorded was 6.86 mg/l. The seasonal variation of DO in water depends upon the temperature of the water body which influences the oxygen solubility in water.

Biochemical Oxygen Demand

The biochemical oxygen demand, abbreviated as BOD, is a test for measuring the amount of biodegradable organic material present in a sample of water. In present study the BOD was ranged between 2.8 mg/l to 6.3 mg/l with minimum at S II in the month of December and maximum at S II in the month of August (Fig. 9.5). The mean value of the Biological Oxygen Demand (BOD) 4.28 mg/l similar observations were confirmed by many other workers such as Pathak and Mudgal (2005), Khanna (2003). The high level of BOD might have been attributed to the discharge of pollutants into the river through washing, sewage contamination, industrial affluent and a like.

Total Hardness

Total hardness is the parameter of water quality used to describe the effect of dissolved minerals (mostly Ca and Mg), determining suitability of water for domestic, industrial and drinking purposes The observation of total hardness reveals that the monthly variation in the water samples of Kunda river ranged between 71 mg/l to 195 mg/l with minimum at S I in the month of November and Maximum at S IV in the month of November (Fig. 9.6). The mean value of the Total Hardness recorded was 141.04 mg/l. same results were also reported by Sharma *et al.*, 2012.

Alkanity

Alkanity of water is a measure of weak acid present in it and of the cations balanced against them (Sverdrap *et al.*, 1942). The observation of alkanity reveals that the monthly variation ranged from a minimum of 210 mg/l- 415 mg/l. with minimum at S IV in the month of Deceber and maximum at S II in the month of September. (Fig. 9.7) and the mean value of the Total Hardness recorded was 272.87mg/l. same results were also reported by Choubey (1991) and Sharma *et al.*, (2004).

Chloride

Chloride is one of the major inorganic anion in water and waste water. In present study the values of chloride varied between 0.3 mg/l to 50 mg/l with minimum in October at S I and Maximum in August at S IV (Fig. 9.8). The mean value of the Chloride recorded was 30.237 mg/l. seasonally, the values were highest in summer and lower in winter and intermediate values were recorded in rainy season. Similar results have been observed by Ahmad (2004).

Nitrate

Nitrates are the most oxidised forms of nitrogen and the end product of the aerobic decomposition of organic nitrogenous matter. Nitrogen is an essential building block in the synthesis of protein. The evaluation of nitrogen is therefore an important parameter in understanding the nutritional status of water bodies. The concentration of nitrate in Kunda river water was found to be in the range of 0.090 mg/l to 0.890 mg/l. Minimum nitrate concentration was recorded at S IV in the month of January and maximum was also recorded at S II in the month of January (Fig. 9.9) and the mean value of the Nitrate recorded was 0.334 mg/l. Nitrate is attributed mainly due to anthropogenic activities such of run of water from agricultural lands, industrial wastes, discharge of house hold and municipal sewage from the market place and other effluents containing nitrogen. Such observations were also reported by Royer *et al.*, (2004).

Phosphate

Phosphorous is one of the most important nutrients limiting the growth of autotrophs and biological productivity of the system. High phosphorus content causes increased algal growth, often as blooms, till nitrogen becomes limiting. During the present study the values of phosphate fluctuated between 0.16 mg/l to 0.75 mg/l. the maximum phosphate was recorded at S IV in the month of September and minimum was also recorded at S II in the month of November (Fig. 9.10). Similar values were also observed by Jain (2000). The increased use of fertilizers, use of detergents and domestic sewage greatly contribute to the heavy loading of phosphorus in the water.

BENTHIC MACRO-INVERTEBRATES FAUNA

The number of macro-invertebrates obtained during the study period is show in Tables 9.5, 9.6, 9.7, 9.8 and Monthly Variation of Benthic Macro-invertebrates species diversity of Station I, II, III and IV Show in figures 9.11 to 9.40.

A total of forty two (42) species of macro-invertebrates belonging to 3 phyla (Arthropoda, Annelida and Mollusca) were identified. Chironomus species was found to have the highest density with a total number of 142 and 5.42% followed by *Thiara tuberculata* and *Chaoborus species* with a total density of 126 and occurs at 5.61%. The least occurred macro-invertebrates were the oligocheates *Stylaria foesularis species* with a total density of 09 and occurs at 0.40%, Crustaceans *Cypris species* with a total density of 20 and occurs at 0.74% and *Prawn species* with a total density of 21 and occurs at 0.94% and *Neso Cyclopes species* with a total density of 23 and occurs at 0.78% and in Baetidae family *Baetiella species* with a total density of 20 and occurs at 0.89% and in Ephemeridae family *Ephemera species* with a total density of 22 and occurs at 0.74% Other macro-invertebrates with intermediate estimations were the Oligocheates *Tubifex tubifex* with a total of 45 at 2.004%, Crustacians *Pina dubia* with a total of 51 at 2.27%, *Nauplius* with a total of 52 at 2.32%, Gastropods *Pila globosa* with a total of 87 at 3.88% and *Thiara scabra* with a total of 86 at 3.83%, Pelecypoda *Lymnaea acuminate* with a total of 60 at 2.67% and *Lamellidens lamellatus* with a total of 61 at 2.72% and Ephimeridae family *Ephemera nadinac* with a total of 55 at 2.45% and the Heptageniidae family *Heptagenia nubile* with a total of 49 at 2.18% and *Chironomus species* that has the total of 84 and occur at 3.74% out of the forty two (42) macro-invertebrates. (Tables 9.5, 9.6, 9.7 and 9.8).

This result was similar to the findings of Lang-Bertalot (1979). The result further revealed that of the 3 phyla identified, Arthropods were dominant. This conforms to the research findings of Mellanby (1997) that arthropods are adapted to life diverse habitats due to their mode of feeding, behaviour, physiology and physicochemical parameters. The monthly variation in the density of macro-invertebrates as observed from the study could be to the variation in the physic-chemical factors which also indicates the presence of dissolved organic matter at Kunda River. The population density of living organisms in aquatic environment usually various with the variation of environmental parameters.

Table 9.5: (Station- I) (DEJLA-DEVADA DAM): Results of Benthic Macro-invertebrates Identified from Kunda River Shows the Number Species and Percentage of Occurrence of Aquatic Benthic Macro-invertebrates Recorded during the Study Period

Name of Group and Species	August	September	October	November	December	January	Total No.	Relative Abundance (% Number)
Oligocheates								
Tubifex tubifex	Nil	10	12	08	12	03	45	2.00
Limmodrilus hoffmeisteri	Nil	04	09	05	03	02	23	1.02
Telmatodrilusmultispinosus	Nil	04	10	05	12	08	39	1.74
Dero dorsalis	Nil	05	07	10	15	06	43	1.92
Stylaria fossularis	Nil	–	03	02	–	04	09	0.40
Branchiodrillus hortensis	Nil	09	10	07	05	08	39	1.74
Tubifex albicola	Nil	15	20	25	22	10	92	4.09
Dero digitata	Nil	09	10	15	14	08	56	2.49
Dero cooperi	Nil	05	03	07	05	12	32	1.43
Crustacians (1)								
Daphnia cercinata	Nil	06	02	04	08	03	23	1.02
Pina dubia	Nil	06	08	11	14	12	51	2.27
Cypris	Nil	06	08	10	15	12	51	2.27
Cyclopes	Nil	05	07	12	10	08	42	1.87
Neso cyclopes	Nil	07	07	09	12	11	46	2.05
Nauplius	Nil	02	07	14	17	12	52	2.32
Prawn	Nil	03	04	05	06	03	21	0.94

(Contd...)

Name of Group and Species	August	September	October	November	December	January	Total No.	Relative Abundance (% Number)
Gastropoda(/M²)								
Pila globosa	–	12	14	18	20	23	87	3.88
Thiara scabra	–	12	15	14	20	25	86	3.83
Bellamya bengalensis	–	05	10	15	12	20	62	2.76
Thiara lineata	–	10	12	12	15	24	73	3.25
Thiara tuberculata	–	13	22	29	32	30	126	5.61
Vivipara bengalensis	–	10	12	12	16	12	62	2.76
Digiostana pulchella	–	08	12	15	18	20	73	3.25
Pelecypoda (/M²)								
Lymnaea acuminate	–	10	11	13	12	14	60	2.67
Lymnea auricularia	–	08	10	12	11	13	44	1.96
Lamellidens corricaunus	–	08	12	10	13	15	58	2.58
Lamellidens consobrinus	–	04	05	10	12	18	49	2.18
Lamellidens lamellatus		08	11	12	15	15	61	2.72
Pisidium clarkeanum	–	05	08	11	15	14	53	2.36
Corbicula striatella	–	10	12	15	14	20	71	3.16
Melanoides tuberculates	–	05	09	12	17	20	63	2.81

(Contd…)

Name of Group and Species	August	September	October	November	December	January	Total No.	Relative Abundance (% Number)
Baetidac -								
Baetiella sp.	–	05	02	04	06	03	20	0.89
Baetis sp.	–	02	08	05	04	08	27	1.20
Baetis simplex	–	01	05	08	02	07	23	1.02
Baetis festivus	–	05	07	09	10	14	45	2.00
Caenoidac -								
Caehis sp.	NIL	05	12	14	15	11	57	2.54
Ephemeridac -								
Ephemera Nadinac	NIL	06	10	17	10	12	55	2.45
Heptageniidac -								
Epeorus sp.	–	05	06	08	09	07	35	1.56
Epeorus sp.	–	01	05	07	09	10	32	1.43
Heptagenia nubile	–	05	07	10	12	15	49	2.18
chironomus sp.	10	11	17	18	13	15	84	3.74
Chaoborus sp.	12	12	20	27	25	30	126	5.61

Table 9.6: (Station- II) (Confluence with Undri River): Results of Benthic Macro-invertebrates Identified from Kunda River Shows the Number Species and Percentage of Occurrence of Aquatic Benthic Macro-invertebrates Recorded during the Study Period

Name of Group and Species	August	September	October	November	December	January	Total No.	Relative Abundance (% Number)
Oligocheates								
Tubifex tubifex	Nil	15	20	25	22	10	92	3.12
Limmodrilus hoffmeisteri	Nil	09	10	15	14	08	56	1.89
Telmatodrilusmultispinosus	Nil	10	12	10	14	18	64	2.16
Dero dorsalis	Nil	06	15	20	25	30	96	3.24
Stylaria fossularis	Nil	10	13	12	18	14	67	2.26
Branchiodrillus hortensis	Nil	05	03	07	05	12	32	1.08
Tubifex albicola	Nil	07	03	05	12	18	45	1.52
Dero digitata	Nil	06	08	06	20	19	59	1.99
Dero cooperi	Nil	03	08	12	13	15	51	1.72
Crustacians (1)								
Daphnia cercinata	02	10	15	20	10	15	72	2.43
Pina dubia	–	3	7	18	3	7	38	1.28
Cypris	05	8	14	22	8	14	66	2.23
Cyclopes	01	7	9	10	7	9	42	1.42
Nesc cyclopes	03	3	5	7	3	5	23	0.78
Nauplius	01	8	6	9	8	6	37	1.25
Prawn	02	10	15	20	10	15	70	2.36

(Contd...)

Name of Group and Species	August	September	October	November	December	January	Total No.	Relative Abundance (% Number)
Gastropoda (/M²)								
Pila globosa	02	12	15	18	19	20	86	2.90
Thiara scabra	01	08	10	12	18	15	63	2.13
Bellamya bengalensis	02	10	12	18	13	20	73	2.46
Thiara lineata	–	08	12	17	19	22	78	2.63
Thiara tuberculata	–	05	17	13	15	25	75	2.53
Vivipara bengalensis	01	06	09	10	15	20	61	2.06
Digiostana pulchella	–	10	12	15	12	15	64	2.16
Pelecypoda (/M²)								
Lymnaea acuminate	–	20	30	35	25	20	130	4.39
Lymnea auricularia	02	15	20	24	35	40	136	4.59
Lamellidens corricaunus	05	19	27	30	35	40	156	5.27
Lamellidens consobrinus	02	10	20	20	30	42	124	4.19
Lamellidens lamellatus	02	10	12	15	20	35	94	3.17
Pisidium clarkeanum	02	10	14	17	29	35	107	3.61
Corbicula striatella	08	12	18	20	25	30	113	3.81
Melanoides tuberculates	02	12	18	20	25	30	107	3.61

(Contd…)

Name of Group and Species	August	September	October	November	December	January	Total No.	Relative Abundance (% Number)
Baetidac -								
Baetiella sp.	NIL	04	07	08	10	12	41	1.38
Baetis sp.	–	02	04	07	09	10	32	1.08
Baétis simplex	–	02	06	08	10	09	35	1.18
Baetis festivus	02	08	09	07	10	12	48	1.62
Caenoidac -								
Caehis sp.	–	02	05	08	10	07	32	1.08
Ephemeridac ´-								
Ephemera Nadinac	NIL	02	03	05	07	05	22	0.74
Heptageniidac -								
Epeorus sp.	02	03	05	09	10	12	41	1.38
Epeorus sp.	–	05	10	10	12	15	52	1.75
Heptagenia nubile	01	03	07	11	14	17	53	1.78
Chironomus sp.	14	15	17	18	13	15	92	3.11
Chaoborus sp.	20	15	20	27	25	30	137	4.63

Table 9.7: (Station- III) (Khargone): Results of Benthic Macro-invertebrates Identified from Kunda River Shows the Number Species and Percentage of Occurrence of Aquatic Benthic Macro-invertebrates Recorded during the Study Period

Name of Group and Species	August	September	October	November	December	January	Total No.	Relative Abundance (% Number)
Oligocheates								
Tubifex tubifex	–	5	12	9	17	18	61	2.33
Limmodrilus hoffmeisteri	–	7	4	9	15	20	55	2.10
Telmatodrilusmultispinosus	–	12	15	20	23	35	105	4.01
Dero dorsalis	–	08	20	25	30	35	118	4.51
Stylaria fossularis	–	15	12	14	12	18	71	2.71
Branchiodrillus hortensis	–	06	15	18	19	20	78	2.98
Tubifex albicola	–	10	12	15	18	20	75	2.86
Dero digitata	NIL	NIL	NIL	NIL	NIL	NIL	NIL	NIL
Dero cooperi	NIL	NIL	NIL	NIL	NIL	NIL	NIL	NIL
Crustacians (1)								
Daphnia cercinata	03	08	09	10	18	12	60	2.29
Pina dubia	03	02	05	07	10	12	39	1.48
Cypris	04	02	03	04	02	05	20	0.76
Cyclopes	05	08	02	06	10	12	43	1.64
Neso cyclopes	08	06	12	15	18	20	79	3.02
Nauplius	05	10	17	12	18	12	74	2.83
Prawn	NIL	NIL	NIL	NIL	NIL	NIL	NIL	NIL

(Contd…)

Name of Group and Species	August	September	October	November	December	January	Total No.	Relative Abundance (% Number)
Gastropoda(/M^2)								
Pila globosa	05	12	13	17	20	24	91	3.47
Thiara scabra	–	10	15	14	15	20	74	2.83
Bellamya bengalensis	02	05	10	12	13	15	57	2.18
Thiara lineata	01	06	10	15	18	21	71	2.71
Thiara tuberculata	–	10	12	14	19	20	75	2.86
Vivipara bengalensis	–	10	13	14	17	20	74	2.83
Digiostana pulchella	05	14	13	20	25	27	104	3.97
Pelecypoda (/M^2)								
Lymnaea acuminate	04	18	16	19	24	29	110	4.20
Lymnea auricularia	02	10	12	19	25	26	94	3.59
Lamellidens corricaunus	04	10	13	17	20	24	88	3.36
Lamellidens consobrinus	05	12	17	13	25	30	102	3.89
Lamellidens lamellatus	04	12	20	23	30	25	114	4.35
Pisidium clarkeanum	10	20	18	24	25	17	114	4.35
Corbicula striatella	NIL	NIL	NIL	NIL	NIL	NIL	NIL	NIL
Melanoides tuberculates	03	10	12	15	12	18	70	2.67

(Contd…)

Name of Group and Species	August	September	October	November	December	January	Total No.	Relative Abundance (% Number)
Baetidac -								
Baetiella sp.	NIL	NIL	NIL	NIL	NIL	NIL	NIL	NIL
Baetis sp.	NIL	02	04	07	10	08	31	1.18
Baetis simplex	NIL	01	05	08	10	12	36	1.37
Baetis festivus	NIL	NIL	NIL	NIL	NIL	NIL	NIL	NIL
Caenoidac -								
Caehis sp.	NIL	NIL	NIL	NIL	NIL	NIL	NIL	NIL
Ephemeridac -								
Ephemera Nadinac	NIL	02	04	08	12	15	41	1.57
Heptageniidac -								
Epeorus sp.	NIL	05	07	08	06	04	30	1.15
Epeorus sp.	NIL	NIL	NIL	NIL	NIL	NIL	NIL	NIL
Heptagenia nubile	NIL	02	03	05	06	08	24	0.92
Chironomus sp.	16	19	25	27	30	25	142	5.42
Chaoborus sp.	10	15	18	19	20	24	106	4.05

Table 9.8: (Station- IV) (SIPTAN): Results of Benthic Macro-invertebrates Identified from Kunda River Shows the Number Species and Percentage of Occurrence of Aquatic Benthic Macro-invertebrates Recorded during the Study Period

Name of Group and Species	August	September	October	November	December	January	Total No.	Relative Abundance (% Number)
Oligocheates								
Tubifex tubifex	02	14	13	12	21	25	87	4.99
Limmodrilus hoffmeisteri	06	08	12	15	19	21	81	4.65
Telmatodrilusmultispinosus	NIL	NIL	NIL	NIL	NIL	NIL	NIL	NIL
Dero dorsalis	–	04	08	10	11	12	45	2.58
Stylaria fossularis	–	02	03	05	08	10	28	1.61
Branchiodrillus hortensis	NIL	NIL	NIL	NIL	NIL	NIL	NIL	NIL
Tubifex albicola	NIL	08	10	11	12	10	51	2.93
Dero digitata	NIL	NIL	NIL	NIL	NIL	NIL	NIL	NIL
Dero cooperi	NIL	NIL	NIL	NIL	NIL	NIL	NIL	NIL
Crustacians (1)								
Daphnia cercinata	NIL	NIL	NIL	NIL	NIL	NIL	NIL	NIL
Pina dubia	NIL	NIL	NIL	NIL	NIL	NIL	NIL	NIL
Cypris	NIL	NIL	NIL	NIL	NIL	NIL	NIL	NIL
Cyclopes	NIL	NIL	NIL	NIL	NIL	NIL	NIL	NIL
Neso cyclopes	NIL	NIL	NIL	NIL	NIL	NIL	NIL	NIL
Nauplius	NIL	NIL	NIL	NIL	NIL	NIL	NIL	NIL
Prawn	NIL	NIL	NIL	NIL	NIL	NIL	NIL	NIL

(Contd...)

Name of Group and Species	August	September	October	November	December	January	Total No.	Relative Abundance (% Number)
Gastropoda(/M²)								
Pila globosa	–	05	12	14	18	19	68	3.91
Thiara scabra	–	04	15	12	19	18	68	3.91
Bellamya bengalensis	–	03	13	14	16	20	66	3.79
Thiara lineata	–	06	10	13	14	13	56	3.22
Thiara tuberculata	–	04	08	12	15	12	51	2.93
Vivipara bengalensis	02	08	10	11	12	14	57	3.27
Digiostana pulchella	–	05	08	10	14	13	50	2.87
Pelecypoda (/M²)								
Lymnaea acuminate	–	04	08	12	10	15	49	2.81
Lymnea auricularia	–	02	07	12	11	10	42	2.41
Lamellidens corricaunus	01	04	07	10	13	18	53	3.04
Lamellidens consobrinus	NIL	NIL	NIL	NIL	NIL	NIL	NIL	NIL
Lamellidens lamellatus	–	08	10	13	12	15	58	3.33
Pisidium clarkeanum	02	06	11	14	16	12	61	3.50
Corbicula striatella	NIL	NIL	NIL	NIL	NIL	NIL	NIL	NIL
Melanoides tuberculates	–	06	10	11	14	15	56	3.22

(Contd...)

Name of Group and Species	August	September	October	November	December	January	Total No.	Relative Abundance (% Number)
Baetidac -								
Baetiella sp.	NIL	05	07	09	12	14	47	2.69
Baetis sp.	NIL	04	05	09	10	12	40	2.29
Baetis simplex	NIL	03	10	12	15	10	50	2.87
Baetis festivus	NIL	02	04	08	11	10	35	2.01
Caenoidac -								
Caehis sp.	NIL	05	10	11	13	12	51	2.93
Ephemeridac -								
Ephemera Nadinac	NIL	03	05	08	10	11	37	2.13
Heptageniidac -								
Epeorus sp.	NIL	02	04	08	11	13	38	2.18
Heptagenia nubile	–	05	08	09	12	10	44	2.53
Chironomus sp.	05	06	09	10	12	10	52	2.98
Chaoborus sp.	3	4	9	2	8	2	28	1.61

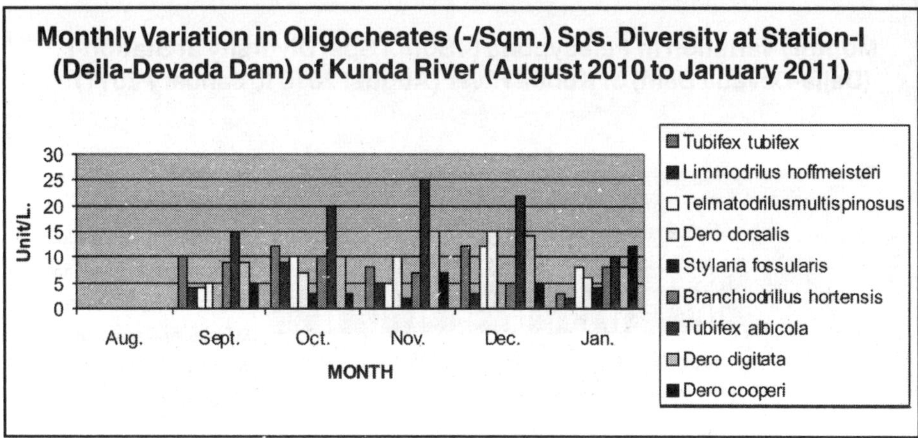

Fig. 9.11

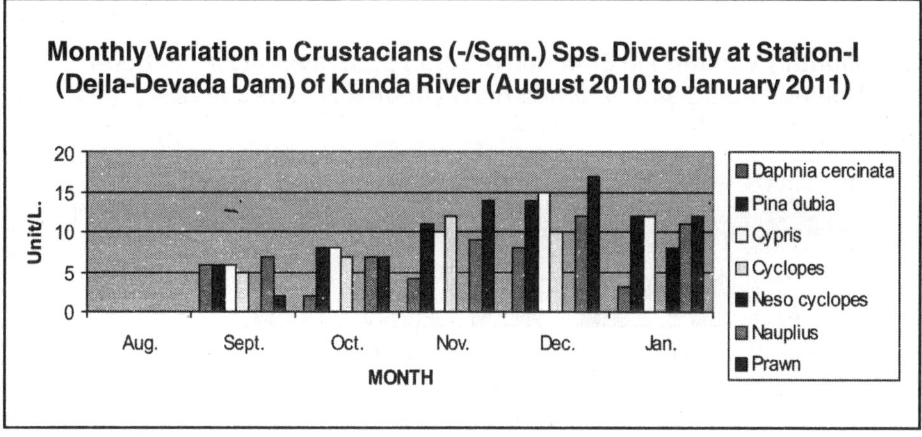

Fig. 9.12

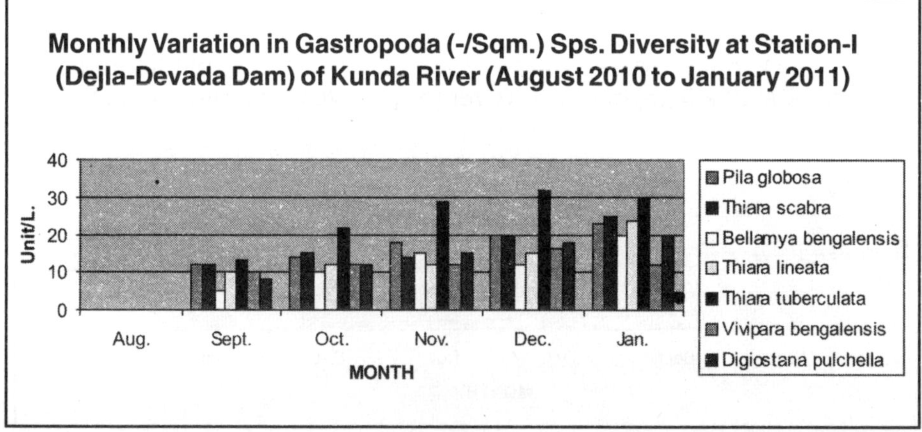

Fig. 9.13

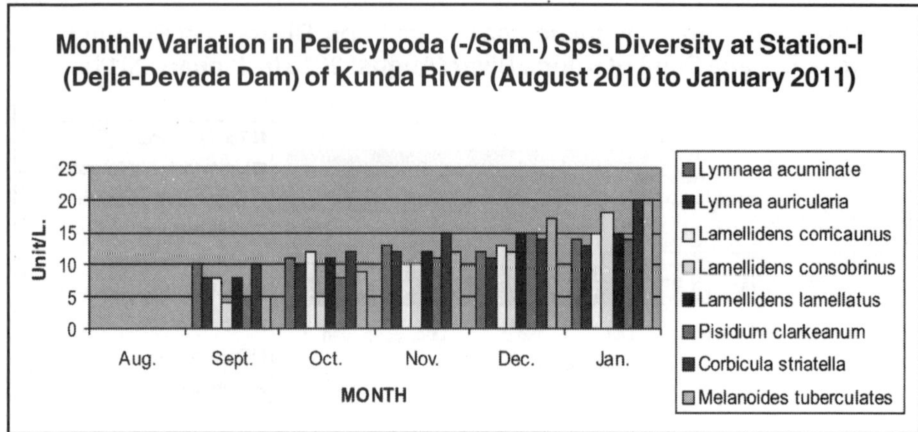

Fig. 9.14

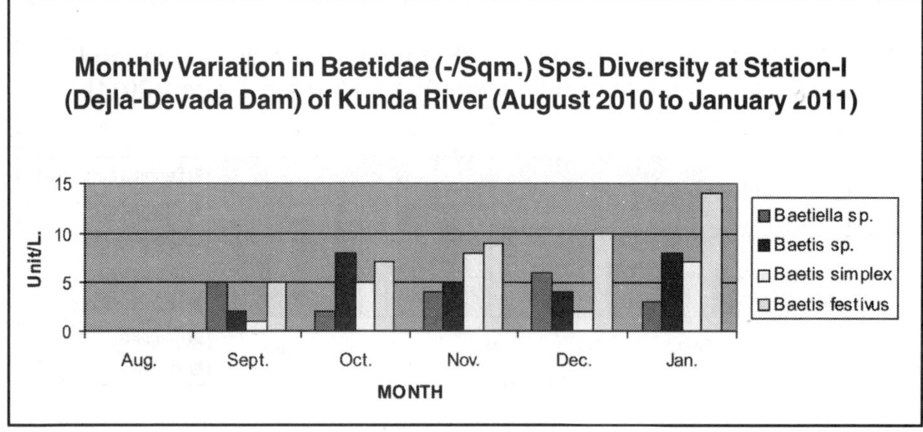

Fig. 9.15

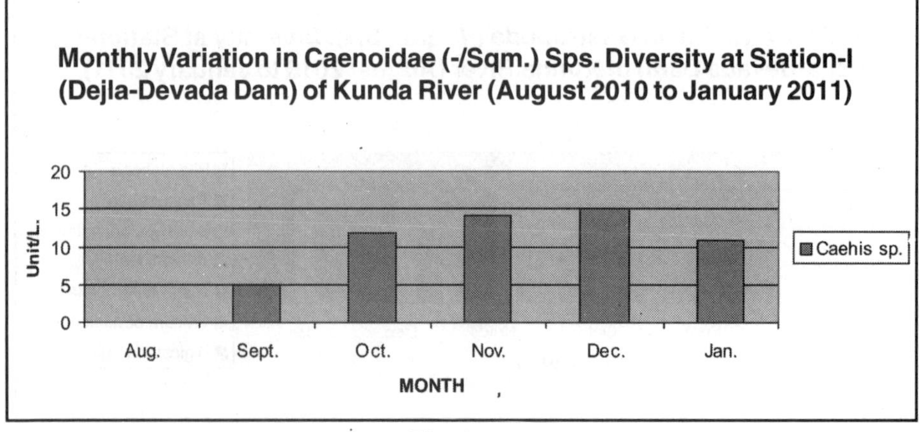

Fig. 9.16

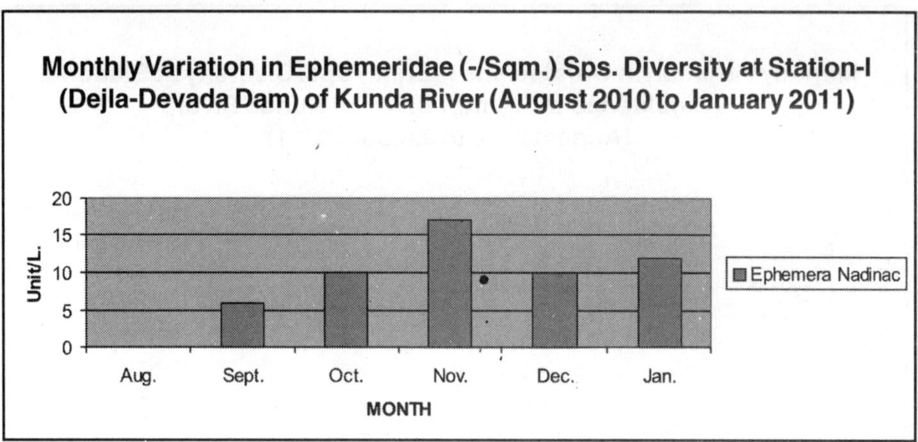

Fig. 9.17

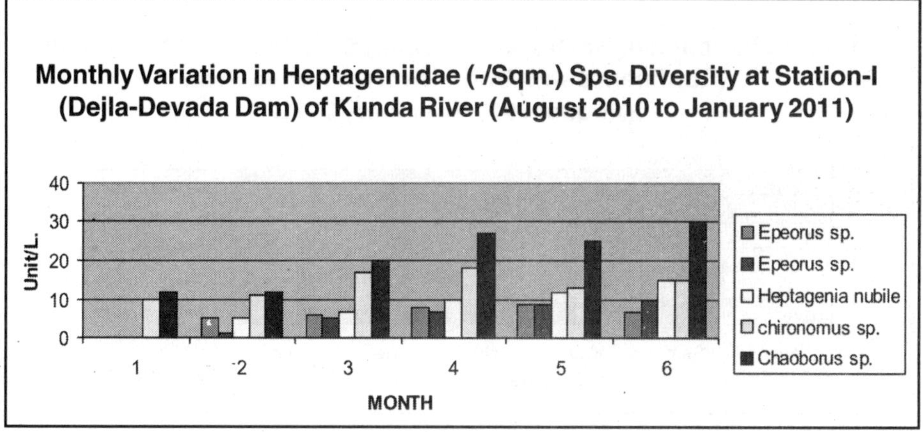

Fig. 9.18

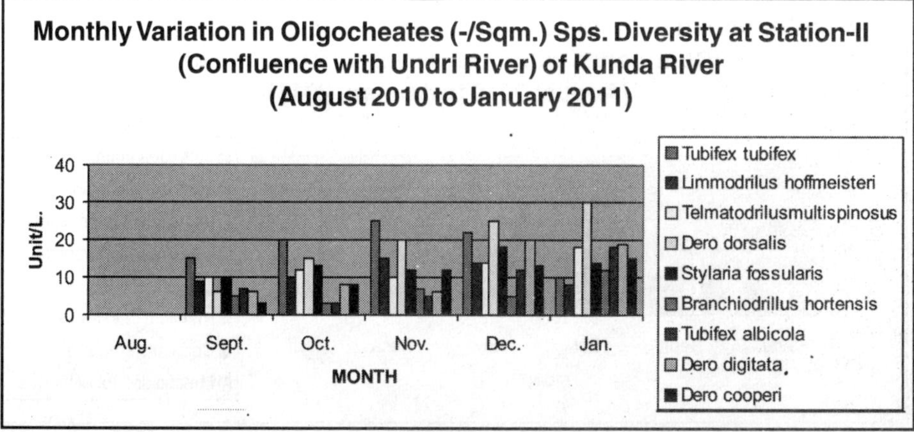

Fig. 9.19

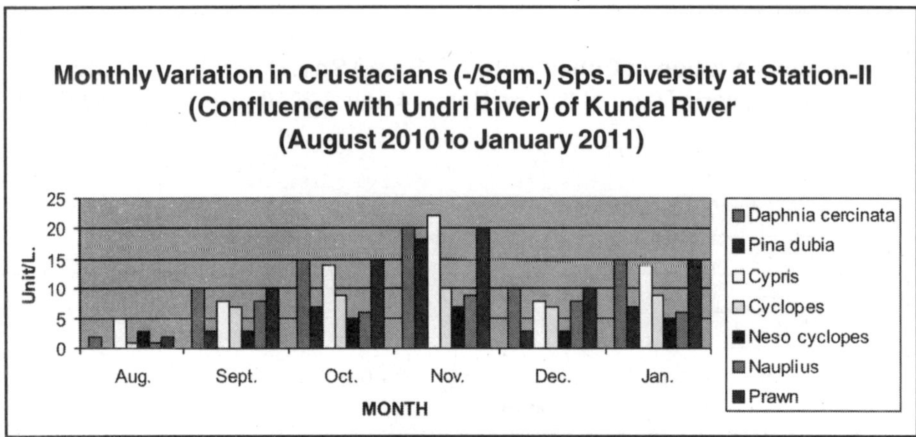

Fig. 9.20

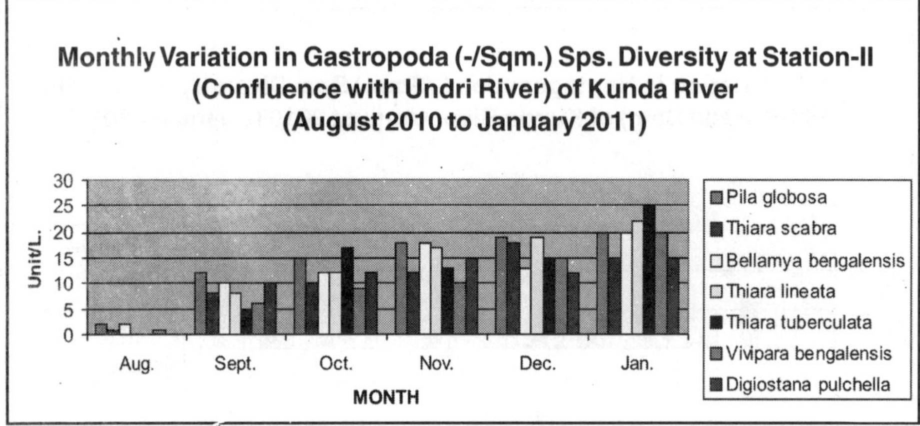

Fig. 9.21

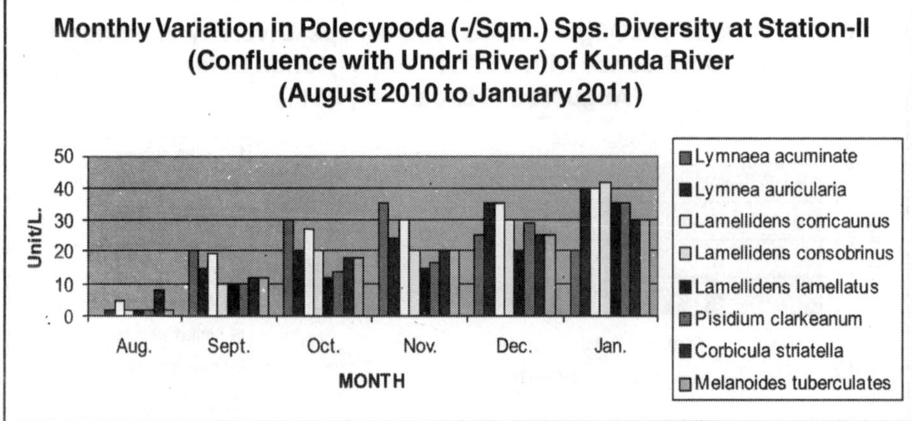

Fig. 9.22

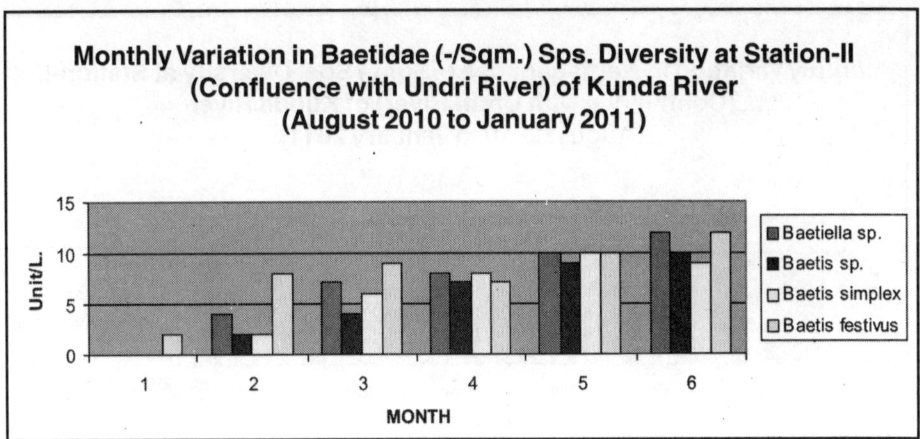

Fig. 9.23

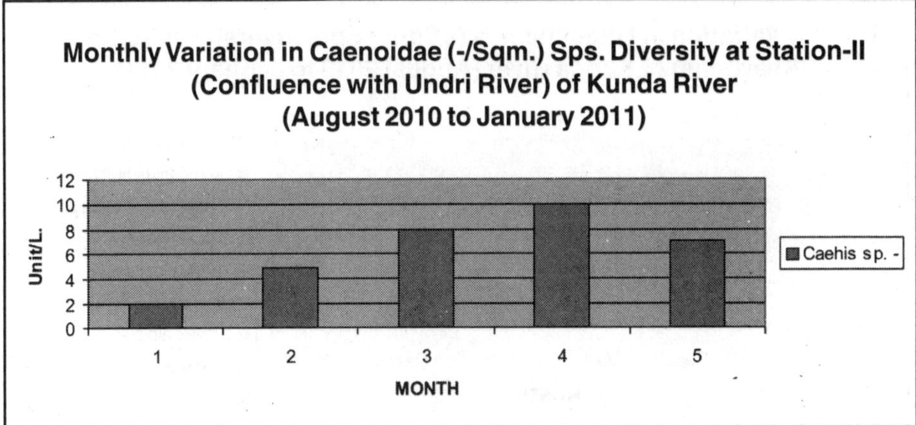

Fig. 9.24

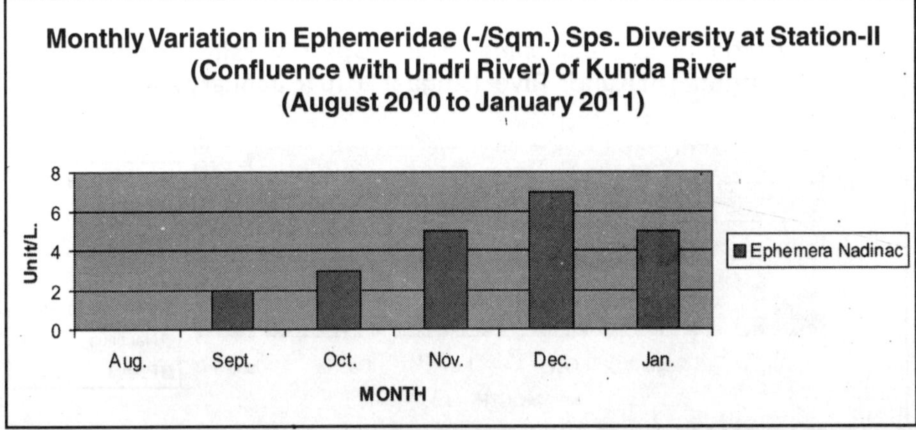

Fig. 9.25

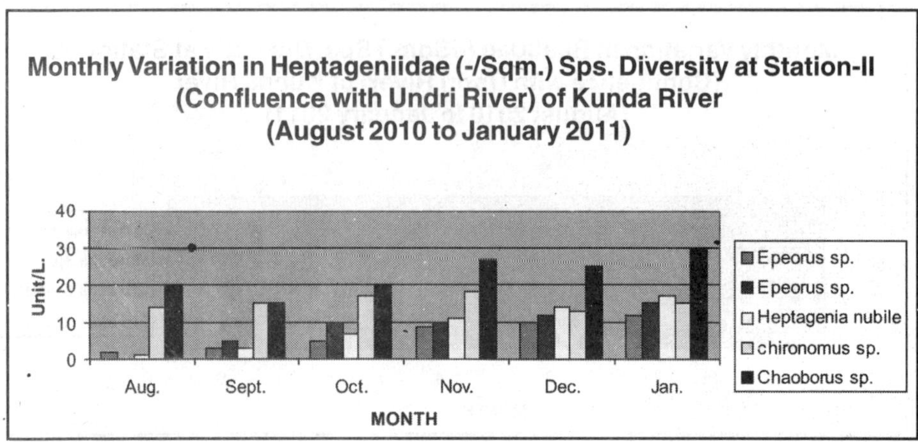

Fig. 9.26

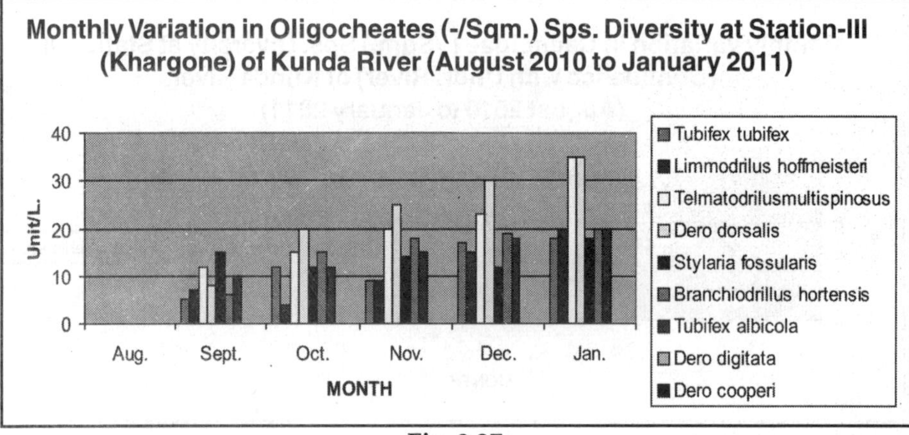

Fig. 9.27

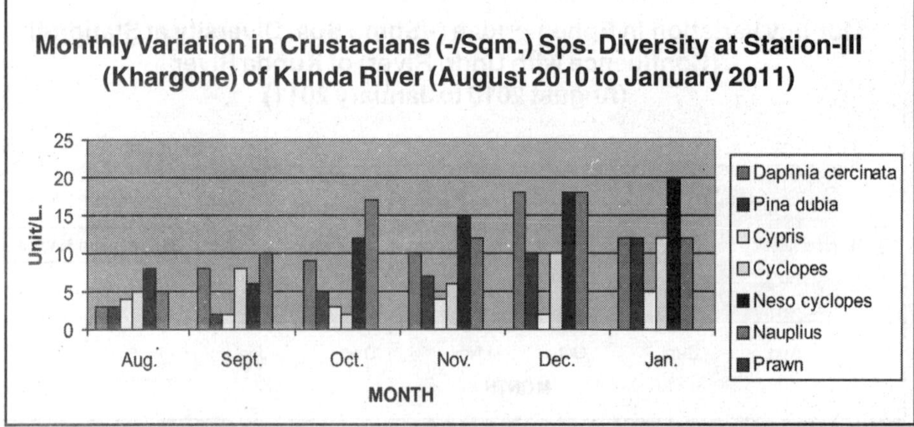

Fig. 9.28

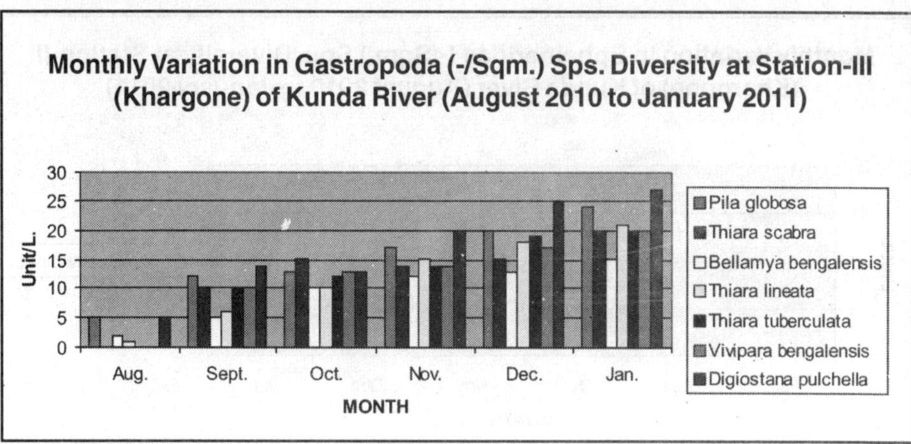

Fig. 9.29

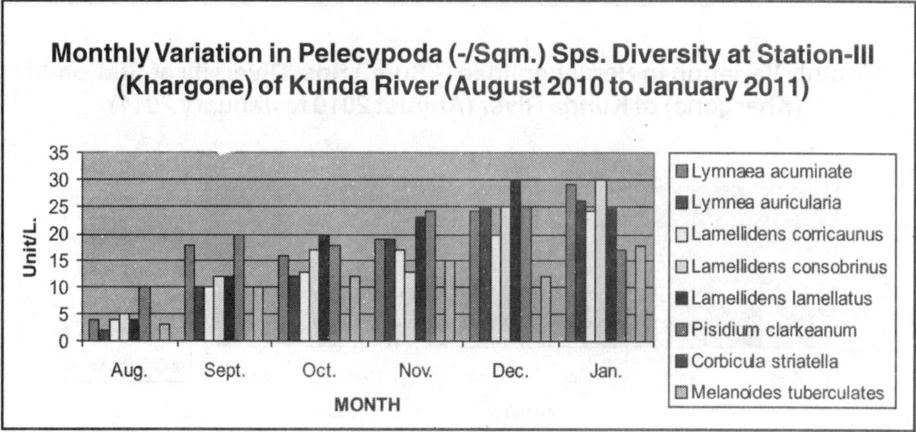

Fig. 9.30

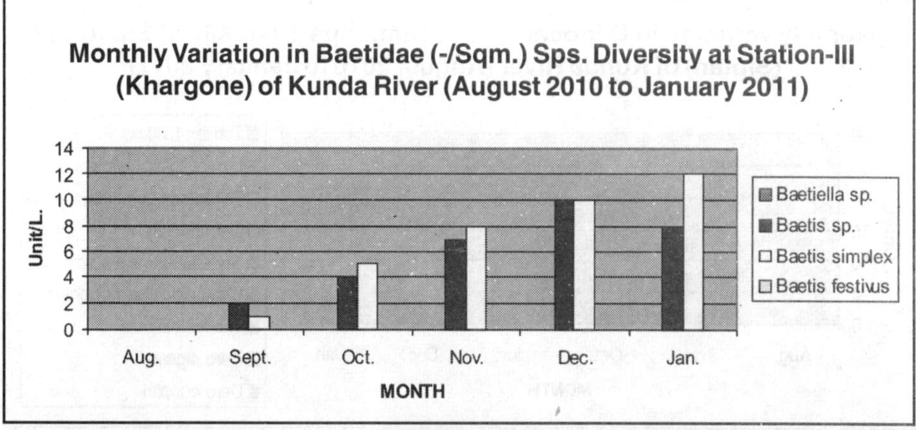

Fig. 9.31

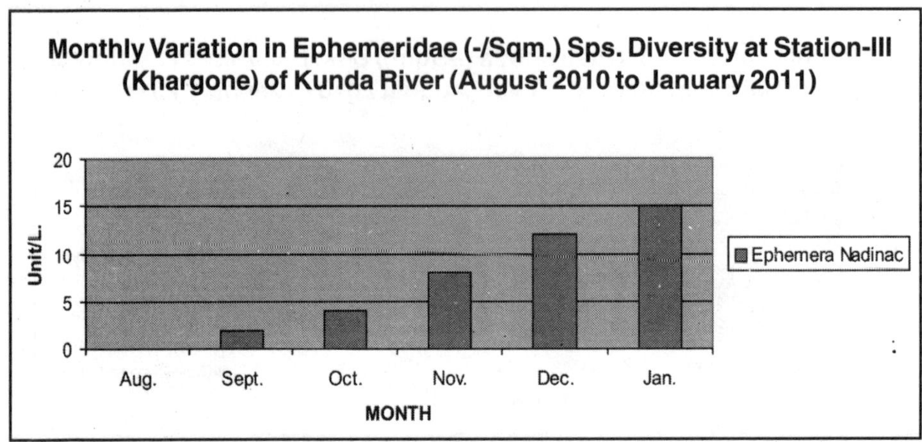

Fig. 9.32

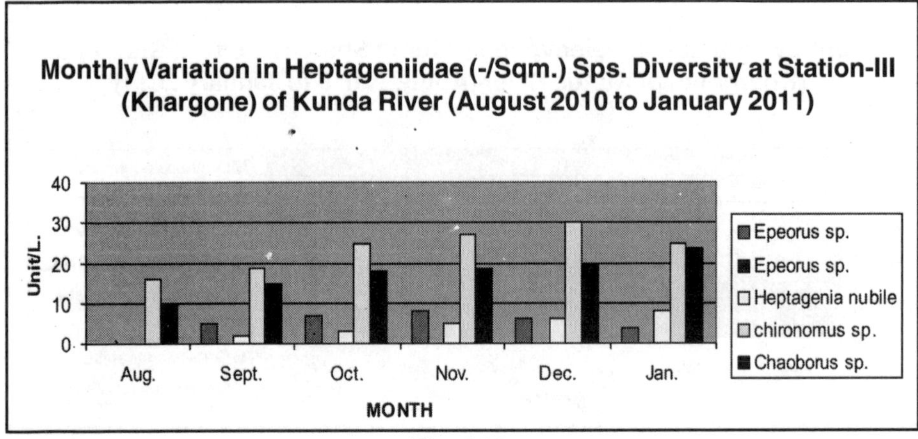

Fig. 9.33

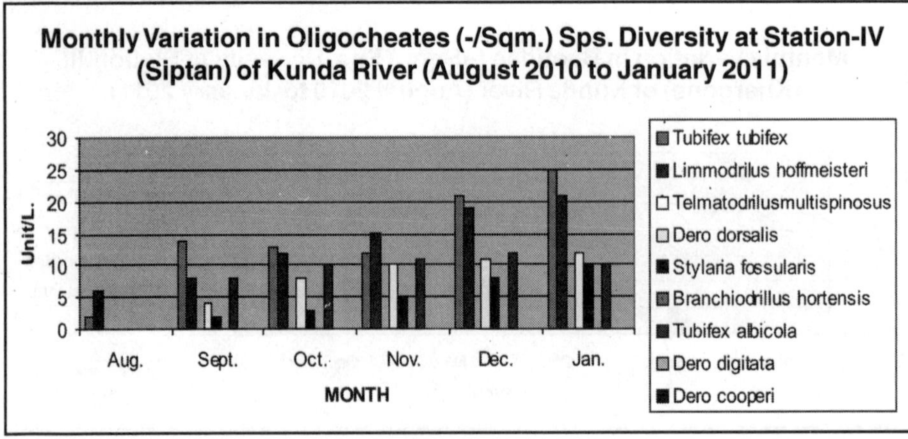

Fig. 9.34

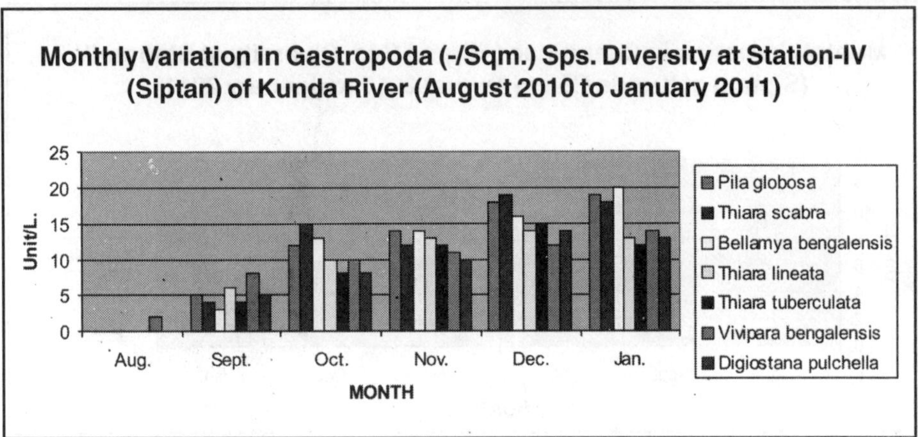

Fig. 9.35

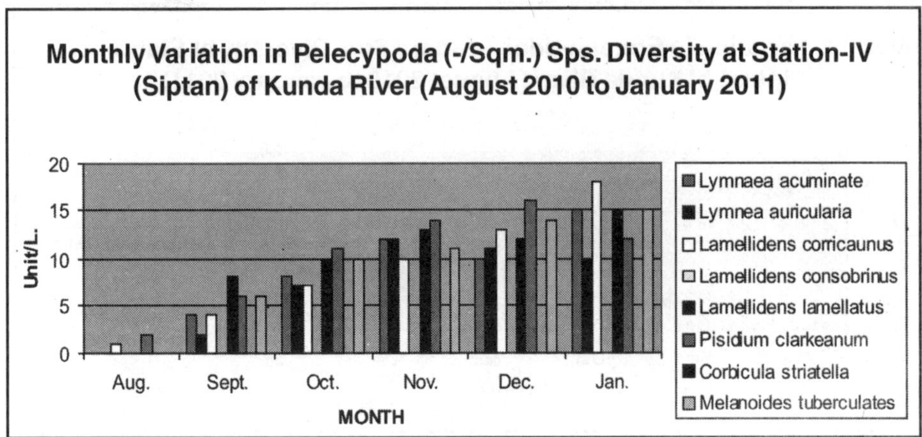

Fig. 9.36

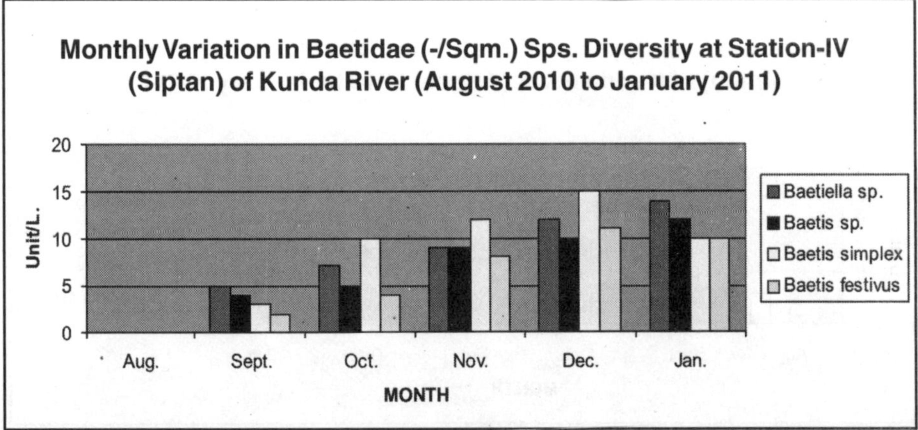

Fig. 9.37

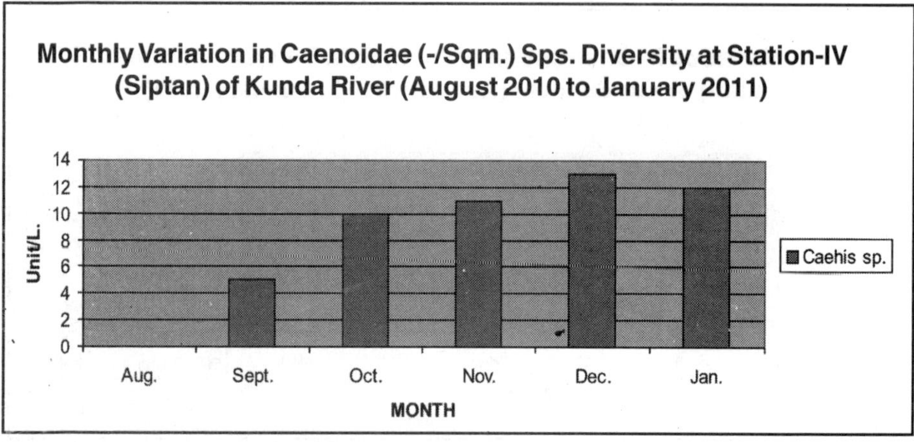

Fig. 9.38

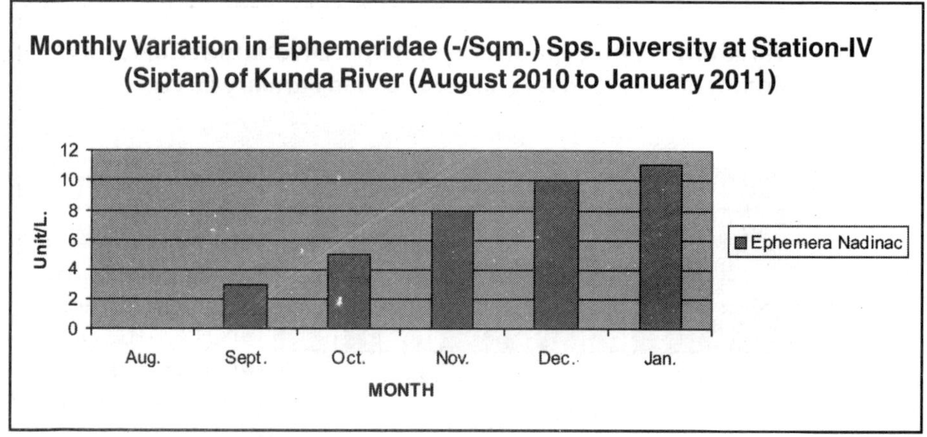

Fig. 9.39

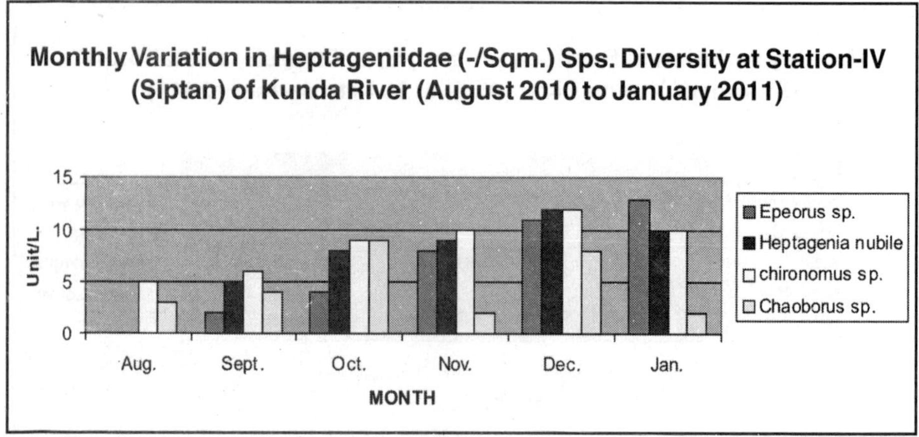

Fig. 9.40

The presence of pollution-tolerant macroinertebrate such as *Chironomus sp., Lymnaea truncatula* and *Lymnaea glabra* could be attributed to the effect of domestic and industrial wastes in the river. The low DO and high BOD values recorded in the present study may have favour the presence of these pollution indicator species. The adaptations of *Chironomus sp.* include possession of pigment hemoglobin which gives it a high affinity for oxygen (Mason, 1981), hence their tolerance of low DO. These are characteristic species in water showing some degree of change due to anthropogenic activities in the river. Their high presence is a common feature of organically polluted water bodies (Chindah *et al.*, 1999; Miserendino and Pizzolon 2000; Ogbogu and Olajide 2002; Tyokumbur *et al.*, 2002; Dyer *et al.*, 2003; Negishi and Richardson 2003; Atobatele *et al.*, 2005; Arimoro and Osakwe 2006).

The weak correlation of some of the fauna to water quality parameters can be attributed to their physiological adaptations to the unfavorable environmental conditions. This assertion agrees with earlier works of Tyokumbor *et al.*, 2002. Ansa (2005) reported that the presence of bivalve and polychaete in her benthic collection in the Andoni mud flats was due to their ability to inhabit sandy and loamy substrates with or without vegetation.

The low diversity of benthic macrofauna in this study is not unusual in the Niger Delta. Hart (1994) reported forty-three species from mangrove swamp of Port Harcourt area of the Niger Delta. Also Umeozor (1995) recorded twenty three species in the New Calabar river; Ansa (2005) in her study of Adoni flats reported twenty eight families, six classes and five phyla, Hart and Zabbey (2005) recorded thirty taxa belonging to twenty families and five classes of macro-invertebrates in Woji Creek in the upper reaches of Bonny River in the Lower Niger Delta; while Sikoki and Zabbey (2006) Identified fourteen species representing eleven families of macro-invertebrates in Imo River.

Studies on Ogunpa River were on physico-chemical parameters and macro-invertebrates fauna (Atobatele *et al.*, 2005; Adeyemo *et al.*, 2008 and Ogidiaka Efe 2012). Same results were also reported by (George *et al.*, 2009; Indabawa 2010 and Tampus *et al.*, 2012).

CONCLUSION

The study revealed that Kunda River at Khargone district Madhya Pradesh, India is polluted as indicated by low DO, high BOD and abundance of pollution tolerant benthic macro-invertebrate hence proper management of the river.

REFERENCES

1. Adakole, J.A. and Anunne, P.A. (2003): Benthic Macroinvertebrates as Indicators of Environmental Quality of an Urban Stream, Zarie, Northern, Nigeria. J Aquat. Sc. 18 (2), 85-92 pp.

2. Adeyemo, O. k., Adedokun O.A., Yusuf, R.K., Adeleye, E.A. (2008): Seasonal Changes in Physico-chemical Parameters and Nutrient Load of River Sediments in Ibadan City, Nigeria.Global Nest Journal, Vol. 10, No. 3. pp. 326-336.

3. Ahmed, A.M. (2004): Ecological Studies of the River Padma at Mawa Ghat, Munshiganj Physico-chemical Properties. Pakistan Journal of Biological Sciences. 7(11): 1865-1869 pp.

4. Ansa, E.J., (2005): Studies of the Benthic Macrofauna of the Andoni Flats in the Niger Delta Area of Nigeria. Ph.D Thesis, University of Port Harcourt, Port Harcourt, Nigeria, pp: 242.

5. APHA (2002): Standard Method for Examination of Water and Waste Water, American Public Health Association Inc. New York 22nd Ed.

6. Arimoro, F.O. and Osakwe, E.I. (2006): 'The Influence of Sawmill Wood Wastes on the Distribution and Population of Macroinvertebrates at Benin River, Niger Delta Area, Nigeria. Chemistry and Biodiversity, 3, 578-592 pp.

7. Atobatele, O.E., Morenikeji, O.A., & Ugwumba, O.A. (2005): 'Spatial Variation in Physical and Chemical Parameters of Benthic Macroinvertebrate Fauna of River Ogunpa, Ibadan'. The Zoologist, 3:58-67 pp.

8. Beqiraj S., Licaj P., Luotonen H., Adhami E., Hellsten S., Pritzl G., (2006): Situation of Benthic Macroinvertebrates in Vjosa River- Albania and Their Relationships with Water Quality and Environmental State. http:/ / balwois.com/balwois/ administration /full-paper/ffp-1190.pdf.

9. Boyd, C.E. (1982): Water Quality in Warm Fish Ponds, Auburn University Agricultural Experiment Station. Auburn University Agricultural Experiment Station. Auburn, Alabama United States of America. 9-44 pp.

10. Chindah, A.H., Hart, A.I. and Atuzie, B. (1999): 'A Preliminary Investigation on the Effects of Municipal Waste Discharge on the Macrofauna Associated with Macrophytes in a Small Freshwater Stream in Nigeria'. African Journal of Applied Zoology, 2: 29-33 pp.

11. Choube U (1991): Studies on Physico-chemical and Biological Parameters of Gandhi Sagar Reservoir, Mandsaur District MP. Ph.D Thesis, Vikram University Ujjain.

12. Danes, K.W., Hynes, H.B.N. (1980): Some Effects of Agricultural Land Use on Stream Insect Communities. Environ. Pollut. Ser. A 22, 19-28 pp.

13. Edmunds, J. (1978): Sea Shells and Other Molluscs Found on West African Coast and Estuaries. Ghana University Press, Accra. 146 pp.

14. Edokpayi, C.A., J.C. Okenyi, A.E. Ogbeibu and E.C. Osimen, (2000): The Effect of Human Activities on the Macrobenthic Invertebrates of Ibiekuma Stream, Ekpoma, Nigeria. Biosci. Res. Commun. 12: 79-87 pp.

15. Emere M.C. (2000): A Survey of Macroinvertebrate Fauna Along River Kaduna, Kaduna, Nigeria, J. Basic and Applied Sci. 9: 17-27 pp.

16. Esenowo I.K. and Ugwunba A.A.A. (2010): Composition and Abundance of Macrobenthes in Majidun River Ikorodu Lagos State. Nigeria. Research Journals of Biological Science 5(8): 556-560 pp.

17. George A.D.I., Abowei J.F.N. and Daka E.R. (2009): Benthic Macro Invertebrate Fauna and Physico-chemical Parameters in Okpoka Creek Sediments, Niger Delta, Nigeria International Journal of Animal and Veterinary Advances, ISSN; 2041- 2908 1(2): 59-65 pp.

18. Golterman, H.L. (1991) Physiological Limnology: An Approach to the Physiology of Lake Ecosystem. Elsvier Scientific Publication Comp. Amsterdam. Oxford, New York, 249- 277 pp.

19. Hart, A.I., (1994): The Ecology of the Communities of Benthic Macro Fauna in the Mangrove Swamp of Port Harcourt Area of the Niger Delta. Ph.D. Thesis, University of Port Harcourt, Rivers State, pp: 262.

20. Hart, A.I. and Zabbey, N. (2005): Physico-chemistry and Benthic Fauna of Woji Creek in the Lower Niger Delta, Nigeria. Environment and Ecology 23(2): 361-368 pp.

21. Holme, N.A and McIntyre, A.D. (1984): Methods for the Study of Marine Benthos. Blackwell Scientific Pub. Oxford London Edinburgh UK. 387 pp.

22. Idowu, E.O. and A.A.A. Ugwumba, (2005): Physical, Chemical and Benthic Faunal Characteristics of a Southern Nigeria Reservoir. The Zoologist, 3: 15-25 pp.

23. Indabawa I.I. (2010): The Assessment of Water Quality at Challawa River via Physico-chemical and Macro Invertebrate Analysis, Bioscience Research Communications Vol. 22, 227-233 pp.

24. Jain R. and Sharma D. (2000): Water Quality of Rampur Reservoir of Guna District (M.P. India) Environ. Cons. J. 1(2): 99-102 pp.

25. Khanna DR and Bhutani R. (2003): Limnological Status of Satikund Pond at Hardiwar. Indian J. Environ. Sci 7(2): 131-136 pp.

26. Lange-Bertalot, H. (1979): Pollution Tolerance as Criteria for Water Quality Estimation. Nova Hed wigia 64: 285-304 pp.

27. Lydeard, C., R.H. Cowie, W.F. Ponder, A.E. Bogan and P. Bouchet, (2004): The Global Decline of Non-marine Mollusks. Bioscience, 54: 321-330 pp.

28. Macan, T.T. (1959): A Guide to Freshwater Invertebrate Animals. Longman, England. 118 pp.

29. Mason, C.F. (1991): Biology of Freshwater Pollution. Longman Scientific Technical, New York, USA. pp. 350.

30. Mellanby, H (1997): Animal Life in Freshwater, Printed by Prentice-Hall of Canada 593 pp.

31. Miserendino, M.L. and Pizzolon, L.A. (2000): 'Macroinvertebrates of a Fluvial System in Patagonia: Altitudinal Zonation and Functional Structure'. Archiv Fur Hydrobiol. 150(1), 55-83 pp.

32. Negishi, J.N. and Richardson, J.S. (2003): Responses of Organic Matter and Macroinvertebrates to Placement of Boulder Clusters in a Small Stream of Southwestern British Columbia, Canada. Canadian Journal of Fisheries & Aquatic Sciences, 60(3), 247-258 pp.

33. Ogbeibu A.E. (2001): Distribution Density and Diveristy of Dipterans in a Temporary Pond in Okomu Forest Reservoir, Southern Nigeria. J. Aqu. Sci. 16: 43-52 pp.

34. Ogbogu, S.S., & Olajide, S.A. (2002): Effect of Sewage Oxidation Pond Effluent on Macroinvertebrate Communities of a Tropical Forest Stream, Nigeria. Journal of Aquatic Science, 17(1), 22-27 pp.

35. Ogidiaka Efe (2012): Physico-Chemical Parameters and Benthic Macro-invertebrates of Ogunpa River at Bodija, Ibadan, Oyo State European Journal of Scientific Research ISSN 1450-216X Vol. 85 No. 1, 89-97 pp.

36. Olomukoro J.O. and Egborge, A.B.M. (2003): Hydrobiological Studies on Warri, River, Nigeria Part 1: The Composition, Distribution and Diversity of Macrobenthic Fauna. Biose. Res. Commun. 15: 279-296 pp.
37. Pathak SK., Mudgal LK., (2005): Limnology and Biodiversity of Fish Fauna in Virla Reservoir, MP India. J. Comp. Toxicol. Physiol. 2(1) 86-90 pp.
38. Pennak, R.W., (1978): Freshwater Invertebrates of the United States, 2nd Edn., John Wiley and Sons, New York. pp: 810.
39. Rosenberg, D.M. and Resh, V.H. (1993): Freshwater Biomonitoring and Benthic Invertebrate. Chapman and Hall, New York. Chapman & Hall. 488 pp.
40. Royer T.V. Tank J.L David M.B. (2004): Transport and Fate of Nitrate in Headwater Agriculturalstreams in Illinois. J.Environ. Qual. (33):1296-1304 pp.
41. Sharma D. and Jain R. (2001): Duirnal Variation in Some Aspects of Limnology of Gopalpura Tank of District Guna (M.P.) India Environ. Cons. J. 2(1): 41-44 pp.
42. Sharma A., Mudgal L. K., Sharma A., Sharma S. (2004): Fish Diversity of Yashwant Sagar Reservoir Indore M.P. Him J. Environ. Zoology. 18(2) 117-119 pp.
43. Sharma S., Tali I., Pir Z., Siddique A., Mudgal L.K. (2012): Evaluation of Physico-chemical Parameters of Narmada River, MP, India Researcher 4(5): 13-19 pp. (ISSN: 1553-9865) http://www.science pub.net/researcher.
44. Tampus Anneielyn D., Tobias Ermelinda G., Amparado Ruben F., Bajo Lydia and Sinco Astrid L. (2012): Water Quality Assessment Using Macroinvertebrates and Physico-chemical Parameters in the Riverine System of Iligan City, Philippines, Advances in Environmental Sciences (AES) International Journal of the Bioflux Society Volume 4, Issue 2. 59-68 pp. http:// www.aes.bioflux.com.ro.
45. Tyokumbur, E.T., T.G. Okorie and O.A. Ugwumba, (2002): Limnological Assessment of the Effects of Effluents on Macroinvertebrates Fauna in AWBA Stream and Reservoir, Ibadan, Nigeria, The Zoologist, 1(2): 59-69 pp.
46. Umeozor, O.C., (1995): Benthic Fauna of New Calabar River, Nigeria. Trop. Freshwater Biol., 4: 41-51 pp.
47. Welch P.S. (1998): Liminological Methods Mcgran Hill Book Co. New York.
48. Wetzel R.G., Likens G.E. (2006): Limnological Analysis. 3rd ed. Springer-Verlag, New York, 391 pp.
49. WHO, (1978): A Field Guide to African Freshwater Snails. WHO Snail Identification Center, Danish Bilharziasis Lab. Jaegersborg, Charlottenlund Denmark, pp. 30.
50. World Health Organisation (1993): Guidelines for Drinking Water Quality-I, Recommendations, 2nd Ed. Geneva.
51. Yogesh S. and Pendse D.C. (2001): Hydrological Study of Dahikhura Reservoir. J. of Environmental Biology. 22(1) 67-70 pp.
52. Zabbey, N., (2006): An Ecological Survey of Benthic Macroinvertebrates of Woji Creek, off the Bonny River System Rivers State. M.Sc. Thesis, University of Port Harcourt, pp: 102.

Assessment of Ambient Air Quality Status in Urbanization, Industrialization and Commercial Centers of Uttarakhand (India)

Avnish Chauhan

ABSTRACT

Development in industrialization, urbanization and expansion of the Haridwar city has resulted in increase of air pollution like SO_2, NO_x, SPM and RSPM in urban and industrial areas of Haridwar (Uttarakhand), India. This investigation represented the assessment of ambient air quality with respect to PM_{10} (RSPM), SPM, oxides of nitrogen (NO_x) and sulphur dioxide (SO_2) at four sites namely Shivalik nagar, SIDCUL, Clock Tower, and Bhadrabad. Meteorological parameters like temperature, relative humidity, wind speed and rainfall were also recorded simultaneously during the sampling period. Monthly and seasonal variation of these pollutants have been observed and recorded. The annual average and range values have also been calculated.

It has been observed that the concentrations of the pollutants are high in winter in comparison to the summer or the monsoon seasons. Investigation results elucidates that industrial activities, indiscriminate open air burning of coal by the local inhabitants for cooking as well as

1. Department of Zoology and Environmental Sciences, Gurukula Kangri University, Haridwar - 249 404, (Uttarakhand), India.

2. Department of Applied Science, Phonics group of institutions, Roorkee, Haridwar (Uttarakhand), India.

cooking purpose, vehicular traffic etc. are responsible for the high concentration of pollutants in this area. In the present study, it was noticed that the SPM and RSPM levels at residential and industrial areas exceeds the prescribed limits as stipulated by Central Pollution Control Board (CPCB) New Delhi, India. Apart from this the SO_2 and NO_x levels in residential and industrial areas remain under prescribed limits of CPCB.

INTRODUCTION

Air pollution is one of our most serious problems, faced by developing as well as developed countries. Most of the cities in developing countries suffer from serious outdoor air pollution due to poor control of industrial emission and improper maintenance of vehicles (Ravindra, et al., 2003). The advent of industrial revolution and increase demand of vehicles has increase the air pollutants concentration all over the world. The release of air pollutants in atmosphere is the direct effect of industrialisation and urbanisation which are essential to meet the growing demands to the increasing population. Such activities can not be stopped as they are directly related to the development of the society (Varma *et al*., 1994). Industrialization and urbanization bring with them the unwanted adverse air pollutants, namely suspended particulate matter (SPM), sulphur dioxide (SO_2) and nitrogen dioxide (NO_2) (Reddy and Suneela, 2001). Suspended particulate matter (SPM) refers to the mixture of solid and liquid particles in air. In a broader sense the term applies to matter in the atmosphere classed into particles having a lower size limit of the order of 10^{-3}µm and an upper limit of 100 µm. SPM, a complex mixture of organic and inorganic substances, is a ubiquitous air pollutant, arising from both natural and anthropogenic sources. Particulate matter (PM) that is 10µm or less in diameter is called as Respirable suspended particulate matter (RSPM) or PM10, it penetrates the respiratory system. RSPM is generally grouped into three modes: ultra fine (size range less than 0.1µm), fine (0.7-1µm) and coarse (1-10µm) (Fenger, 1999; Mohanraj and Azeez, 2004). Respirable dust particle is the term for particles found in the air, including dust, dirt, soot, smoke and liquid droplets. Particles can be suspended in the air of long periods (Senthlinathan, 2005). Most of cities in Northern India are afflicted with the presence of unusually high concentration of PM10 in the ambient environment posing a serious risk to human health (Tandon et al., 2008).

The issue of urban air quality is receiving increasing attention as a growing share of the world's population is now living in urban centers and demanding a cleaner urban environment (Gurjar et al., 2008). Air pollution is a serious public health problem in most of the metropolitan areas in India. The increased air pollutant concentrations in urban area are responsible for deficits in pulmonary functions, cardiovascular disease, neurobehavioral effects, morbidity and mortality (WHO, 1987). According to the United Nations report (UN, 2003) the global urban population continues to grow faster than the total population of the world. About, 3 billion people are living in urban settlements. In, number of urban centers has grown from 1827 in 1901 to 5161 in 2001. The population residing in urban areas has also increased from 25.8 millions in 1901 to 285.3 millions in 2001 (Sri Muruganandam and Shiva Nagendra, 2007). The United Nations (UN) estimates that 4.9 billion inhabitants out of 8.1 billion will be living in cities by 2030 (UNCSD, 2001). Rapid industrialization followed by consequential population and economic growth surrounding industrial nuclei have often serious concern for the environmental deterioration on surrounding areas (Reddy et al., 2004).

The major anthropogenic sources of air pollutants are industrial emissions, domestic fuel burning, emissions from power plants and transportation activities. In India, specifically in Delhi, vehicular pollution contributes 67% of the total air pollution load, which is approximately 3,000 metric tones per day (Central Pollution Control Board, 1999). It is estimates that diesel combustion emits 84 g/km of particulates as compared to 11 g/km in CNG (Nylund and Lawson, 2000). An air quality index is one of the important tolls available for analyzing and reprinting air quality status uniformly (Swamee and Tyagi, 1999).

MATERIALS AND METHODS

Study Area

Haridwar is one of the most important holy cities of India, located in newly carved state of Uttaranchal. Haridwar is extended from latitude 29° 58′ in the north to longitude 78°13′ in the east and has subtropical climate. It is about 60 km in length from east to west and about 80 km in width from north to south. District Haridwar lies in the foot hills of Shivalik ranges. Total area of district Haridwar is 2,360 km^2 with a population of 14, 44,213 (as per 2001 census). It receives millions of tourists every month. The study was carried out at three different sites of Haridwar, namely Shivalik nagar (referred to as site-1), industrial area in SIDCUL (referred to as site-2) and Control Area (referred to as site-4) and one site from Dehradun which is residential area (referred to as site-3).

Concentration of air pollutants viz. NO_x, SO_2, SPM and RSPM was measured with the help of RDS APM 460 by sucking air into appropriate reagent for 24 hours at every 30 days and after air monitoring it procured into lab and analysis for the concentration level. The SPM and RSPM were analyzed using Respirable Dust Sampler (RDS) APM 460 and operated at an average flow rate of 1.0-1.5 m^3 min^{-1}. Preweighed glass fiber filters (GF/A) of Whatman were used as per standard methods. SO_2 and NO_x were collected by bubbling the sample in a specific absorbing (sodium tetrachloromercuate of SO_2 and sodium hydroxide for NO_x) solution at an average flow rate of 0.2-0.5 min^{-1}. The impinger samples were put in ice boxes immediately after sampling and transferred to a refrigerator until analyzed. The concentration of NO_x was measured with standard method of Modified Jacobs- Hochheiser method (1958), SO_2 was measured by Modified West and Geake method (1956), SPM and RSPM using filter paper methods. The apparatus was kept at a height of 2 m from the surface of the ground.

RESULTS AND DISCUSSION

Figure 10.1 represents the monthly variation of PM_{10}, RSPM, NO_x and SO_2 at four monitoring sites. The seasonal variation of PM_{10}, RSPM, NO_x, SO_2 and AQI in terms of range and the average values are depicted in Table 10.3. The annual ambient air quality status in the form of the arithmetic mean and geometric mean are shown in Table 10.4. The meteorological data with respect to temperature, humidity, rainfall and wind speed were collected from the study sites.

It was observed from the meteorological data that the highest temperature attained was during the month of May at site 1, 2 and 4, whereas highest temperature during June at site 3 and the lowest in the month of December at site 1, 2 and 4, while lowest during January at site 3.

Highest humidity was recorded during the month of December at site 1, 2 and 4, whereas highest humidity during August at site 3 and the lowest in the month of May at site 1, 2 and 4, while the lowest during April at site 3.

Highest rainfall was recorded during July at site 1, 2 and 4, however at site 3 during August. In the case of wind speed, highest observed during June at site 1, 2 and 4, while highest during April and October.

RSPM or PM_{10}

It is observed from figure 10.1 and Table 10.3 that the average PM_{10} concentration was found to be much higher during winter (November-February) in comparison with the monsoon (July-October) and the summer (March-June). This trend is the same in all the four monitoring stations. In winter, anti-cyclonic conditions prevails, which characterized by calm or light winds and restrict mixing depth due to stable or inversion atmosphere lapse rate, resulting in little dispersion or dilution of pollutants, which, in turn, helps in the build-up of pollution concentrations to higher levels. Monsoon experiences the lowest SPM levels at four monitoring sites (except site-2), which is because of the dust by intermittent precipitation.

SPM

From figure 10.1 and Table 10.3 it is elucidate that annual average of SPM values were maximum as per standard set by CPCB during the study period at site 1, 2 and 3. The average SPM levels were relatively high during winter in comparison with monsoon and summer at all four monitoring sites. During winter at all selected sites were experienced calm or light winds, resulting in little dispersion of pollutants causes higher levels of SPM.

NO_x

The annual average of NOx concentration levels are comparable at the four monitoring sites (Table 10.4), but did not cross the reference levels of 80/120 μgm^{-3} at any four sampling sites.

SO_2

From Table 10.4 it is observed that the annual average of SO_2 values were higher than the prescribed limit of CPCB at site 1, 2 and 3. The average SO_2 levels were relatively high during winter (Table 10.3) in comparison with both the summer and monsoon. Lower levels of SO_2 during monsoon can be attributed to the prevalence of high wind speeds and precipitation.

Above results shows that concentration of particulate matter (SPM and RSPM) were higher than the prescribed limits by CPCB, whereas NO_x and SO_2 remained under prescribed limit.

Rajasekhar *et al.*, (1999) reported that the higher concentration of SPM exceeds the permissible limits, this may be attributed of automobile pollution. The major sources of SO_2 are combustion, metallurgical industries such as smelting, automobile exhaust and automobiles. Jain *et al.*, (2004) reported the suspended particulate matter has found to higher that of CPCB standards. Apart from the emission factors of vehicles, the SPM concentration would be mainly affected by the moving vehicles, wind and the thermal turbulence produced by the hot vehicle exhaust gas. Another factor that can affect the particulate matter concentration is rainfall (Lam *et al.*, 1999). Many studies indicated that the total and respirable suspended particulate matter in the ambient air would be affected by various meteorological factors like wind speed, wind direction, solar radiation, relative humidity as well as source conditions (Leung and Lam 1993, Monne *et al.*, 1995, Prendiz *et al.*, 1995). The natural sources of particulate matter in the atmosphere are the erosion of soil by wind, salt particles from oceans, forest fires, volcanic residues, plant pollen and seeds. Manmade sources are households grates, automobile exhaust, thermal power stations, iron and steel plants, foundries, cement factories, petrochemical refineries, paper mills, agricultural operations and so on (Gurtu *et al.*, 2001). The diesel engine produces high level of very small particles (Gupta, 1999). Sandhu *et al.*, (2004) reported that the high concentration of RSPM in all commercial site due to plying of diesel vehicles. Motor vehicles also generate a range of particulate matter through the dust produced from brakes, clutch plates, tires and indirectly through the ré-suspension of particulates on road surfaces through vehicles – generate turbulence (Watkins, 1991). Joshi *et al.*, (2006) found that the concentration of gaseous pollutants viz SO_x and NO_x was under the permissible limits as per CPCB while the concentration of particulate pollutants (SPM and RSPM) was higher the permissible limits as per CPCB in Haridwar city.

Table 10.1: Characterization of Four Monitoring Sites

Sampling Station Location	Zonal Activities	Major Sources of Pollution in 2 km Radius
Shivalik Nagar (Site-1)	Residential/Commercial	• Transportation activities • Coal burning • Spray painting works • Poor road conditions • Construction works • Poor maintained vehicles • Very close and surrounded by two industrial areas
SIDCUL (Site-2)	Industrial	• Coal burning • Spray painting works • Poor road conditions • Construction works • Steel and Iron Plant • Soap manufacturing works • Biscuit factory • Oil mill • Polythene factory • Bricks factory • Battery and Generator factory • Glass factory • Scrub factory • Transportation activities • Poor maintained vehicles
Clock Tower (Site-3)	Commercial	• Transportation activities • Poor maintained vehicles
Control Area (Site-4)	Agricultural land	• Unpaved road • Agricultural activities

Table 10.2: Concentrations PM10, SPM, NO_X and SO_2 at Selected Sites in Haridwar District

Sl. No.	Months March 2007 - Feb. 08	PM10 (μgm^{-3})				SPM (μgm^{-3})				NO_X (μgm^{-3})				SO_2 (μgm^{-3})			
		Site-1	Site-2	Site-3	Site-4	Site-1	Site-2	Site-3	Site-4	Site-1	Site-2	Site-3	Site-4	Site-1	Site-2	Site-3	Site-4
1.	March	138.40	162.56	103.32	34.37	401.14	546.10	251.01	94.57	16.10	20.33	28.35	2.34	8.64	13.33	26.21	1.42
2.	April	122.30	169.54	109.04	28.50	404.50	568.40	267.25	103.40	16.55	19.46	28.41	2.44	11.88	16.72	26.99	1.43
3.	May	118.34	158.49	108.21	22.83	398.44	512.70	264.25	101.30	13.24	18.46	28.96	2.37	8.90	14.88	26.90	1.34
4.	June	110.23	165.25	97.38	29.88	403.22	532.12	245.89	95.50	17.67	22.23	29.31	2.12	11.43	17.47	28.01	1.28
5.	July	100.60	171.66	79.98	20.88	375.11	509.11	193.89	98.47	15.36	22.48	28.81	2.29	11.67	19.46	26.56	1.39
6.	August	112.68	164.23	88.11	18.34	390.00	524.74	216.31	101.38	16.87	21.33	27.56	2.54	9.08	18.30	24.45	1.48
7.	September	118.22	173.24	76.71	19.57	407.12	534.88	187.19	109.40	16.80	22.67	23.66	2.12	10.44	18.12	23.38	1.38
8.	October	119.70	170.33	91.25	22.49	404.50	540.12	191.17	110.22	17.12	23.50	27.28	2.23	11.32	15.63	21.72	1.22
9.	November	121.55	172.59	109.42	23.31	410.28	510.19	286.42	109.54	18.24	24.54	30.19	2.34	11.77	14.88	26.78	1.89
10.	December	130.26	178.50	140.32	24.50	414.52	522.25	320.20	111.32	17.44	23.32	28.78	2.57	12.30	17.90	27.00	1.93
11.	January	128.59	177.83	149.43	25.90	410.87	507.43	338.56	106.00	18.40	21.47	30.37	2.36	11.79	18.68	28.17	1.87
12.	February	125.12	180.12	142.81	21.96	412.47	509.24	312.12	109.46	15.44	25.49	27.63	2.40	11.12	20.12	25.52	1.80

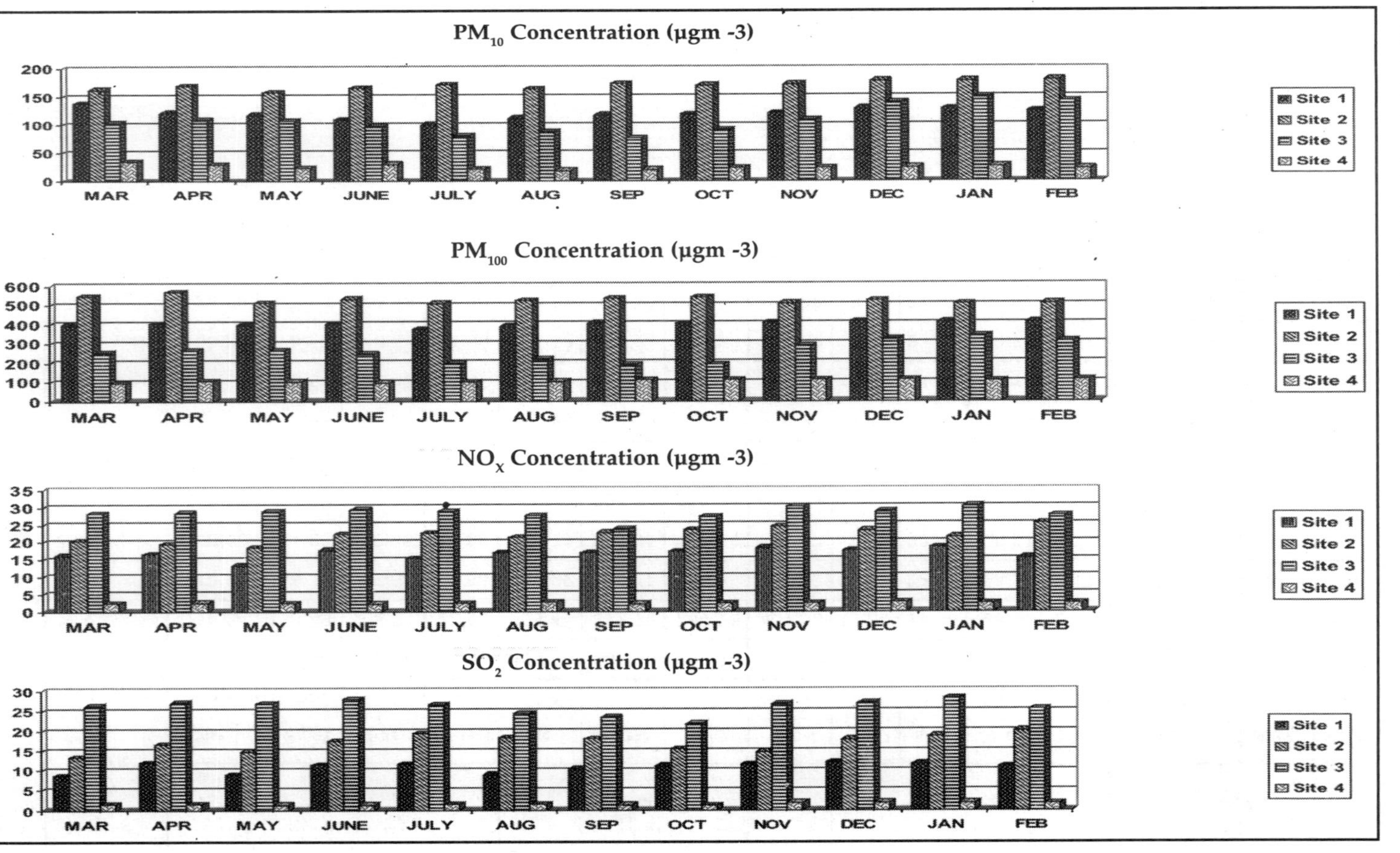

Fig. 10.1: Monthly Variation of RSPM, SPM, NO_x and SO_2

Table 10.3: Seasonal Variation of $PM_{2.5}$, PM10, NO_X, SO_2 and AQI at Three Selected Sites in Haridwar District

Air Pollutants	Site I			Site II			Site III			Site IV		
	Summer	Monsoon	Winter	Summer	Monsoon	Winter	Summer	Monsoon	Winter	Summer	Monsoon	Winter
PM10 (μgm⁻³)	110.23-138.40 [122.32]	100.60-119.70 [112.80]	121.55-130.26 [126.38]	158.49-169.54 [163.96]	164.23-173.24 [169.87]	172.59-180.12 [177.26]	97.38-109.04 [104.49]	76.71-91.25 [84.01]	10943-149.43 [135.50]	22.83-34.37 [28.90]	18.34-22.49 [20.32]	21.96-25.90 [23.92]
SPM (μgm⁻³)	398.44-404.50 [401.83]	375.11-407.12 [394.18]	410.28-414.52 [412.04]	512.70-568.40 [539.83]	509.11-540.12 [527.21]	507.43-522.25 [512.28]	245.89-267.25 [257.10]	187.19-216.31 [197.14]	286.42-338.56 [314.33]	94.57-103.40 [98.69]	98.47-109.40 [104.87]	106.00-111.32 [109.80]
NO_x (μgm⁻³)	13.24-17.67 [15.89]	15.36-17.12 [16.54]	15.44-18.40 [17.38]	18.46-22.23 [20.12]	21.33-23.50 [22.50]	21.47-25.49 [23.71]	28.35-29.31 [28.76]	23.66-28.81 [26.38]	27.63-30.37 [29.24]	2.12-2.34 [2.32]	2.12-2.54 [2.30]	2.34-2.57 [2.42]
SO_2 (μgm⁻³)	8.64-11.88 [10.21]	9.08-11.67 [10.63]	11.12-12.30 [11.75]	13.33-17.47 [15.60]	15.63-19.46 [17.88]	14.88-20.12 [17.90]	26.21-28.01 [27.03]	21.72-26.56 [24.03]	25.52-28.17 [26.87]	1.28-1.43 [1.37]	1.22-1.48 [1.37]	1.80-1.93 [1.87]
AQI	75.63-79.63 [77.85]	73.78-79.27 [77.02]	78.81-88.88 [82.56]	43.44-47.94 [45.91]	45.59-46.99 [46.36]	44.32-46.62 [45.64]	64.67-68.33 [67.08]	51.00-57.67 [54.08]	74.33-80.67 [75.75]	17.33-23.47 [20.57]	17.95-19.81 [19.01]	19.43-20.43 [19.97]

Range values and average values of PM10, SPM, NO_X, SO_2 and AQI

Table 10.4: Annual Ambient Air Quality Status at Three Monitoring Sites

Sampling Sites	PM10 (μgm⁻³)			SPM (μgm⁻³)			NO_x (μgm⁻³)			SO_2 (μgm⁻³)			AQI		
	Range	Arithmetic Mean	Geometric Mean	Range	Arithmetic Mean	Geometric Mean	Range	Arithmetic Mean	Geometric Mean	Range	Arithmetic Mean	Geometric Mean	Range	Arithmetic Mean	Geometric Mean
Site I	100.60-138.40	120.50	120.12	375.11-412.47	402.68	402.54	13.24-18.40	16.60	16.54	8.64-12.30	10.86	10.79	73.78-88.88	79.14	79.06
Site II	158.49-180.12	170.36	170.24	507.43-568.40	526.44	526.14	18.46-25.49	22.11	22.02	13.33-20.12	17.12	17.01	43.44-47.94	45.97	45.96
Site III	76.71-149.43	108.00	105.58	187.19-338.56	256.19	251.29	23.66-30.37	28.28	28.22	21.72-28.17	25.97	25.91	51.00-80.67	65.64	64.96
Site IV	18.34-34.37	24.38	24.00	94.57-111.32	104.21	104.05	2.12-2.57	2.34	2.34	1.22-1.93	1.54	1.52	17.33-22.65	19.85	19.78

Table 10.5: Monthly Variation in Temperature and Humidity as Recorded from Different Study Sites during 2007-08

Sl. No.	Months (March 2007 - Feb. 08)	Temperature (°C)				Humidity (%)				Rainfall (m.m.)				Wind Speed (m/sec)			
		Site-1	Site-2	Site-3	Site-4	Site-1	Site-2	Site-3	Site-4	Site-1	Site-2	Site-3	Site-4	Site-1	Site-2	Site-3	Site-4
1.	March	24.0	24.5	18.9	24.0	79	78	67	79	49	49	82	49	0.6	0.6	0.7	0.8
2.	April	36.0	36.6	26.6	36.0	61	63	49	62	36	36	16	36	0.5	0.5	0.8	0.6
3.	May	37.4	37.7	27.6	37.0	57	59	53	58	40	40	22	40	0.6	0.9	0.7	0.8
4.	June	36.0	36.3	28.9	36.0	70	71	65	70	176	176	79	176	1.7	1.6	0.8	1.5
5.	July	33.0	33.4	26.6	32.8	86	87	85	88	287	287	792	287	1.4	1.3	0.7	1.2
6.	August	32.6	32.6	26.2	32.6	84	85	87	85	273	273	846	273	0.4	0.6	0.4	0.6
7.	September	29.0	29.3	25.9	29.0	81	83	79	81	43	43	255	43	0.6	0.6	0.3	0.5
8.	October	20.2	20.4	21.9	20.0	79	80	67	80	0.0	0.0	10	0.0	0.3	0.3	0.8	0.2
9.	November	17.0	17.3	17.3	16.8	89	88	72	90	0.0	0.0	0.0	0.0	0.1	0.2	0.6	0.4
10.	December	9.6	9.0	12.4	10.0	90	89	71	94	7	7	6	7	0.3	0.4	0.6	0.2
11.	January	14.0	13.1	11.6	14.5	85	84	69	93	12	12	13	12	0.4	0.5	0.7	0.3
12.	February	13.0	12.2	13.9	13.2	89	88	67	91	0.0	0.0	19	0.0	0.5	0.6	0.7	0.4

REFERENCES

Central Pollution Control Board (1999). *Parivesh*: Newsletter. Ministry of Environment and Forests.

Fenger, J. 1999. Urban Air Quality. *Atmos. Environ.* 33, 4877-4900.

Gupta, A.B. 1999. Vehicular Air Pollution and Asthma. *Asthma Sanjeevani* 5(2), 3-5.

Gurjar, B.R., Butler, T.M., Lawrence, M.G. and Lelieveld, J. 2008. Evaluation of Emissions and Air Quality in Megacities. *Atmospheric Environment*, 42, 1593-1606.

Gurtu, D., Vaidya, M. and Gajghate, D.G. 2001. World Scenario of Particulate Matter, NO_2 and SO_2: A Review. *IJEP* 21(2), 683-695.

Jacob, M. B. and Hochheiser, S.: 1968. Continuous Sampling and Ultra-micro Determination of Nitrogen Dioxide in air. *Annal. Chem.* 32, 426.

Jain, R., Dwivedi, D.K. and Gupta, A.B. 2004. Status of Air Quality at Selected Traffic Junctions of Jaipur City. *Nature Environment and Pollution Technology* 3 (4), 435-442.

Joshi, P.C., Swami, A. and Gangwar, K.K. 2006. Air Quality Monitoring at Two Selected Traffic Junctions in the City of Haridwar. *Him. J. Env. Zool.* 20 (2), 219-221.

Krichstrtter, T.W., Harly, R.A., Kreisberg, N.M., Stolzenburg, M.R. and Hering, S.V. 1999. On Road Measurement of the Fine Particles and Nitrogen Oxide Emissions from Light and Heavy Duty Motor Vehicles. *Atmospheric Environment* 33, 2955-2968.

Lam, G.C.K., Leung, D Y.C., Niewiadomski, M., Pang, S.W., Lee, A.W.F. and Louie,P.K.K. 1999. Street Level Concentration of Nitrogen Dioxide and Suspended Particulate Matter in Hong-Kong. *Atmospheric Environment* 33, 1-11.

Leung, Y.C. and Lam, G.C.K. 1993. Development of a Coal Stockpile Dust Suppression System. International Journal of Storing, Handling and Technology Bulk 13, 513-515.

Monne, C.H., Branedli, O., Schaeppi, G., Schindler, C.H., Asckermannm, U., Leuenberger, P.H. and Sapaldia, Team. 1995. Particulate matter < 10 μm in urban, Rural and Alpine air in Switzerland. *Atmospheric Environment*, 29, 2565-2573.

Mohanraj, R. and Azeez, P.A. 2004. Health Effects of Airborne Particulate Matter and the Indian Scenario. *Current Science* 87(6), 2004.

Nylund, N.O. and Lawson, A. (2000). *Exhaust Emissions from Natural Gas Vehicles.* Helsinki: International Association of Natural Gas Vehicles, VTT Energy.

Prendez, M.M., Egido, M., Tomas, C., Seco, J., Calvo, A. and Romero, H. 1995. Correlation Between Solar Radiation and Total Suspended Particulate Matter in Santigo, Chile. *Atmospheric Environment* 29, 1543-1551.

Rajasekhar, R.V. J., Samy, I.K., Sridhar, M., and Muthusubramanian, P. 1999. Estimation of Suspended Particulate Matter in the Ambient air of Madurai City by Sedimentation and Filtration Methods. *IJEP*, 21(8), 673-676.

Ravindra, K., Mor, S., Ameena, Kamyotra, J.S. and Kaushik, C.P. (2003). Variation in Spatial Pattern of Criteria Air Pollutants Before and during Initial Rain of Monsoon. *Environment Monitoring Assessment*, 87, 145-153.

Reddy, M.K. and Suneela, M. 2001. Status of Ambient Air Quality at Hazira with Reference to Modified Air Quality Index. *IJEP*, 21(8), 707-712.

Reddy, M.K., Rao, K.G. R. and Rao, I.R. (2004). Air Quality Status of Visakhapatnam (India)-indices Basis. *Environment Monitoring Assessment*, 93, 1-12.

Sandhu, P.S., Patel, U. and Gupta, A.B. 2004. Exposure to Airborne Particles and Their Physical Characterisation in Ambient Environment of Jaipur City. *Nature Environment and Pollution Technology*, 3 (4), 509-514.

Senthilnathan, T. (2005). Status of Respirable Dust Particle (RDP) Concentration–A Case Study in Chennai City. *Journal of Environmental Biology*, 20 (2 suppl), 425-428.

Sri Muruganandam, B. and Shiva Nagendra, S.M. (2007). Air Quality in Chennai City. Proceeding of the Brainstorm Workshop on Urban Air Pollution in India held at IIT Roorkee, pp. 35-39.

Tandon, A., Yadav, S. and Attri, A.K. (2008). City-wide Sweeping a Source for Respirable Particulate Matter in the Atmosphere. *Atmospheric Environment*, 42, 1064-1069.

UNCSD, 2001. Protection of the Atmosphere-Report to the Secretary General. E/CN.17/2001/2, Commission for Sustainable Development, New York, USA.

Varma, P.C., Jha, C., Mian, S., Sinha, S.B. and Gupta, V.S. 1994. Air Quality Studies in an Industrial and Urban Township of Jharia Coal Field, Dhanbad. *IJEP* 14 (4), 301-306.

Watkins, L.H. 1991. Air Pollution from Road Vehicles. Transport and Road Research Laboratory, London, U.K.

West, P.W. and Gaeke, G.C.: 1956, 'Fixation of Sulphur Dioxide as Sulfitomercurate III and Subsequent Colorimetric Determination', *Annal. Chem.*, 28, 1816.

Index

D

E

F

G

H

I